STUDIES IN LAW, POLITICS, AND SOCIETY

STUDIES IN LAW, POLITICS, AND SOCIETY

Series Editor: Austin Sarat

Previous Volumes:

Volumes 1–2:	Edited by Rita J. Simon
Volume 3:	Edited by Steven Spitzer
Volumes 4–9:	Edited by Steven Spitzer and Andrew S. Scull
Volumes 10–16:	Edited by Susan S. Sibey and Austin Sarat
Volumes 17–33:	Edited by Austin Sarat and Patricia Ewick
Volumes 34–77:	Edited by Austin Sarat
Volume 78:	Edited by Livia Holden and Austin Sarat
Volume 79:	Edited by Austin Sarat
Volume 80:	Edited by Austin Sarat

STUDIES IN LAW, POLITICS, AND SOCIETY VOLUME 81

LEGAL INTERMEDIATION: A PROCESSUAL APPROACH TO LAW AND ECONOMIC ACTIVITY

EDITED BY

AUSTIN SARAT

Department of Law, Jurisprudence and Social Thought, and Political Science, Amherst College, USA

SPECIAL ISSUE EDITORS

SEBASTIAN BILLOWS

Max Planck Institute for the Study of Societies, Germany

LISA BUCHTER

Emlyon Business School, France

JÉRÔME PÉLISSE

Sciences Po, France

emerald PUBLISHING

United Kingdom – North America – Japan
India – Malaysia – China

Emerald Publishing Limited
Howard House, Wagon Lane, Bingley BD16 1WA, UK

First edition 2019

British Library Cataloguing in Publication Data
A catalogue record for this book is available from the British Library

ISBN: 978-1-83867-860-9 (Print)
ISBN: 978-1-83867-859-3 (Online)
ISBN: 978-1-83867-861-6 (EPub)

ISSN: 1059-4337 (Series)

Printed and bound by CPI Group (UK) Ltd, Croydon, CR0 4YY

CONTENTS

LIST OF CONTRIBUTORS

Sebastian Billows	Max Planck Institute for the Study of Societies, Germany
Lisa Buchter	Emlyon Business School, France
Camille Herlin-Giret	Centre d'études et de recherches administratives, politiques et sociales (CERAPS), France.
Jérôme Pélisse	Center for the Sociology of Organizations, CNRS, Sciences Po Paris, France
Alexis Spire	Institut de recherche interdisciplinaire sur les enjeux sociaux (IRIS), France
Alina Surubaru	Centre Emile Durkheim (CNRS), Université de Bordeaux, France
Fanny Vincent	Centre de recherche sur l'expérience, l'âge et les populations au travail (CREAPT), France and Centre d'études de l'emploi et du travail - Conservatoire national des arts et métiers (CNAM), France

EDITORIAL BOARD

INTRODUCTION: THE MICROFOUNDATIONS OF LEGAL INTERMEDIATION IN ORGANIZATIONAL CONTEXTS

Sebastian Billows, Lisa Buchter and Jérôme Pélisse

Keywords: Legal intermediation; regulation; economy; labor; legal tools; neo-institutionalism; France

Law, public policy, and economic activity are intimately tied to each other. State policies and the legal system have often worked in favor of private economic interests. For instance, core features of the US legal system of the nineteenth century were designed to protect the interests of the capitalist class (Horwitz, 1992). Nowadays, narrow definitions of responsibility and privileged access to formal legal institutions still help the "haves" to "come out ahead" (Galanter, 1974, 2013; Sutton, 2001). Conversely, law has also been used (successfully or not) to coerce economic interests. Due to rules governing industrial relations and giving workers more power vis-à-vis their employers, corporations have become "legalized" settings (Selznick, 1969), where labor unions have gained leverage to shape workers' rights and accommodations (Chappe, 2015; Dixon & Martin, 2012; Guillaume, Pochic, & Silvera, 2015; Pélisse, 2007). Some laws mandated corporations to participate in broader societal change, such as the inclusion of discriminated minorities (Bereni & Revillard, 2007; Burstein, Paul, 1985; Dobbin, 2009; Edelman, 2016; Heyer, Baudot, Borelle, & Revillard, 2013; Lempert & Sanders, 1986; Stryker & Pedriana, 2004) or, in France, the

Legal Intermediation: A Processual Approach to Law and Economic Activity
Studies in Law, Politics, and Society, Volume 81, 1–9

ISSN: 1059-4337/doi:10.1108/S1059-433720190000081001

fight against unemployment through the reduction of working time (Pélisse, 2004, 2011). Finally, the rise of the "regulatory state" (Thatcher, 2014) or "regulatory capitalism" (Levi-Faur, 2005) has led to even more interactions between law and economic activity. Despite popular belief that regulation was abandoned due to the diffusion of neoliberalism throughout the Western world in the 1980s, empirical evidence suggests that privatization, deregulation, and the promotion of market-based solutions under neoliberal governments expanded and extended business regulation in many national contexts (Braithwaite, 2009; Vogel, 1996) and even on a transnational basis (Bartley, 2007, 2010). In other words, the alleged deregulation and move toward free markets led to a slow re-regulation of free markets in the form of soft regulation allegedly perfecting market performance (Levi-Faur, 2005; Majone, 1997).

A more and more prevalent phenomenon, the interplay between law, public policy, and economic activity has become a core part of socioeconomic and socio-legal scholarship (Edelman & Stryker, 2005; Stryker, 2003; Bessy, Delpeuch & Pélisse, 2011; Edelman, 2016).[1] A major outcome of this literature is that public policy goals, legal norms, and the ensuing enforcement measures are inherently ambiguous (Dobbin, 2009; Edelman, 1992), especially as we shift from "government" to a "governance" model where multiple stakeholders design and implement regulations (Ansell & Gash, 2008; Braithwaite, 1982; Freeman & Minnow, 2009; Kagan, Gunningham, & Thornton, 2003). Due to normative ambiguity and to the organizational clout of economic interests (Perrow, 1991), legal mandates always go through some degree of reinterpretation by economic and organizational actors, which impacts the reach of regulatory authorities (Edelman, 2016; Edelman, Krieger, Eliason, Albiston, & Mellema, 2011). Our argument is that this ongoing process of legal intermediation is shaped by a diverse set of actors and relies on hybrid tools and instruments, which have differential effects (either positive or negative) on organizational routines, compliance monitors, as well as judicial and legislative forces. The process leading from a new regulation to new organizational and business routines involves specific actors whom we call "legal intermediaries." While some economic actors and organizations turn to external and highly specialized corporate services, such as tax advisers or business lawyers, others rely on various types of "in-house" legal or non-legal specialists. A significant aspect of their work is to design specific devices, such as contracts, guidelines, or any other type of formalized procedures. Those legal devices, which stand halfway between the regulatory and the managerial sphere, shape the legal consciousness of laypeople who undertake economic activities or who work in large organizations (Ewick & Silbey, 1998; Pélisse, 2005).

Our processual, intra-organizational approach departs from other accounts of legal intermediation (Talesh & Pélisse, 2018). Regulation scholars are now taking "regulatory intermediation" seriously (Abbott, Levi-Faur, & Snidal, 2017). However, because they focus on formal institutions such as international bodies or rating agencies, their approach overlooks subtler and more local forms of intermediation affecting organizations and economic activity (Gray & Pélisse, 2019). Despite using at times a different terminology, the neo-institutional literature on "legal environments" has already researched legal intermediation at length (Dobbin, 2009; Edelman, 2016; Talesh, 2015). This literature's main findings can be summarized as follows: by infusing "managerial logics" into law, organizational fields are capable of mitigating the impact of legislation targeted at them. In a second step, which is referred to as "endogenization," managerialized law "subsequently influences understandings of law and legal actors and legal institutions" (Edelman, 2016, p. 19). Although we build on core insights of the neo-institutional approach, such as the managerialization of law and legal endogeneity, our approach to legal intermediation departs from the latter in four respects: (1) we challenge the current portrayal of legal intermediaries (primarily seen as legal experts or compliance professionals) by studying actors who are neither legal professionals nor corporate managers and who nonetheless deeply influence the interpretation of the law; (2) we emphasize the multiple roles of legal devices in shaping compliance or non-compliance; (3) from a methodological standpoint, we use an intra-organizational and intra-industry perspective rather than a field-based perspective; and (4) we investigate the relationship between law and economic activity within more varied social settings: in countries outside the United States and in other areas of regulation than anti-discrimination law, both of which are overwhelmingly represented in the neo-institutional literature.

Our first difference with the neo-institutional approach is that we provide a more detailed account of legal intermediaries' work and profile. Proponents of the neo-institutional approach have shown how different types of "compliance professionals" (Edelman, 2016) reinterpreted US laws fighting employment discrimination. Compliance professionals include lawyers, consultants, human resource professionals, and insurance staff. By contrast, our symposium describes a wider range of legal intermediaries, such as legal counsels, civil rights activists, judicial experts salespeople, hospital directors, union members, managers, health and safety specialists, or even street level bureaucrats, who may or may not belong to established professions. In his contribution, Jérôme Pélisse presents a systematic comparison of these actors, which helps understanding and contrasting the different ways through which they contribute to legal intermediation. In particular, he stresses the importance of what he calls non-legal professionals acting as legal intermediaries within organizations.[2] They contribute to the framing of ordinary legality on the workplace and in other areas of economic activity. Their contribution to legal intermediation depends on different types of constraints and resources, such as their relational profile, their hierarchical status or their local reputation.

Our second departure from the neo-institutional literature is our consideration of legal devices. Legal intermediaries design specific devices that shape economic activity and, in some cases, have feedback effects on regulation. Legal devices are a core feature of the neo-institutional approach to legal intermediation: in response to Equal Employment Opportunity law, organizations set up legal devices such as grievance procedures or guidelines which "symbolically demonstrate attention to law while maintaining sufficient flexibility to preserve managerial prerogatives that are seen as advancing business goals"

(Edelman, 2016, p. 31). However, we argue that the symbolic legitimacy of legal devices (Bourdieu, 1987, p. 4) is only one of three different ways in which they shape economic activity and regulatory outcomes. This symposium puts forth two other channels by which legal devices exercise their influence. The first is instrumental: the mere presence of rules means that economic actors can play with them (Lascoumes & Le Bourhis, 1996). The scholarship at the crossroads of social movement and organizations has showed how activists use symbolic devices put forth by companies to hold firms accountable for their pro-social claims and monitor their practices (McDonnell, King, & Soule, 2015). The second effect of legal devices is constitutive. As Robin Stryker wrote, "law provides tools that help actors attribute meaning, existence, desirability or undesirability to their economic environment" (Stryker, 2003, p. 349). Weber provided empirical evidence of this a long time ago: from a historical standpoint, legal devices changed the way economic actors calculate economic returns and made strategic business decisions (Weber, 1978). By shaping legal consciousness, legal devices may create new opportunities for certain disadvantaged groups to claim more rights (McCann, 1994). To capture the diverse effects of legal devices on economic activity and organizations, we define the act of crafting objects such as contracts, guidelines, grievance procedures, collective agreements, or any other type of formalized procedures, as a social process. As Suchman has shown, such objects "possess both symbolic and technical properties," which arise from the interactions between experts and laypeople (Suchman, 2003, p. 91). Similar to Macaulay's work on contracts (1963), we adopt a "law in action" approach to find how and whether those objects are used in economic and organizational contexts. However, in contrast to Suchman and Macaulay's work, which tends to ignore institutional factors, we never lose sight of regulation and the institutionalized practices that might prevail at the level of an industry.

A third difference lies in the methods we use to study legal intermediaries and legal intermediation. Neo-institutional sociologists have collected evidence of legal intermediation by reading the professional literature (such as magazines), observing professional gatherings (such as conferences or "webinars"), and conducting statistical surveys about organizational practices across a large number of organizations. While these empirical strategies are useful to map out the diffusion of managerialized rules and procedures across the entire organizational field, it fails to account for how legal intermediaries craft and deliver advice within specific organizations and sectors. Yet, as most of the contributions in this special issue show, legal intermediation is particularly salient in the case of industry-specific regulation. To provide a much needed finer-grained view of legal intermediation, our contributions outline the "division of labor [...] in the cubicle" (Abbott, 2005). Similar to the research conducted by Nelson and Nielsen (2000), for example, we investigate the daily interactions between laypeople and the legal intermediaries who assist them in complying with regulation. While the literature has insisted on how professional groups "frame" the law, we take into account both institutional factors and the informal micropolitics that give rise to local compromises between laypeople and legal intermediaries (Huising, 2015). The use of qualitative research methods enables us to capture not only the specific challenges faced by different actors, but also the impact of their status – formal and informal power, authority, position within the company, ability to speak out (Hirschman, 1970) – on their ability to leverage social change. Additionally, this microsociological perspective helps us to explore cases where legal intermediation is a contentious issue. The neo-institutional literature tends to equate contentiousness with litigation (Revillard, 2017). Our contributions show that even when litigation is absent, the internalization of law by organizations may turn into a contentious social process where different groups of actors defend conflicting interpretations of the law.

The last difference between our approach and previous neo-institutional research lies in the empirical scope of our investigations. While virtually all existing neo-institutional research is centered on US anti-discrimination law,[3] we expand the scope and the types of organizational environments where legal intermediation is analyzed, as Talesh and Pélisse (2018) did recently to find out how legal intermediaries impact social change. We believe that legal intermediation is virtually ubiquitous and holds true not only across countries, but also across types of organizations, whether it is private businesses, schools (Hallett, 2010), hospitals (Kellogg, 2009), or scientific laboratories (Huising & Silbey, 2013; Pélisse, 2017). Our contributions use this conceptual framework to address responses to different types of law. While Lisa Buchter's contribution addresses anti-discrimination law in the French context, the rest of our contributions describe areas of regulation that the literature has overlooked so far, such as tax law, competition law, labor law, or health and safety procedures. Moreover, our contributions focus on European cases. This goes against some neo-institutional claims arguing that legal intermediation is unlikely outside the US. More specifically, we reject the claim that compared to the "weak" US federal state and its "vague" law, the "French legal system doesn't permit expansive reinterpretation" (Dobbin, 2009, pp. 6–7). First, the alleged weakness of the US federal state and its legal system has been contested by political scientists, historians, and sociologists alike (Carpenter, 2001, 2010; Lieberman, 2015; Stryker & Pedriana, 2004). Second, besides the contributions showcased in our symposium, there is already a wealth of empirical evidence showing how private actors reinterpret, managerialize, and endogenize the French legal environment (Bereni, 2011; Billows, 2016; Pélisse, 2004, 2011).

Thanks to our approach that focuses on the contingent and processual aspects of legal intermediation, we find patterns of compliance that differ from those predicted by the existing literature. In the neo-institutional approach, legal intermediation is a one-way street by which the profit-oriented logic of private business systematically taints the "legal logic," a sphere where "principles such as due process, equal access to law, and equal protection of law" dominate (Edelman, 2016, p. 23). Lauren Edelman claims that the "managerialization of the law" (or the infusion of the law with managerial ideals) is so prevalent that it led the US to become a "symbolic civil rights society" (Edelman, 2016), while Frank Dobbin claims that diversity practices are adopted regardless of their efficacy, primarily to protect firms in courts (Dobbin, 2009, p. 209). We argue that this perspective on legal intermediation is too monolithic, and multiple case studies in this symposium corroborate this idea.

We find instances where legal intermediation actually succeeds in fulfilling the initial goals of regulation. Lisa Buchter's contribution, for instance, shows how activists co-opted French large corporations, and imposed an interpretation of anti-discrimination law that at times made a difference in the lives of the minorities whom legislation sought to protect. Camille Herlin and Alexis Spire show that professional intermediation of law does not always succeed in institutionalizing new interpretations of regulation and that the laypeople who buy their legal services sometimes contest their legitimacy. In her contribution on French hospitals, Fanny Vincent analyzes a contentious process of managerialization of labor law, where nurses and hospital managers clash over a legal rule allowing 12-hour work shifts. Jérôme Pélisse's contribution addresses the diversity of legal intermediation in a systematic way by identifying the factors that allow legal intermediaries to influence legality and impact the legal consciousness of their audience. Their ability to do so depends on the legal frame and legal instruments that they can harness, the profile of the legal professionals and/or the laypeople with whom they interact, and their relative power in their organizations. Finally, our findings also reevaluate the role of the legal devices that organizations set up to comply with regulation and illustrate their diverse impact on legality and legal consciousness in organizations and in economic life. Sebastian Billows shows that, depending on the audience, a single legal device can bear many different meanings and shape different legalities within the same organizational context, a feature which gives large corporations more autonomy in interpreting how they should comply with regulation. Alina Surubaru goes even further and outlines the intra-organizational conflicts that arise from complex legal instruments such as contracts, which weakens their ability to constrain future business behavior.

NOTES

1. While part of this literature describes the relation between law and economic activity as a top-down process, we focus our attention on the scholarship that views legal intermediation as a bottom-up process. The work on "regulatory capture" (Carpenter & Moss, 2014) constitutes an example of the top-down approach. This perspective situates legal intermediation as a chain link between laws and regulation – which have to be applied to the economic world – and the economic and social relations embedded in organizations, as if law and economy or organizations were two separate spheres, of which we have to study the interrelations. A bottom-up approach does not only start from the social relations but is anchored in a constitutive perspective, where law and organizations are conceived together, shaping mutually one another through, notably, the activities of such legal intermediaries.

2. This does not preclude us from analyzing borderline cases such as the French judicial expert, who stands in between laypeople and the legal profession, or the safety engineer working in a scientific institution, who must translate safety regulations into concrete rules readily usable by the scientists who conduct experiments.

3. Talesh is among the few exceptions (Talesh, 2009, 2015).

REFERENCES

Abbott, A. (2005). Sociology of work and occupations. In N. J. Smelser & R. Swedberg (Eds.), *Handbook of economic sociology* (pp. 307–330). Princeton, NJ: Princeton University Press.

Abbott, K., Levi-Faur, D., & Snidal, D. (2017). Theorizing regulatory intermediaries: The RIT model. *The Annals of the American Academy of Political and Social Science, 670*(1), 13–35.

Ansell, C., & Gash, A. (2008). Collaborative governance in theory and practice. *Journal of Public Administration Research and Theory, 18*(4), 543–571.

Bartley, T. (2007). Institutional emergence in an era of globalization: The rise of transnational private regulation of labor and environmental conditions. *American Journal of Sociology, 113*(2), 297–351.

Bartley, T. (2010). Transnational private regulation in practice: The limits of forest and labor standards certification in Indonesia. *Business and Politics, 12*(3), 1–34.

Bereni, L. (2011). Le Discours de la Diversité en Entreprise: Genèse et Appropriations. *Sociologies pratiques, 23*, 9–19.

Bereni, L., & Revillard, A. (2007). Des Quotas à la Parité: "Féminisme d'État" et Représentation Politique (1974–2007). *Genèses, 67*, 5–23.

Bessy, A., Delpeuch, T., & Pélisse, J. (2011). Droit et régulations des activités économiques. *Perspectives sociologiques et institutionnalistes*. Paris: LGDJ Editions.

Billows, S. (2016). La Politique de l'ambiguïté Juridique. Quand l'Etat Tente de Réguler Les Échanges Entre La Grande Distribution et Ses Fournisseurs. *Sociologie Du Travail, 58*(1), 8–31.

Bourdieu, P. (1987). The force of law: Toward a sociology of the juridical field. *The Hastings Law Journal, 38*(1971), 805–853.

Braithwaite, J. (1982). Enforced self-regulation: A new strategy for corporate crime control. *Michigan Law Review, 80*, 1466–1507.

Braithwaite, J. (2009). *Regulatory capitalism: How it works, ideas for making it work better*. London: Edward Elgar Publishing.

Burstein, P. (1985). *Discrimination, jobs, and politics: The struggle for equal opportunity in the United States since the new deal*. Chicago, IL: University of Chicago Press.

Carpenter, D. (2010). *Reputation and power: Organizational image and pharmaceutical regulation at the FDA*. Princeton, NJ: Princeton University Press.

Carpenter, D., & Moss, D. A. (2014). *Preventing regulatory capture: Special interest influence and how to limit it*. New York, NY: Cambridge.

Carpenter, D. P. (2001). *The forging of bureaucratic autonomy. Reputations, networks, and policy innovation in executive agencies, 1862–1928*. Princeton, NJ: Princeton University Press.

Chappe, V.-A. (2015). Les discriminations syndicales saisies par le droit à PSA. *La nouvelle revue du travail, 7*. Retrieved from https://journals.openedition.org/nrt/2324.

Dixon, M., & Martin, A. W. (2012). We can't win this on our own: Unions, firms, and mobilization of external allies in labor disputes. *American Sociological Review, 77*(6), 946–969.

Dobbin, F. (2009). *Inventing equal opportunity*. Princeton, NJ: Princeton University Press.

Edelman, L. (2016). *Working law: Courts, corporations, and symbolic civil rights*. Chicago, IL: The University of Chicago Press.

Edelman, L. B. (1992). Legal ambiguity and symbolic structures: Organizational mediation of civil rights lawl. *American Journal of Sociology, 97*(6), 1531–1576.

Edelman, L. B., Krieger, L. H., Eliason, S. R., Albiston, C. R., & Mellema, V. (2011). When organizations rule: Judicial deference to institutionalized employment structures. *American Journal of Sociology, 117*(3), 888–954.

Edelman, L. B., & Stryker, R. (2005). A sociological approach to law and the economy. In *The handbook of economic sociology* (pp. 527–551). Princeton, NJ: Princeton University Press.

Ewick, P., & Silbey, S. (1998). *The commonplace of law: Stories from everyday life*. Chicago, IL: University of Chicago Press.

Freeman, J., & Minnow, M. (2009). *Government by contract: Outsourcing and American democracy*. Cambridge, MA: Harvard University Press.

Galanter, M. (1974). Why the "Haves" come out ahead: Speculations on the limits of legal change. *Law & Society Review*, *9*(1), 95–160.

Galanter, M. (2013). Pourquoi les mêmes gardent l'avantage ? Introduction à la traduction française. *Droit et société*, *85*(3), 559–574.

Guillaume, C., Pochic, S., & Silvera, R. (2015). Dans Les Syndicats: Du Volontarisme à La Contrainte Légale. *Travail, Genre et Sociétés*, *34*(2), 193–198.

Gray, G., & Pélisse, J. (2019). Frontline workers and the role of legal and regulatory intermediaries, *Paper Presented at the Law and Society Association Annual Meeting*.

Hallett, T. (2010). The myth incarnate: Recoupling processes, turmoil, and inhabited institutions in an urban elementary school. *American Sociological Review*, *75*(1), 52–74.

Heyer, K., Baudot, P.-Y., Borelle, C., & Revillard, A. (2013). Droits Ou Quotas ? L' American with Disabilities Act (ADA) Comme Modèle Des Droits Des Personnes Handicapées. *Terrains & Travaux*, *23*(2), 127.

Hirschman, A. O. (1970). *Exit, voice and loyalty. Responses to decline in firms, organizations and states*. Cambridge, MA: Harvard University Press.

Horwitz, M. (1992). *The transformation of American law: The crisis of legal orthodoxy*. Oxford: Oxford University Press.

Huising, R. (2015). To hive or to hold? Producing professional authority through scut work. *Administrative Science Quarterly*, *60*(2), 263–299.

Huising, R., & Silbey, S. (2013). Constructing consequences for noncompliance: The case of academic laboratories. *Annals of the American Academy of Political and Social Science*, *649*, 157–177.

Kagan, R., Gunningham, N., & Thornton, D. (2003). Explaining corporate environmental performance: How does regulation matter. *Law & Society Review*, *37*(1), 51–90.

Kellogg, K. (2009). Operating room: Relational spaces and microinstitutional change in surgery. *American Journal of Sociology*, *115*(3), 657–711.

Lascoumes, P., & Le Bourhis, J.-P. (1996). Des 'Passe-Droits' aAux Passes Du Droit. La Mise En Oeuvre Socio-Juridique de l'action Publique. *Droit et Société*, *32*(1), 51–73.

Lempert, R., & Sanders, J. (1986). *An invitation to law and social science: Deserts, disputes and distribution*. Philadelphia, PA: University of Pennsylvania Press.

Levi-Faur, D. (2005). The global diffusion of regulatory capitalism. *The Annals of the American Academy of Political and Social Science*, *598*(1), 12–32.

Lieberman, R. C. (2015). Private power and American bureaucracy: The state, the EEOC, and civil rights enforcement. In J. T. Sparrow W. J. Novak, & S. W. Sawyer (Eds.), *Boundaries of the state in US history* (pp. 259–286). Chicago, IL: The University of Chicago Press.

Macaulay, S. (1963). Non-contractual relations in business. *American Journal of Sociology*, *28*(1), 55–67.

Majone, G. (1997). From the positive to the regulatory state: Causes and consequences of changes in the mode of governance. *Journal of Public Policy*, *17*(02), 139–167.

McCann, M. (1994). *Rights at work. Pay equity reform and the politics of legal mobilization*. Chicago, IL: University of Chicago Press.

McDonnell, M.-H., King, B. G., & Soule, S. A. (2015). A dynamic process model of private politics: Activist targeting and corporate receptivity to social challenges. *American Sociological Review*, *80*(3), 654–678.

Nelson, R. L., & Nielsen, L. B.. (2000). Cops, counsel, and entrepreneurs: Constructing the role of inside counsel in large corporations. *Law & Society Review*, *34*(2), 457–494.

Pélisse, J. (2004). *A la recherche du temps gagné. Sens et usages sociaux des règles autour des 35h*, Thèse de sociologie, Centre d'Etudes de l'Emploi, Université Marne la Vallée, p. 668.

Pélisse, J. (2005). A-t-on conscience du droit? Autour des legal consciousness studies, summary. *Genèses*, *59*(2), 114–130.

Pélisse, J. (2007). 7. Les Usages Syndicaux du Droit et de la Justice. In Jacques Commaille, J., & Kaluszynski, M. (Eds.), *La fonction politique de la justice* (pp. 165–189). Paris: La Découverte.

Pélisse, J. (2011). La Mise En OEuvre Des 35 Heures: D'une Managérialisation Du Droit à Une Internalisation de La Fonction de Justice. *Droit et Société*, *77*, 39–65.

Pélisse, J. (2017). Gérer les risques par le droit: articulation et intermédiation dans les laboratoires de nanosciences en France et aux Etats-Unis. *Droit et société*, *96*(2), 321–336.
Perrow, C. (1991). A society of organizations. *Theory and Society*, *20*(6), 725–762.
Revillard, A. (2017). Social movements and the politics of bureaucratic rights enforcement: Insights from the allocation of disability rights in France. *Law & Social Inquiry*, *42*(2), 450.
Selznick, P. (1969). *Law, society, and industrial justice*. New York, NY: Russell Sage Foundation.
Stryker, R. (2003). Mind the gap: law, institutional analysis and socioeconomics. *Socio-Economic Review*, *1*(3), 335–367.
Stryker, R., & Pedriana, N. (2004). The strength of a weak agency: Enforcement of title VII of the 1964 civil rights act and the expansion of state capacity, 1965–1971. *American Journal of Sociology*, *110*(3), 709–760.
Suchman, M. C. (2003). The contract as social artifact. *Law and Society Review*, *37*(1), 91–142.
Sutton, J. (2001). *Law/society: Origins, interactions, and change*. New York: Sage.
Talesh, S. (2009). The privatization of public legal rights: How manufactures construct the meaning of consumer law. *Law & Society Review*, *43*, 527–562.
Talesh, S. (2015). Legal intermediaries: How insurance companies construct the meaning of compliance with antidiscrimination laws. *Law & Policy*, *37*(3), 209–239.
Talesh, S., & Pélisse, J. (2018). How legal intermediaries facilitate or inhibit social change. *LIEPP Working Paper* no. 73.
Thatcher, M. (2014). From old to new industrial policy via economic regulation. *Rivista Della Regolazione Dei Mercati*, *2*, 6–22.
Vogel, S. K. (1996). *Freer markets, more rules: Regulatory reform in advanced industrial countries*. Cornell, NY: Cornell University Press.
Weber, M. (1978). *Economy and society*. Berkeley, CA: University of California Press.

"COMPANIES CAN DO BETTER THAN THE LAW": SECURING RIGHTS FOR MINORITIES AS AN INSIDER ACTIVIST IN FRENCH CORPORATIONS

Lisa Buchter

ABSTRACT

Previous theories discuss how corporate managers can stir anti-discrimination laws away from their initial social goal by managerializing the law. Yet, other actors – notably insider activists – can contribute to move corporate regulations beyond merely symbolic compliance. I demonstrate this influence of activists with three cases studies: (1) LGBT activists for same-sex parental leave; (2) disability rights activists for implementing a quota; and (3) Muslim activists to secure accommodations in French workplaces. Through these cases, I show how activists can move corporate laws beyond compliance, pressure firms to go from merely symbolic to substantive compliance, and analyze mechanisms that explain their unequal success. Bringing together insights from the legal endogeneity theory and social movements theory, I analyze these activist legal intermediaries as actors faced with unequal structure of opportunities, and examine what factors hinder or favor an activist-driven legal endogeneity. I demonstrate the impact of more prescriptive regulations, the institutional power of union representatives (and their alignment with activists' claims), reputational stakes for companies, and the resources of activists themselves (legal expertise, ability to reframe laws, and informal power within their organizations). Last, I show how activists

Legal Intermediation: A Processual Approach to Law and Economic Activity
Studies in Law, Politics, and Society, Volume 81, 11–44

ISSN: 1059-4337/doi:10.1108/S1059-433720190000081002

leverage organizational and legal tools (collective agreement, diversity policies) to induce recoupling between formal commitments and informal practices.

Keywords: Insider activists; legal endogeneity; anti-discrimination laws; social movements; diversity policies; legal intermediation

INTRODUCTION

Sociologists have explained how corporations attempt and succeed to circumvent their legal mandates. They identified a plethora of mechanisms – managerialization of the law, legal endogeneity of "merely symbolic compliance," or rebranding of human resources programs – that accounted for how corporate managers and personnel experts protected their firms from lawsuits while depoliticizing the laws they were subjected to (Dobbin, 2009; Edelman, 1991, 1992; Edelman, Fuller, & Mara-Drita, 2001). The employees, who interpreted how to comply with the law within corporations, usually tried to minimize corporate disruption by resisting both lawsuits and organizational change. By rebranding old practices without changing them, they acted against the spirit of the law they claimed to implement – anti-discrimination laws (Dobbin & Sutton, 1998; Kelly & Dobbin, 1998). While this theory is crucial in explaining the mediating role of employees in compliance design and in demonstrating why anti-discrimination laws fail to achieve their goals, it obscures some variability among corporations, and fails to explain why some private internal regulations achieve or surpass legal mandates.

This research starts with an empirical puzzle: French corporations developed varied and evolving responses to anti-discrimination laws. Corporations have ignored the disability quota in France for decades, paying the fine for non-compliance[1] (Barnay, Duguet, Clainche, & Videau, 2016). Starting in the late 1990s, and intensifying consequently after the 2005 law, a movement initiated in firms – and spearheaded by workers with disabilities – led to proactive compliance with this law in an increasing number of firms. Similarly, paid parental leave for same-sex couples was spearheaded by lesbian gay bisexual and trans (LGBT) affinity groups as a gender equality measure, and became institutionalized in large private corporations before the state secured it as a national right – providing a concrete example of activist-led legal endogeneity. While religious minorities initially received structurally similar legal protections as LGBT minorities within companies, they failed to secure comparable accommodations in the workplace.

These different responses to the law – from non-compliance to substantive compliance, or from symbolic compliance to granting rights and accommodations beyond compliance – show how the current theory that emphasizes the managerialization of the law and its tendency to dampen civil rights is insufficient to explain empirical variations. My analysis draws on Edelman's legal endogeneity theory, which contends that "law acquires meaning from (and thus becomes in part endogenous to) the social arenas that it seeks to regulate" (Edelman, Krieger, Eliason, Albiston, & Mellema, 2011, p. 890). I take the idea of social arena seriously by contending that the production of legal compliance to social policies is not only in the hands of corporate managers, but also involves other "legal intermediaries" (activists, union representatives) through both institutional and political processes.[2] The involvement of legal intermediaries promoting social change can account for why some companies go beyond sustaining an old arsenal of practices decoupled from political change (Berrey, 2015; Dobbin, 2009; Edelman, 2016).

The kind of legal intermediaries at the heart of my analysis was conceptualized in social movements' theory as "insider activists" – or employees acting for a social agenda to change their own hiring organization (Briscoe & Gupta, 2016). These insider activists also wish to take part in the production of private regulation in companies and in endogenizing new understanding of law and legal compliance, in this case anti-discrimination laws. This research will focus on insider activists who promoted new rights for minorities (i.e., gaining LGBT paid parental leave, developing hiring targets for workers with disabilities, securing halal food option for Muslim workers, etc.). I distinguish here two types of insider activists: (1) insiders activists claiming rights for minorities; and (2) union activists, because their agenda, institutional power and resources are different in nature.[3] While insider activists could argue that such rights could benefit the corporation – therefore making a business case for diversity (Noon, 2007)[4] – their primary goal was to secure rights, regardless of whether this was beneficial for the company or not.

I show how the structure of opportunities of these insider activists – that is their chances of success to acquire rights and accommodations within the workplace and take part in the design of private regulation – is the product of both the corporate legal environment and the broader social environment. Firms, indeed, attempt to appear legally compliant but also to sustain a good social reputation by supporting prosocial claims (King, 2008; McDonnell, King, & Soule, 2015), which sometimes led them to commit themselves beyond legal mandates.

From a theoretical standpoint, I will demonstrate that (1) insider activists can influence their organization through their involvement in the endogenous production of corporate regulations; (2) they rely on different mechanisms and legal devices (e.g., collective agreements) to influence these regulations according to legal and institutional contexts; and (3) the different power of insider activists (status, institutionalization of their cause, informal authority) strongly changes their ability to influence private regulations. My analysis relies on three case studies that show how minority activists have unequal success in securing rights for their groups through collaborating with unions in their firms. I analyze the high success of disability rights activists, the relative success of LGBT workers after the use of different strategies, and the failure of Muslim workers.

MANAGERIALIZATION OF THE LAW AS A DEPOLITICIZING FORCE

Many scholars wrote about the complexity of enforcing laws within corporations. When the state issues new laws, the means of compliance to these laws are unclear, ambiguous or too vague (Dobbin & Sutton, 1998; Edelman, 2016; Pedriana & Stryker, 2004). There is no such thing as a direct, straightforward enforcement of legal obligation. Studying the impact of anti-discrimination laws, these authors demonstrate that corporate managers mediate the response to the law by creating formal structure of compliances that change the laws' meaning (Dobbin, 2009, p. 131; Dobbin & Sutton, 1998; Edelman, 1992, p. 1532). Diversity programs are a form of "managerialization of the law" that "refashion[s] legal ideas that challenge traditional managerial prerogatives and suggest new ideas, which they claim are more innovative, more rational, and more progressive" (Edelman et al., 2001, p. 1596). These programs are employer-sponsored formal structures that aim to demonstrate firms' commitment to anti-discrimination.[5] Yet, this managerialization of the law often "undermine[s] legal ideals as managers shift the focus of attention from law to management" (Edelman et al., 2001).

The literature on legal endogeneity oftentimes points to how companies tend to depoliticize and dejudicialize the content of regulations and thus minimize corporate constraints (Edelman, Leachman, & McAdam, 2010, p. 658). Companies "creat[e] token or symbolic structures that pay tribute to this environmental pressure, while in practice transforming the meaning of law" (Edelman, Leachman, & McAdam, 2010, p. 667; Edelman et al., 2001). Similarly, Dobbin analyzes diversity programs as a rebranding of pre-existing practices – the personnel arsenal – that just changed names and justification to resonate with a new political climate (Dobbin, 2009, p. 226). Personnel experts justified them through a business case that was "building on executives' dual worries about increasing efficiency and avoiding lawsuits" (Dobbin, 2009, p. 134), thus far from anti-discrimination concerns (Dobbin, 2009, p. 112). As Dobbin concludes, there is still little evidence that the programs designed were efficient in neutralizing discrimination; their goal was to formally pick up best practices to avoid lawsuits (Dobbin, 2009, pp. 232–233).

The mechanisms explored by these authors account well for how corporate managers resist social change. Avoiding lawsuits and increasing efficiency replaced the social agenda of ensuring equality, undermining legal ideals and favoring a managerial vision of the law spearheaded by middle managers.

BRINGING ACTIVISTS BACK IN

While this article acknowledges the depoliticizing impact of the some managerialization of the law, I claim that other mechanisms influence legal endogeneity, in particular the goals and strategies of other oftentimes non-professional legal intermediaries shaping these regulations (cf. intro). While some research has started to show how the political commitment of managers affects the efficiency of diversity programs, therefore opposing a reified analysis of managers (Dobbin, Kim, & Kalev, 2011; Dobbin, Kim, & Kalev, 2012; Kalev, Kelly, & Dobbin, 2006), I focused my attention on the impact of insider activists. In the social movement literature, "insider activists" refer to employees who try to challenge their hiring companies to defend social claims (Briscoe & Gupta, 2016; Scully & Segal, 2002). Here, my analysis focuses on workers belonging to a minority and who claim new rights for this minority.[6] I argue that these activists may see diversity offices as an opportunity to challenge corporate regulations. Their actions oppose symbolic compliance, as they attempt to secure substantive rights and accommodations and refuse the depoliticization of legal ideals.

Scholars often assume that challenging companies from within is problematic and that resulting changes are "piecemeal" (Scully & Segal, 2002). Briscoe and Gupta describe how, because they are more dependent on the targeted organization than outsider activists, insiders cannot use disruptive, extra-institutional tactics such as boycotts or public shaming to pressure corporations to change (Bartley & Child, 2014; Briscoe & Gupta, 2016; King, 2008; King & Pearce, 2010). Meyerson and Scully describe them as "tempered radicals" to the extent that their multiple allegiances can lead to feelings of isolation and pressure to cooperate (Bell, Meyerson, Nkomo, & Scully, 2003; Meyerson & Scully, 1995; Scully & Segal, 2002). Yet, insider activists have the benefit of knowing the corporation well, which may help them to strategically appeal to corporate interests or weaknesses (Briscoe & Gupta, 2016). Such inner knowledge might be even more useful if activists call out the unsubstantiated symbolic claims of their companies and claim concrete rights and accommodations.

The role of insider activists in influencing private regulation remains under-investigated. Scholars have often portrayed identity movements' activists, such as the civil rights movement, as a purely external and preliminary force that has hardly any say in designing compliance (Dobbin, 2009, pp. 1–3). They described the actors involved in the endogenous interpretation of the law as a "counter-movement" resisting "social movements [and] legal and normative pressure" (Edelman et al., 2010, p. 658). Dobbin does refer to the demographic shift in the equal employment opportunity offices: "personnel was transformed from a bastion of white men with backgrounds in labor relations to a bastion of white women attracted by equal opportunity goals" (Dobbin, 2009, p. 9). Yet, he stresses how their primary goal was professional and not social, describing them as a "social movement [that morphed] into a professional project" (Dobbin, 2009). More recent research has explored the impact of "internal advocacy" on diversity programs, but their proxy for this advocacy was the presence of "white women in management" (Dobbin et al., 2011, pp. 388–389), therefore emphasizing narrow identity markers and occupational status. By contrast, I studied the strategies of insider activists who claimed to be activists and mobilized inside their companies (creation of a LGBT advocacy group, requests to unions). I differentiate identity-based activists from union organizers, because the case of union organizers is liminal in many respects. While union organizers also attempt to challenge their hiring companies to fulfill a social agenda, their high level of protection in France gives them more leverage to challenge companies (and they can therefore use disruptive tactics). In France, labor unions are pivotal in securing rights and monitoring the achievement of substantive equality in the workplace because they negotiate legally binding collective agreements, which are powerful legal devices.

If we can classify union organizers in France as insider activists, they would be insider activists with a high degree of power and institutionalization, so much so that they mediate the opportunity of identity-based activists to influence corporate regulation. As we will demonstrate in the analysis, union organizers are not equally sensitized to the identity-based claims of all minorities. They would, therefore, collaborate with some minorities to secure legally binding collective agreements but refrain from doing so with other minorities. In this sense, union organizers also constitute unequal resources for identity-based insider activists to secure new rights: they do not negotiate equal rights for all minorities, and they do not accept identity-based activism evenly within their ranks.[7] This difference between insider activists who are inside or outside of a union shows that there exist unequal status and institutional power of insider activists within companies. I, therefore factor in my analysis, the role of the status and legitimacy of insider activists by looking at the interaction between identity-based activists and union organizers, as well as the impact of making claims with unequal approval from the public opinion and the media.

The social movement literature explores how firms developed "impression management," and "social management devices[8]" to deflect social movements' attention without responding to activists' claims (McDonnell & King, 2013; McDonnell et al., 2015). They also theorized how such symbolic commitments might turn against firms as they increased activists' scrutiny and monitoring, and reinforced corporate accountability.[9] I argue that the same mechanism plays out with symbolic compliance to anti-discrimination laws. While middle managers hoped that creating diversity offices and adopting formal "best practices" would be enough to deter lawsuits, it also created new leverage for activists who wished to monitor and influence corporate practices (Baron, 2001). While the literature has stressed how activists monitor and influence corporations from outside (Baron, 2003, 2005; Bartley, 2007, 2010; Luders, 2006; Mena & Waeger, 2014), I study how insider activists challenge the managerialization of the law from within, bringing a new light on how social movements can influence companies (Edelman et al., 2010, p. 656).

My research answers the neo-institutionalist call for further research on which mechanisms could create effective anti-discrimination compliance that would enhance social reform (Edelman, 2016, p. 237). Since corporate compliance is produced endogenously, insider activists are well-situated challengers of symbolic compliance and impression management. By taking part in the definition of private regulation (corporate policies, collective bargaining), they can compel corporations to move toward more substantive compliance (cf. enforcing a still unenforced quota, case 2), or even toward securing new rights for minorities (cf. same-sex parental leave, case 1). Edelman envisioned the possibility for such influence, stating that "movements may motivate change more directly when compliance professionals within organizations become normative entrepreneurs, promoting social movement goals" (Edelman et al., 2010, p. 659), but did not acknowledge that such intermediaries needed not be legal professionals. Similarly, recent research explores how the feminization of diversity offices leads to more progressive reforms and argues that "identity groups successfully lobby for progressive social policies only when they win representation in powerful positions within a firm" (Dobbin et al., 2012, p. 22). Yet, the actual mechanisms through which identity groups gain leverage to influence diversity policies have not been empirically investigated.

BACKGROUND

The case of anti-discrimination in French corporations provides an opportunity to understand how the unequal status of insider activists affects their ability to influence legal endogeneity processes. To provide some context, I will discuss French anti-discrimination laws and give information about the specific status of unions in France, since French unions serve as an institutionalized pathway for endogenous regulation.

Anti-discrimination policies in France: France prides itself on a universalist model of formal anti-discrimination that is indifferent to differences and dismisses both the recording and measurement of difference and disparate treatment, such as positive discrimination, which are often considered as "reverse discrimination" (Calvès, 2016; Sabbagh & Peer, 2008). This explains why official statistics ignore race and ethnicity and why the main tool to fight racial bias in professional settings has been an unsuccessful attempt to implement anonymous resumes (that would take out the name, picture, age, and any identity markers from the CV of job applicants) – which is symptomatic of how equality is disconnected from the recognition of difference in France (Fraser, 2000). For all those reasons, French organizations have traditionally been a challenging environment for those promoting minorities' rights in the workplace through identity politics.

Yet, some social movements have challenged this ideology of "indifference to difference" as an unjust fiction (Bereni, Debauche, Latour, & Revillard, 2010; Bereni & Lépinard, 2004; Scott, 1997, 2009). Under the pressure of these activists, the French state has granted different exceptions to the principles of universalism. Parity laws are being expanded in France, monitoring of gender equality is strongly mandated in large corporations, and there is a quota of workers with disabilities. More subtly, the paradigm of diversity – an open and direct promotion of potentially discriminated minorities in the workplace – is progressively pervading French corporations (Bereni, 2011; Calvès, 2016; Doytcheva, 2009; Sénac, 2012). Diversity offices are a cultural and organizational tool designed to testify a firm's commitment to diversity that often focus on specific minorities, segmenting their actions in response to the legal trends perceived by personnel experts and diversity managers (Bereni, 2011; Dobbin, 2009; Doytcheva, 2009). Both the diversity paradigm and these new waves of anti-discrimination laws skyrocketed after 2000 (Bereni, 2011; Bereni & Lépinard, 2004; Doytcheva, 2009;

Maggi-Germain, 2010; Scott, 1997), providing an ideal site to study corporate responses to changes in their legal environments.

Unions: legitimate institutional pathway and pitfalls for identity politics: In the French context, the main pathway for involving insider activists in the endogenous regulation of companies is unions. They are the legitimate actors to buttress new rights and policies for employees within their corporations.[10] As the French labor code prescribes, the main mission of workers' representatives is to:

> present to employers all the claims – individual or collective – as they relate to wage, implementation of the Labor code and other regulations regarding social protection, health, security, as well as collective bargaining and agreements applicable in the company. (Labor Code, article L.2 313-1)

They have the legal and institutional legitimacy to engage in collective bargaining with firms' boards and to set objectives, implement policies and monitor compliance with the negotiated policies within companies (Bethoux, Desage, Mias, & Pélisse, 2013; Maggi-Germain, 2010; Pélisse, 2007, 2011). These collective negotiations give them opportunities to secure rights beyond the scope of the current legal system according to the "favor principle" (*principe de faveur*), which states that, whenever there is a discrepancy between the law and collective agreements signed with unions, the one that is the most favorable to employees needs to be implemented and respected.[11] Their leverage to bring about change in corporations is thus legally enforced, making them a crucial resource for social movements promoting minority rights.

Yet, there are limits to the unions' power: it depends largely on their legal expertise in different areas, and they do not invest in all issues equally. For example, unions do not work extensively on anti-discrimination and only slowly develop tools for monitoring compliance with collective bargaining (Pélisse, 2007, p. 178). Unions are also imbued with French cultural frames to address minority rights. For instance, they are historically meant to defend at once the rights of all employees (Pélisse, 2007, p. 169), according to a class-based logic rather than an identity politics logic[12] (Bernstein, 2005, p. 48; Piore & Safford, 2006).[13] The State historically provided them with a "representativeness presumption" (Nadeau, 2012; Pélisse, 2007) that served as ground for their power and has only been recently contested by emerging identity claims (Piore & Safford, 2006). These growing challenges to representativeness presumption led to a change through the law from August 2008, which required the election of union representatives (Bevort, 2011). Traditionally, unions mirrored the respect of formal anti-discrimination, and did not promote special treatment for certain identity categories, except for labor-based categories, to align with the French ideology that promotes "indifference to difference" (Monchatre, 2014; Sénac, 2012, p. 201), color blindness (Sabbagh & Peer, 2008) and the eviction of religion from the public sphere through Laïcité (Scott, 2009).

Yet, in the last decade, unions have evolved toward becoming a new social institution mimicking "interest groups" (Andolfatto & Labbé, 2006). If they do embrace some aspects of identity politics, these aspects are largely selective and legally-endorsed. Consequently, unions are a privileged place to study the potential institutional roadblocks faced by some minority insider activists within corporations. Looking at the claims that unions receive from minority groups and how they respond to them – as well as the type of identity-based claims that they support by allowing workers from minority in their rank – are a rich signal of unequal status and unequal treatment of different minorities.

CASE STUDIES AND METHODS

This chapter relies on three case studies of insider activists negotiating rights within their companies for the minorities they belong to: LGBT workers, disabled workers, and Muslim workers. I focused on activists working for large French corporations, because these companies were the most likely to give leverage to activists, as they are concerned with their social reputation and needed to have union representatives (Dobbin et al., 2012; King, 2008; King & Pearce, 2010; McDonnell & King, 2013; McDonnell et al., 2015).

I analyze identity claims as the rights and accommodations that minority groups seek to obtain in the workplace based on their identity, similarly to studies about the feminist movement in France, which was highly investigated.[14] I cast a new light on how other minority movements succeeded or failed to secure similar types of rights and social provisions within the workplace, and deliberately chose movements with unequal level of success to explore the types of mechanisms that could explain their different outcomes. I created a typology to classify and identify these claims and make them commensurable across categories. The main categories of claims relate to workforce representation, workplace accommodations, work hours' flexibility, and arenas for self-expression. Table 1 provides substantive examples of what these claims look like for each minority in the workplace. The claims that are underlined are the ones that

Table 1. Claims' Categorizations and Substantive Examples Across Social Groups.

	Employees with Disabilities	LGBT Employees	Muslim Employees
Workforce presence	Quota of 6%*	Prohibited discrimination	Prohibited discrimination
Workplace accommodation	Office accommodation*, accessibility of the workspace*	Space and time for affinity groups within the workplace, LGBT and allies breakfast	Prayer space at work, halal meals
Work hours flexibility	Flexible hours for adjusting therapy*, days off*, remote work*	Parental leave for same-sex parents*, day off for LGBT day, AIDS awareness day	Religious holidays day off, flexible hours during Ramadan, break for prayers
Arenas for self-expression at work	Week for disability inclusion*, conferences*, awareness day*, handouts*	LGBT inclusion posters, two yearly days of awareness campaign in France	Poster – Muslim calendars in locker room, hours of prayers

activists spearheaded in my case study. The other claims – not underlined – were claims mentioned in other interviews that I conducted with activists but that were not cited in the three case studies fleshed out in this chapter. The ones followed by a * are the ones secured by these activists.

This research assumes that it is not only scientifically sound, but also theoretically fruitful to compare these different types of workplace accommodations claimed by social groups as different as Muslims, LGBT employees, and workers with disabilities. This assumption relies on Brubaker's method to study identity (Brubaker, 2016), where he claims that comparison between social categories is an intellectual opportunity to study the micro-politics of identity (Brubaker, 2016, pp. 415–416), and the "policing of identity claims" (Brubaker, 2016, p. 421). By stating that identity claims are comparable regardless of the said identities, Brubaker strips these categories from their normative values and essentialist components. This approach might seem counter-intuitive, as these categories are imbued with normative discourses and essentialist assumptions. The understanding of a category as ascribed or acquired, essential or constructed, visible or not, as a source of pride or of shame, or as a legitimate ground for political action is socially constructed and fluid in history. Pride and political legitimacy, in particular, are not inherent to categories, but are often advocated for by social movements. These dichotomies also operate along a continuum depending on context and on individual case.[15] While I acknowledge that these debates exist, this is not what my analysis will focus on. Comparing rights and accommodation claims enables me to study how these categories are politically constructed, how people can mobilize around them, as well as the inequalities of legitimacy and resources available to each.

This research is based on more than 40 in-depth interviews with insider activists and union representatives working to secure rights and accommodation in the workplace,[16] as well as textual analysis of the texts (union literature, newspaper coverage, etc.) covering the claims and actions of insider activists across categories. These interviews were conducted between 2013 and 2018, as a subsection of a larger research project about the impact of social movements on workplace rights and accommodations, as being an "insider activist" in only one of the ways through which social movements can attempt to influence corporate practices. While my findings are consolidated by interviews with several activists, I chose to focus my case studies on fleshing out the different strategies of a single activist for each category, because doing so, helped me build heuristic narratives to show how these activists navigated their unequal structure of opportunity through a social constructionist lens. While I discuss each time the extent to which this single narrative reflects, what I observed in other interviews I hold that one of the virtues of qualitative case study is to bring insights into how individual actors navigate their social world, make sense of their goals, their mission, and the roadblocks preventing them to achieve those, which is best captured by fine-grained analysis of individual trajectory and narrative (Daly, 2007; Ch1).

My first case study about LGBT claims describes how a lesbian activist managed a *tour de force*, by creating an advocacy group that opened up opportunities for similar groups in other corporations and culminated in the creation of a national law for paid parental leave for same-sex couples in France in 2012 (case study 1). My analysis will flesh out the strategies of the LGBT activist who endogenously secured new rights in her company, before discussing synthetically the trajectories of other LGBT activists who followed her path during the same period. The negotiation of collective bargaining in favor of the employment of disabled workers (case study 2) is an even more widespread strategy, but I elaborate on one representative case to show how one activist was enough to initiate a full collective agreement process, and how she relied on a complex strategy based on law, diversity offices, and union's cooptation to influence corporate policies and spearhead the implementation and monitoring of changes in favor of disabled workers. Since I could not identify a similar successful case for Islam (case study 3), I used it as a negative case by analyzing newspapers' coverage to show how Muslim claims existed but were being dismissed when brought to the unions. To complement this perspective, I relied on the literature written by the union confederations themselves to demonstrate how the collaboration with Muslim rights activists was perceived as being problematic. This enables me to lay out some conditions for insider activism to successfully influence corporate regulation.

FINDINGS

Case 1: Maternity and Paternity Leave for Gay Parents, a Union-based and Reputation-based Strategy

In the current French legislation, LGBT people's rights in the workplace are only secured under a neutral, formal right for equality, and anti-discrimination. Before 2012, there were no additional provisions for defending specific rights and claims of LGBT employees in the private sector. Yet, in this case study, a lesbian activist, who spearheaded the creation of an LGBT affinity group in her IT company, explains how she navigated both unions and diversity offices to secure maternity and paternity leave for all LGBT couples in her corporation. Her success further triggered the passing of a national law to secure this right for all gay parents in 2012 – a perfect example of the power of endogenous legal change to positively affect national legislation (Edelman et al., 2011).

Martha is a lesbian engineer who worked for more than a decade in the headquarters of her IT company – here called *Technormas*. After having experienced harassment from one of her managers because of her sexual orientation, she started to think about how to be actively involved in the defense of LGBT rights in her workplace. Her commitment led to the creation of *Tech-Homos*,[17] an affinity and advocacy group for the LGBT employees of her company. *Tech-Homos* became a social network and a hotline for discrimination within the whole company. In the following verbatim, Martha recounts how she first got involved in trying to influence the policies of her corporation:

> One day, one female employee called me and said, "I am in a couple with another woman. She will bear our child, and I would like to know whether or not I could benefit from paternity

leave." [...] So I reached out to the diversity manager and he said, "Don't worry, we will make her a special treatment, she will have her leave." And so I answered: "Well, I think you did not really understand me. I don't want any special treatment, no confidentiality, no one-time favor. I want this right to be open." "Oh but the law [...]" So I start launching the unions on the topic. They were not at all acquainted with this cause, except maybe for the CGT[18] because they have a LGBT task force. And so the CGT delegated me to the table of negotiation for the collective bargaining around Professional Equality between men and women. Because I was thinking, "Yes, that's it. If we are going to negotiate it, it should be in a collective agreement. So Women-Men Equality, I thought to myself, perfect: lesbians don't have paternity leave so they are discriminated against, because men have it." (Martha, engineer in *Technormas*, founder of its LGBT network *Tech-Homos*[19])

This first part of the interview shows how joining a union is perceived as a way to secure rights for all workers and avoid individual special treatment or one-time favors. Yet, Martha mentions that few unions had enough expertise about and commitment for LGBT parental rights. Some federal-level unions were aware of the question, but local representatives did not appear to her as equipped or willing to negotiate on the question. Therefore, she asked to join one union and could only manage to be at the table of negotiation by joining an already aware union (they already had a task force specialized on the topic). Second, to make claims for LGBT workers, Martha deliberately connected them with gender equality rights, which are a state-endorsed and even state-mandated topic for negotiation.

In her view, the legal protection of LGBT people was insufficient, and this was used by her interlocutor in the diversity office to deny the importance of this topic of conversation. During the initial meetings for the negotiation of the collective agreements – Martha recounts – her claims for LGBT workers were systematically denied by the executive board. Joining the union was an attempt to rely on legally sanctioned paths of action to claim substantive rights, yet she had no institutional power there:

When I arrived at the negotiation table, everyone tried to kick me out, the diversity manager, the union representatives – from the other [unions]. And they were telling me, "listen, Martha, here we are talking about the important matters: men-women equality, wage equality, promotions. Your topic it will be for a later diversity agreement." I said: "No, I am here, I am staying" [And so how did it end?] Well the manager would only say: "I take your point," and I answered "I could write you the text [for the policy] if that's simpler." (Martha, engineer in *Technormas*, founder of its LGBT network *Tech-Homos*)

This excerpt illustrates the fact that insider activists also managerialize the law by making every effort so that the company could smoothly incorporate their rights into their management practices. A similar phenomenon happened here, as Martha wrote the text to be included in the collective agreement, provided the rationale for a LGBT clause in a gender agreement, and framed it later on as a reputational asset for the companies. This first legally-mediated action did not work though, and Martha used a strategy of action relying widely on this new significance of the company's image and reputation stake to pursue her political agenda. The way she obtained paternity leave for same-sex couples clearly relies on this reputation-mediated mechanism:

> It all started with a meeting with the Human Resource Director – poor lady – who received us, me and the vice-president, to talk about Tech-Homos. She was constrained to meet us by the CEO, whom I came across and who asked for us to be received. And so I took advantage of this opportunity to talk about this request [of same-sex paternity leave], and she told me, "Oh but of course!," I answered "Of course?," and she went on, "But Martha, I would even go further: not only for lesbians, but for gays as well, we don't want to create discrimination!" I answered, "Of course [...]" and she went on, "Companies can do better than law." She is the one who said that, and so when [the vice president and I] got out of there, we glanced at each other, and we said "Press release!" With her quote: "Companies can do better than law." After that I hugged the wall. So we posted a press release, we didn't quote her name but we said the HRD of [Technormas] (laughter). So we said we were thrilled, we obtained an agreement in principles, it's wonderful, everyone loves everyone! The catch is that one week later, the Figaro [French nationwide newspaper] called the HRD for an interview. The Figaro! We couldn't have expected better! (laughter) So I was quietly in my office and I got a call from the directors of the group asking me, "Are you crazy? Do you realize what you just did?!" [...] And eventually she confirmed to the Figaro, and then it became hectic, we could no longer handle all the interviews' requests that we got, from TV channels and all. (Martha, engineer in *Technormas*, founder of its LGBT network *Tech-Homos*)

By quoting the human resource director in a press release, Martha made the company publicly accountable and created a direct relationship between same-sex paternity leave and the company's reputation. This reputational stake – and the potential for the company to appear as socially vanguard and "better than the law" – mediated Martha's success to legally bind the company. As the question became public, the company decided to enact this right through the collective agreement signature and this company became the first one in France to ensure maternity and paternity leave for gay couples. This case shows the intertwining of legal and reputational concerns for corporations, as well as the multiplicity of the tactics used by insider activists – navigating both legal and reputational mechanisms. Labor unions are still pictured, in this story, as the source of legitimate legal change and right acquisition. Yet, this activist does not fully identify with unions. After this collective agreement, Martha left the board of union representatives, as she felt that the defense of LGBT rights was more an encroachment and an exception in the work of the union than the rule.

This section discusses the acquisition of one right through legally sanctioned agreement (parental paid leave for same-sex couples) at the scale of one corporation (work schedule accommodation). Although these are not the center of attention here, the fact that a LGBT affinity group was authorized within the company also constitutes a cultural recognition and workspace accommodation (ability to meet for LGBT awareness events within the headquarters). These two last accommodations were not legally binding rights: they were granted by the diversity office, which is a voluntary corporate structure. The collective agreements offering same-sex parental leave, though, had significant repercussions. Other groups (I interviewed activists in three of them) followed the example of this activist and managed to secure the same right in other corporations, and even in some areas of the public sector. Following this movement, this right was secured through a national law which passed in the same year (2012). We see here, therefore, how different types of mechanisms are used to bind the company to its prosocial commitment: some mechanisms involve agreements that are legally binding (such as the rights encoded in collective bargaining), while others are strengthened by public and media scrutiny (threat of press release, etc.). The latest strategy seems to be frequent in the United States, where labor unions do not have the same institutional power, but where companies are held accountable for their prosocial commitments by activists (McDonnell et al., 2015).

This example shows how LGBT activists remain marginal for unions, but how they could still use unions to secure social rights through collective agreements. Their strategy is not purely legal though, as it plays with the reputation of the corporation attached to its diversity commitment. Here, the final response of the French legal system – endorsing this right at the national level, a couple of months after its acquisition in a couple of public and private organizations – shows the overall support of the state for LGBT claims. This adds to Edelman's theory of endogenous production of regulation (Edelman et al., 2011) by showing that endogenous regulation is indeed impactful, but that it is not solely at the hands of managers trying to restrict the scope of the law. In this case, the endogenous change propelled national rights after having been secured in private companies by insider activists.

Case 2: Joining a Union to Create Collective Agreements and Disability Department

This second case study shows how one insider activist – Annie – managed to use unions to negotiate a full collective agreement on disabled workers' rights and inclusion in her company. In contrast with the first case, the activist here managed to secure a whole collective agreement (versus one right), and subsequently obtained a position as a "disability manager" to oversee and implement the agreement's many accommodations that she negotiated. She then spearheaded the disability office, which is a specialized and structurally equivalent version of the diversity offices studied by different authors (Dobbin, 2009). This case, therefore, shows the interplay between union-secured rights and diversity offices' works.

The legal context of this success story is different. Since 1987, companies have had a legally mandated quota of employing 6% of workers with disabilities. Yet companies have ignored this quota consistently for over 20 years and would rather pay the fine for non-compliance than hiring more workers with disabilities (Barnay et al., 2016; Blatge, 2010). In 2005, the State designed a new disability law that both drastically increased the fine for not meeting the quota,[20] and provided further blueprints on the different ways this legal obligation could be met. One of the ways this obligation can be met is to design a collective agreement on disability inclusion, validated by union representatives and by a state agency (Maggi-Germain, 2010). Even though this collective bargaining is not mandated as in the case of women, I contend that it is state-incentivized, as it enables corporations to not pay the fine for not meeting their quota.

This case study shows how disability rights activists played a crucial role in moving corporations from "paying the fine" (Barnay et al., 2016) to actually negotiating collective agreements, developing accommodations and implementing policies for the inclusion of workers with disabilities. While in the first case, the role of insider activists was to secure a right that was not yet secured at the national level, the role of insider activists for disabled workers was to enforce laws by pushing companies to go beyond paying the fine for not meeting their quota.

Annie had been working in her company – a consulting firm with over 10,000 employees – for more than 15 years. She was diagnosed with a degenerative and invisible disease early in her career, but it did not hinder her ability to work for several years. At the time of the interview, though, she had to resign from her job because she could no longer maintain part-time employment. She saw her company, and her close managers, as very understanding and supportive of her situation. In the last seven years of her career in the company, she was the head of the disability office that she created in order to support disabled workers. In the following interview quote, Annie recounts how she decided to promote both the signature of a collective negotiation for disabilities and the creation of a disability office in her company:

> I think my interest in disability in companies came before my own health issue got too tricky. I was hanging out with some union organizers who told me: "You know, the 2005 law, there is this new law that recommends a collective agreement on disabilities in companies." And so I said: "Hell that's new, that's great. What an evolution!" And so I started digging into this and I must say, it was like in 2007, before it got, you know. Because between the time the law gets passed and people hear about it you always have some lag, right? So it took two big years. And what really got me interested is that there was this new occupation in company, that would enable you to take care of disability in the corporation. It was not HR, it was not was not [...] It was a new occupation. And you still did not have any training in this area. You would become disability coordinator – they called it like this at this point. They were advising the negotiation of a collective agreement, to appoint a disability coordinator, and this position, I told myself: "I want it." I said I want to do that. (Annie, disability manager, disabled herself, creator of the disability office of her IT company)

In this quote, we can see how the 2005 law is really at the origin of Annie's initiative to promote the creation of a disability office. This leads us to wonder about the existence of an organizational-level form of legal consciousness. In this narrative, Annie tells how the law came to her knowledge late after its creation – a two-year gap – through the intermediation of union representatives who knew such collective agreements was a increasingly interesting option and therefore reached out to her because of her commitment to disability rights. The following excerpt shows how the companies themselves did not seem knowledgeable about these legal changes and stakes, and stresses the role that activist insiders played in diffusing the knowledge of this law within their hiring corporation:

> They [the executive directors] didn't realize this was a stake? No clue! They had never heard about, neither the agreement, nor anything! And so it was [...] When I am telling you I was

> doing politics, I went to defend this at the direction board [...] Yet [...] Well the asset I had, to give you a little bit of context, my asset was that I was part of the top management in my branch in the West. So when I want to talk about the HR director about the necessity of a corporate agreement, I did not talk from a moral standpoint. I truly sold her the thing by saying: "here we are, today, you don't realize this but I can tell you that you are paying a 3 million euros tax per year. So what I am offering you is to stop paying it. If you follow me, we can establish this collective agreement, etc [...] I am taking care of everything, I take this position, I make it work and this way [...]" So yes, they followed. But because first I was bugging them. But also because it was difficult to say no, given the way I presented the thing, and knowing that they did not know anything. They had no clue what they were getting into. No clue! And the asset it gave me, is that they gave me carte blanche, in terms of how to spend the budget, in a way that very little disability office have had. [...] So I would say they trusted me, but behind it, if you asked me about law [...] Regarding disability, I knew everything by heart, because since 2007, when I started to think about creating this agreement, I only thought about this. (Annie, disability manager, herself disabled, creator of the disability office of her company)

This excerpt demonstrates again how activists can contribute to the managerialization of the law. In this case, we see how disability managers developed a lay expertise (Epstein, 1995) in the legal requirements of corporations in order to promote an active enforcement of the law within their firms.[21] In other cases, my interviewees reported taking part in networks for sharing good practices to garner organizational knowledge about how to enforce such quotas through private regulation within corporations. Annie used the law to build a case for enforcing disability employment policies within her corporation. Because not respecting the law was associated with a fine, she also built a business case for being proactive about disability inclusion. It also underlines how she had an active role in the diffusion of the legal consciousness of this law within her corporation, and how she took part in the process of endogenous creation of compliance policies (Edelman et al., 2011, p. 890). Looking at how one's identity and previous activist commitments play out in the choice of who creates compliance policies within a corporation could add more complexity in the stories of compliance design. This story is indeed quite different from the one recounted by Dobbin (Dobbin, 2009, p. 41) about how personnel managers recycled their professional arsenal to meet new compliance needs, regardless of the spirit of the law. Here, the tools for compliance have been missing for decades, and the involvement of activists have produced tools of compliance that were institutionally new and also substantively improved the situation for workers with disabilities (secure a budget for workplace accommodation, agree with remote work and schedule accommodation, awareness campaigns, recruitment targets, etc.).

Yet, as in the LGBT case above, Annie's strategy was largely mediated by the role of unions. She gained leverage and legitimacy by articulating her claims to the regime of collective bargaining. The stronger leverage for enforcing performative disability policies – collective negotiation – was in the hand of union representatives. For this reason, most of the disability managers I interviewed got involved in unions to make sure that a collective agreement was negotiated, and thus on their terms. In the next interview excerpt, Annie explained why she joined a union in order to be better seated at the table of negotiation before she was appointed disability manager:

> And so you joined the union at some point? I had to in order to [...] So it was the sine qua non condition for me to be the one to negotiate the agreements. Because I was not interested in a shitty agreement, and what you have to understand is that in the union world, they did not understand anything either: like what is an agreement, what we should have in a collective agreement for disability inclusion? They had no clue. There was no available example. Afterwards examples came out for ideal collective agreements, but at that time there were none. So I thought to myself, I have to do it. If that's me, that's better. We are our own best advocates. (Annie, disability manager, insider activist, creator of the disability office of her IT company)

In this case, Annie points to her own expertise about the question of disability inclusion to claim her place in the unions and be at the table of negotiation. Even as a disability manager later in time, she used this strategy as a way to make sure that the agreements were moving forward as fast as she wanted to:

> I joined the union a second time, within my company, because I wanted it to move forward faster, and I wanted an agreement at the national level. And, it was a fertile ground in my company, because they just moved the HR directory in a single juridical unit, so they needed an election of union representatives, and I raised my hands. I said: "this way, group-wide agreement: this is all I want. The other negotiation, you have the hand, this is not my thing. But I want to negotiate the group-level disability agreement." All this knowing that the offer from the company's side, I am the one who has written it. At some point, I was wearing two hats, it was nice. But thanks to that I managed to get at 95% the things I wanted to have in this agreement. (Annie, disability manager, insider activist, creator of the disability office of her IT company)

This excerpt is enlightening in different respects. It shows how insider activists interested in disability rights could navigate the union-centered opportunity structure to defend their claims. To be involved in the negotiation process of collective agreement, they stress that they have better knowledge of disability needs and of the stakes of negotiation than their peers in unions. They defend the implementation of collective agreements – not mandatory but recommended by the law – because those agreements appear compelling as they create a structure that is monitored annually by the State and requires incremental improvement of the inclusion of workers with disabilities.

As I asked further questions regarding the terms and rights secured through this collective agreement, Annie told me that it encompassed a target of yearly recruitments of workers with disabilities (workforce claims), a budget allocated to accommodate the workspace of disabled workers, a safe space for them to exchange with her on their challenges (workplace accommodation), possibility for telecommuting or potential days off for health purposes (work schedule accommodation), and training and awareness campaigns for managers in order to better accommodate their new disabled colleagues (cultural recognition). All these rights were legally sanctioned as they were part of collective agreements subjected to yearly monitoring by unions and needed to be renewed by a State agency every three years. This collective agreement was initially negotiated within one of the firm's branches before being expanded to the whole corporation.

Here, the connection between endogenous regulation and national law is different from the LGBT case above: the role of insider activists was mainly to enforce a pre-existing right. Annie, along with most of my interviewees who were disability managers and identified as "activists," ($n = 17$) claimed that her role was crucial in making these structures not only existing (versus absent when the firms paid the quota), but also substantial and not purely symbolic. She was, for instance, very critical of corporations that used too much of their disability inclusion budget for communication, when it should be geared toward accommodations for the disabled workers.

In her article, Edelman shows how ambiguous legal injunctions "give organizations wide latitude to construct the meaning of compliance," leaving room for mediating mechanisms to move from the legal text to the institutionalization of compliance structures (Edelman, 1992, p. 1532). While Edelman mostly focuses on how middle managers produce the compliance mechanisms that get institutionalized afterwards in the courts by "testing" and "negotiating" forms of compliances (Edelman, 1992, p. 1535), I hope to contend here that activists can become another intermediary of the law and offer alternative forms of compliance that enters into this institutional negotiation. In my analysis, activists are able to push their own agenda by altering the legal consciousness of organizations and offering what they frame as safer or more beneficial compliance strategies.[22] Interestingly, the negotiation of this collective bargaining (legal, formal) gave birth to a disability office (specialized version of diversity office focused on the inclusion of disabled workers). This shows the interplay between union and diversity offices, despite their antagonistic description in the literature (as unions are enforcing rights while diversity offices are perceived as being more the vector of producing "merely symbolic compliance"). Like most of my interviewees who pushed for the negotiation of a collective bargaining, Annie took the direction of this disability office and left the union to implement policies on the employers' side.

The French legal system created an institutional pathway for union representatives to get involved in the designing of private regulation of disability employment, and therefore in the making of compliance structures. What I underlined in this section is how disability rights activists coopted the union network to be involved in this designing process of endogenous regulation. Over a decade, most Fortune 40 companies have attempted to implement collective agreements for disability inclusion. While I cannot claim that activists played a role in all of these local implementations,[23] they defended the institutionalization of collective bargaining and the creation of disability offices in many cases by building a business case for these structures. The case presented here is emblematic of many interviews I conducted with the creators of disability offices.[24] Oftentimes, the first generation of disability managers were themselves disabled and operated as legal and institutional entrepreneurs to create policies for the inclusion of disabled workers and enforce them. Dobbin discusses how adopting formal "best practices" was a low-cost way to avoid lawsuits, and explained the diffusion of such practices (Dobbin, 2009, p. 232). Yet, if activists define what are the best practices in the first place, they can diffuse and institutionalize practices that are more tailored to their social agenda.

Case 3: The Negative Case of Muslim's Rights

Despite thorough research, I could not interview Muslim insider activists who actually managed to secure targeted rights and accommodations visibly and at a large scale in their companies – let alone to secure them through institutional tools like collective agreements.[25] This section will rely on different examples, to show that the failures to secure accommodations and rights for Muslim activists during my fieldwork were not anecdotal but spoke to structural challenges faced by these insider activists when trying to secure similar rights and accommodations as other minorities.

The legislative backdrop for Muslim rights in company was initially similar to the one of LGBT minorities: they are both defended horizontally by one section in the Labor Code preventing discrimination in the workplace.[26] Yet, contrary to the LGBT case, new laws regulating civic life after 2004 became restrictive of religious freedom. For instance, a law in 2004 prohibited the use of "ostentatious" religious signs in schools, a public report stated in 2013 that schools were not responsible for providing halal option for lunch. Laws also restricted the right to religious expression in the workplace, and notably the new 2016 Labor law reinforced the principle of religious neutrality in the workplace and the European court gave more leeway to prohibit religious expression in the workplace.[27] Despite a seemingly horizontal ban of discrimination, these laws therefore send a signal that religious freedom was a contentious issue for companies.

As I inquired further to meet Muslim workers involved for Muslim rights,[28] I found that the ones I met were involved in securing rights outside of their workplace, but did not focus their attention on securing rights within their workplace, or only at the margins:

> My priority would be to make sure that women wearing hijab do not get fired or left behind because of this in my company, but I don't feel like I am in the right position to monitor that. (Mohammed, practicing Muslim employee, otherwise involved for religious rights)

> It would be nice to have an easier schedule during Ramadan, but this seems like a too tense topic as of today. This is the same as praying: I have talked to people who got into trouble to look for possibilities to pray in [name of the company], so even if I would rather do all my prayers, I don't feel like [company's name] is ready for that. (Karim, practicing Muslim employee, otherwise involved for religious rights).

To give more substance to this negative case – Muslim failing to secure ongoing and legally binding rights for their minorities in the workplace – I wish to show how the structure of opportunity to claim rights was not as promising as for the two other studied groups. To demonstrate this, I conducted a review of the newspapers' articles I could find in the last 15 years mentioning simultaneously "Muslim" or "Islam" and "labor unions" in French newspapers[29] as well as and archives from unions and Muslim rights' literature.[30]

First, these data enabled me to identify the existence of Muslim claims in the workplace. The claims mentioned in these articles are numerous: asking for accommodation for Muslims' dietary restrictions – halal meat – claims for a space to pray during the work breaks (workspace accommodation), days off for religious celebrations and more flexible hours during the Ramadan month (working schedule accommodations), non-discrimination for women with headscarves or men with beards (workforce-related claims). Yet, such claims were perceived as threatening, as it was described in a press conference from the *Mouvement des Indigènes de la République* (MIR), the movement of Republique's indigenous:

> Dozen of Muslim employees from the Roissy Airport (security agents, luggage handlers, cleaning staff [etc.]) lost their work badge, delivered by the state administration, which enabled them to access to the zones said "sensitive with regards to security." They are now forbidden to work, and firing processes are under way. Their firing came with humiliating discourses, blackmail, which were univocally racist. The flawed arguments from the state authority claiming that these employees might be "connected to fundamentalist movements with a potential terrorist goal" collapse by themselves. Presumed guilty because they are Muslim, they underwent abominable questioning, which sole purpose was to assess their respect of the principles of the Muslim faith. The questions had no relationship with any security necessity, as was officially stated, unless we accept the idea that the sole fact of being Muslim is crime-inducing. (MIR, press conference, November 14, 2006)

These claims also did not receive similar support from unions as the claims described above for disabled workers or LGBT employees. The strategy of joining a union to secure rights and accommodation did not pay off as well for Muslim workers as it did for these other groups. In the following interview excerpt with a union representative published in a newspaper, we see both that joining a union is a common strategy and that claiming accommodations after joining a union was perceived as highly problematic from the union's perspective:

> I know a high number of Muslim union members in many company, where this does not create any issue, repeats André Milan. However, cronyism, religious entryism, are dangers to which unions are exposed." […] The case of radical leader bringing on silver platter 100 or 200 members to a union in exchange for its commitment to negotiate specific advantages (prayer room, abusive schedule accommodations, separatism) are not rare, and constitute a real pressure on union. (Slate, June 09, 2017)

This excerpt is enlightening, because it shows that the strategy of joining a union to claim rights is used by Muslim insider activists as well as other groups, but it perceived in a quite different light. While one insider activist from LGBT minorities or disability rights movements could join union to negotiate new rights relatively easily, a similar practice, carried on by several Muslim workers, was framed as threatening and abnormal.

In the interviews I conducted, people mentioned being granted rights at an individual level: having a vegetarian option for collective lunch (to avoid non-halal meat), being allowed to skip the lunch break during Ramadan and leave earlier from work. Yet, as was mentioned in the LGBT case, having one-time, voluntary accommodation is not as impactful as securing a right at a collective level, where this would be either legally binding or under public scrutiny, so that the firms could be held accountable. Yet, attempting to secure such accommodations for Muslim workers triggered important backlashes, as one can see in the following case. The provision of halal meat in collective catering did not get secured for a long time when it was offered thanks to a union. The CGT passed it for a short amount of time in 2011 in a company with most Muslim workers, and that this case is now referred to as a "scandal" in many newspapers. The following excerpt of a newspaper article is enlightening to see how this affair was framed in the media:

> Sophie still remembers well the case of halal meat in the Roissy Airport. It was in 2011: "The CGT wanted to impose halal meat in the employees' catering service. There were petitions, outcries. It turned out very bad" [...]. The affair indeed made waves in the airport company. Many other unions, CFDT and CFTC[31] first, entered the fray.[32] They denounced a drift toward communitarianism orchestrated by the powerful federation, for a long time Air France's largest union. (France 24, December 18, 2015)

This "scandal" was mentioned in seven articles from different newspapers in my dataset, and it hurt the position of the CGT union in the corporation. Accused, even by leftwing newspapers, to have been "infiltrated by fundamentalists" (Marianne, 2016), it was compelled to "clean up its ranks" (Marianne, 2016) and therefore excluded some of the most vocal Muslim activists from the union. This action of rejecting Muslim activist was consequential for the union: the CGT claimed to have lost over 500 of its 2000 members in Air France after firing Muslim activists from its board of representatives. The union representatives tried to answer – sometimes in a contradictory way[33] – to this powerful backlash from both other unions and the media. The outcome of this show of strength led the CGT to withdraw their offering of halal meat altogether:

> We did not know that the 250kg of Charolaise and Limousine meat [French regions] that the work council ordered was halal" said David Ricatte – the spokesperson of CGT Air France – to defend himself, "We realized that at the delivery. The comrades might have made a mistake by assessing poorly the outcome of this affair. Today we no longer want halal meat in our canteen," went on the union representative. (Les Echos, February 25, 2013)

This excerpt is symptomatic of how accommodations were more easily secured under the radar for Muslim minorities. In contrast with the two previous cases, where granting accommodation became a reputational asset for the company or the unions (who could demonstrate with those their commitment to diversity), securing accommodations for Muslim workers was highly contentious. Here, endorsing the option of halal meat proved challenging for this union, so much so that they ended up stepping back. In a communiqué of the CGT, they reiterated their support to *Laïcité* and Republican values, denied that they created a halal restaurant – instead adding doner sandwiches, which use halal meat, and offering halal grill – and reframed this religious claim in terms of "restaurants with a social utility for the discovery of culinary cultures" (CGT Air France).[34] This opposition between Republican values and Muslim accommodations led unions to see the defense of Muslim claims as a risky endeavor. The support of Muslim claims are framed in the media as a threat, as we can see in the following excerpt:

> The situation is even more serious in subcontracting agencies, like Servair, one of the branches of Air France where the overwhelming majority of workers are of Muslim culture," said one of the employees of the Paris airport with a concerned tone. "Some union representatives pass on claims for prayers' room, halal catering, and work schedule accommodation to respect their religious practices. (Les Echos, February 25, 2013)

The tone here "even more serious," "overwhelming," to describe claims that relate to workplace accommodation, work schedule accommodation and dietary option, clearly shows how these claims are negatively perceived. Halal meat is therefore no exception in this respect. These claims are associated with an idea of radical practices, sectarianism and the looming fear of terrorism. To demonstrate these associations, the following table summarizes this prevalence of negative connotations of Islam. I constructed this table based on an inductive approach to the texts, looking up at words or expression that frequently collocated; the words "radical" and "radicalization" or "fundamentalism" were often collocated with Muslim claims in the workplace (prayers room, halal meat, etc.). These perceived phenomena of radicalization were often associated with a reminder of the threat of terrorism in France, or to a social critique of Muslim communities to develop a sectarian attitude. In France, the concept of "communautarism" – a derogatory term denoting a negative outlook on communities and their consequences on the division of French Republic – is often used against many forms of identity-based social movement, especially around race and religion[35] (Table 2).

In these situations, union representatives sometimes become a buffer zone between Muslim employees and a broader social condemnation, and therefore are held accountable and asked to explain Muslims' behavior. Yet, the attitude of defending minority claims was not as obvious for Muslim minorities as for other minorities inside unions. The analysis of the union-produced guides to deal with specific minority claims are in this respect enlightening. The guide related to religious claims was mainly aiming at educating union organizers about how to not be discriminatory, as we can see in the following excerpt:

Table 2. Collocation of Muslim Claims and Fundamentalist Critiques.

	Number of Articles Where the Word is Mentioned	Frequency of Mentions in the Corpus	Presence in Articles (%)	Mentioned on Average Per Text
Fundamentalist (Fr: "intégriste")	11	24	37	0.8
Radical	17	69	57	2.3
Terrorism	10	22	33	0.7
Communitarianism	14	46	47	1.5

> Religious discrimination and exercise of members' mandate: pitfalls to avoid: It might seem obvious, but rejecting an employee who wants to join a union on religious grounds is a discrimination that can be criminally sanctioned [...]. A representative, once elected, needs to represent the whole body of workers, in all its diversity, which implies respecting the conviction of all employees and displaying a strict neutrality when examining workers' claims. (Guide CFDT, religious facts in companies, pp. 25–26)

The guide for dealing with religious claims primarily emphasizes that union should be non-discriminatory toward religious minorities. This stands in contrasts with the guides written to respond to LGBT claims in the workplace, for instance, where the union pictures itself as being the defender of LGBT rights:

> Today in France, the substantial equality of LGBT people is not achieved. [...] The intervention of the CGT next to these employees, jobseekers, and retired [LGBT people] remains a significant stake. (Guide for the union action CGT – win the rights' equality of LGBT people in the workplace, p. 11)

This section showed how – when trying to adopt similar strategy (i.e., joining a union) to secure rights and accommodation, Muslim workers were faced with significant challenges (media backlashes, stigmatization of their claims, perception of threat when they were joining a union). While granting official rights to minorities was something that companies and union could value for LGBT people or workers with disabilities, the same approach was threatening their reputation when dealing with Muslim rights. As a result, most rights were granted "under the radar," and there is almost no example of legally binding or publicly celebrated accommodations for Muslim workers.

DISCUSSION AND CONCLUSION

This research bridges a gap between social movement theory and the Law and Society literature and sheds a new light on how socially progressive policies develops inside private companies. It also contributes to social movements theory by analyzing how being an insider activist within a corporation is a strategic choice to leverage change. I contend that the legal endogeneity theory should take into account the involvement of insider activists – especially for policies and regulations that respond to laws that have a social goal, such as anti-discrimination, but also environmental laws – to better account for the variety of ways in which government laws are endogenously reinterpreted and transformed within corporations.

In the three cases discussed here, insider activists in corporations attempt to engage in the endogenous production of corporate regulation. Through this, they can secure new rights (case 1) or enforce pre-existing rights that corporations ignored previously (case 2). These cases show how insider activists positioned themselves as legal intermediaries, as they provided blueprints for the regulatory and organizational changes they hoped to make in their corporations. I show as well how unions were oftentimes mediating the articulation between identity activists and corporations. Yet, as the third case shows, the ability to secure rights within companies through unions was different across cases. This qualitative analysis enabled me to underline some of the mechanisms that could account for this variation: (1) the current scope of state legislation; (2) the mediating effect of corporate reputation (which could be facilitating or deterring, depending on whether the claims are framed as "socially vanguard" or as "scandalous"); and (3) the collaboration of union organizers. Corporate openness to activist engagement in endogenous regulations appears correlated with these different factors.

This study has explored three cases to reveal several mechanisms that activists use to endogenously influence the meaning of the law within private corporations (see Table 3). In the LGBT case, Martha, an activist at the head of an advocacy group within a company has been asked to help a lesbian couple to get paid parental leave, and created a new policy securing paid parental leave for same-sex couples at the scale of the company. To pass this policy, she framed it as a gender inequality issue – a topic on which the State mandates yearly collective bargaining for large companies. She also joined a union, in order to be at the table of negotiation during the design of the collective agreement. To do so, she claimed that she had a specific legitimacy to negotiate this point – being herself lesbian – and that she had an expertise on the topic that other union

Table 3. Activists' Use of Different Mechanisms to Influence Corporate Regulation.

#	Mechanism	Sexual Orientation	Disability	Islam
1	Creating advocacy group within firms	Yes	No	No
2	Pushing for the use of collective agreements	Yes, alignment to gender equality	Yes, activate non-mandatory agreements	No
3	Joining a union to negotiate specific rights	Yes, to include new rights	Yes, to expand the scope of agreements	Yes, to pass changes in union-managed canteen
4	Using reputational pressure to secure new rights	Yes, "doing better than the law"	No	No (media have harmful consequences)
5	Using reputational pressure to hold firm accountable	Yes, press release citing the HRD	No	No
6	Connecting minorities' claim with the diversity commitment of firms	Yes, gender equality	Yes, work with the diversity office	No
7	Making a business case for diversity	Yes, through reputation	Yes, through tax cut	Yes, follow consumption of employees
8	Claiming control of diversity office to monitor the implementation of rights	No	Yes, create disability manager position	No
9	Using activist commitment as a source of legitimacy to influence corporate regulation	Yes	Yes	No

organizers did not have. Martha also claimed her legitimacy as being the president of the LGBT advocacy association of the company. This union-mediated strategy was yet not enough to secure this right. To achieve this goal, she also challenged the company from a reputation standpoint, holding them publicly accountable for the lip service of the HRD by issuing press release. The reputational stake here was yet still enmeshed with legal questions, as the reputation claim that she used was that her company should be "better than the law."

This case therefore shows six different mechanisms: (1) the use of activist advocacy groups within corporations to make claims for minorities and to make sure that these rights are not only granted as a one-time exception but become secured for the minorities through private policies (all the numbers in parentheses in this section are references to the table 3 above); (2) the alignment of activists' rights claims to the mandatory negotiation topics of collective agreements as a way to secure substantive right; (3) the unionization as a way to negotiate the specifics of the private policies; (4) the use of reputational pressure to compel corporations to do better than the law; (5) the use of reputational pressure to hold companies accountable for the commitments they make behind closed doors; and (6) the connection of minorities' claims to the diversity commitment of companies.

The disability rights case relies on slightly different mechanisms because French laws support more strongly disability rights activism through its quota, or, if companies do not meet this quota – which is still often the case – through significant tax cuts for the companies that demonstrate an effort toward disability inclusion. Yet, Annie, a disability rights activist, still had a long way to go to promote disability inclusion and collective agreement in her company. First, she framed it as a stake for her company in order to make sure that they would take concrete steps for the inclusion of disabled workers, thus building a "business case for diversity" (7). Second, she developed an expertise on the ways to implement the law, and designed both a collective agreement blueprint and sets of practices to locally implement this collective agreement within her corporation. Then, she joined a union to compel company to sign the collective agreement, and she joined the union once again later to negotiate an up scaling of the collective agreement. (3) Last, she argued for the creation of a disability manager position to supervise the implementation of the agreement, and renegotiate future iterations of the collective agreement. She also discussed how being at the front line of these negotiations was a way for her to have an impact on how the budget was spent, what the priorities were, in a way that moved away from purely lip service and closer to hands-on improvement for the workforce with disabilities. Annie also influenced the types of objectives included within these agreements to make them more impactful. For instance, by increasing the recruitment target, shifting the budget toward more hands-on action and less communication, deciding to purchase services from more reliable and activists contractors, and mandating more long-term and secured contracts for the job seekers with disabilities hired within the company. A new mechanism through which this activist managed to influence corporate endogenous regulation was to secure a position within the firm devoted to supervise and monitor the implementation of this collective agreement (8). Such positions are blooming in the

CSR departments, like diversity managers or sustainability managers. Being recruited in such positions is certainly a way through which activists might influence deeply corporate practices and policies, as they can offer new programs, set new agendas, secure new rights and policies, and monitor the impact of the programs they set up. To secure this position, Annie leveraged her activist commitment in the disability rights movement as a source of legitimacy.

The negative case in this study reveals how the status of Islam inclusion is different than the other rights secured by minorities. Here, activists did not publicly make claims for Halal meat nor did they associate it overtly with the diversity effort of companies. On the contrary, it seems like this accommodation was rather negotiated "under the table" and then displayed as a scandalous endeavor by other unions. This accommodation did not have the legitimacy to be framed as a "diversity enterprise" for inclusion, and therefore the activists did not have the leverage to use this reputation stake to implement their right. The right was passed under the grid by one union, and then withdrawn as it got pushback.

Last, these activists also frame themselves as being the right interlocutor to handle diversity management (9). In the LGBT case, the activist claimed her legitimacy both to propose this right and to negotiate it through unions through her appointment at the head of the company's LGBT association, and through the demands of one of the association members. In the disability case, the activist discussed her status as being disabled as a source of expertise – both of disabilities' struggles and needs – in order to claim the negotiation of the collective agreement and her appointment as disability manager. She also developed a more practical and legal expertise, garnering knowledge about the specifics of these agreements, in order to claim this legitimacy. Yet, the valuation of this activist identity and this minority expertise did not apply to the Muslim case. None of the actors involved in the promotion of Halal meat made explicit claims for Muslim minorities in relation to the diversity commitment of companies.

The macro-story of how such accommodations and rights do not pass as a progressive effort for inclusion is one of the most intriguing puzzles of this case study. It is certainly entangled with consideration from French history and institutional culture. Yet, there might also be a more microsociological story, about the respective class and social status of the activists involved. Both the LGBT activist and the disability rights activists were top managers in their corporations. They had Masters' degrees in engineering, and started claiming rights after years of working within their corporations, and therefore enhancing their professional status. In the Muslim case, it seems that all the actors involved were from lower social backgrounds, and worked as blue collar workers in the company. Discussing this paradox with some Muslim activists on the ground, I was told that Muslims who wanted to reach the higher ranks of corporations tended to erase their religious belongings, and did not make claims on this basis. By contrast, it seems that other identities (LGBT, gender, disabilities) felt empowered to make claims based on their identity, even – and perhaps even more – within the higher ranks of their hiring corporations. Such insights would need further empirical elaboration.

Activists, therefore, are influencing corporate endogenous interpretation of anti-discrimination laws. The French context reveals this phenomenon in a particularly striking way, probably because of the specific role that unions play in France. Yet, I am convinced that this role of activists as intermediary in the interpretation of laws within companies goes beyond the French case. Depending on contexts, activists might draw differently on the legal or reputational stakes of CSR for companies. In France, the pressure to negotiate with union organizers might stir this mechanism more toward legal leverage. And, it is possible that in contexts where companies feel pressured to display prosocial claims and partake in philanthropy, activists might leverage more the reputational stakes of companies. Yet, because these two mechanisms are so deeply intertwined within social policies of firms, it is likely that activists will attempt to appeal to both. In each case though, they might activate the same mechanisms, claiming that they have the legitimacy to defend the social causes for which they are – according to their personal commitments – stakeholders.

To demonstrate the extent of these mechanisms, future studies could investigate how environmental activists get involved in the local interpretation of environmental policies within private companies, notably in the American context where criticisms of green washing are commonplace. In such case, it is possible to hypothesize that activists can leverage their authenticity as activists legitimate to defend social cause in order to gain control over the services in charge of designing and implementing environment-friendly policies. The role of identity activists, such as feminist groups or organizations defending the inclusion of racial minorities, in designing corporate regulations and diversity programs, would also be a compelling site for research.

By studying how insider activists take part in the endogenous production of regulations within firms, I claim that private regulation is a place where employee activists can hope to make change in companies while being hired by them, because there is a converging interest between being compliant with regulation, demonstrating corporate social commitments (especially with the growing role of CSR and social reputation of companies, notably to respond to the pressure of external social movements – see McDonnell et al., 2013), and defending activists' agendas for social change. It is worth looking at activists' strategies at the front line of organizations to see how they influence the endogenous shift of the law. Their role could be to promote proactive compliance with a law that the corporation previously ignored in order to enforce substantive rights (case 2). In some cases, activists could even produce an endogenous regulation that went beyond legal compliance (case 1). When dealing with private regulation, insider activists are in a powerful position to monitor firms' practices and hold them accountable for their CSR policies, as well as their impending anti-discrimination regulation.

Yet, I argue that the opportunity to promote successfully new regulations within corporations depends on the legitimacy of the claims that activists defend (power of the external social movement, media coverage, public opinion). Union organizers are arguably the type of insider activists with the most institutionalized power within corporations, and this explains why minority activists developed collaboration with them to pass on new regulations. The ability of minorities' rights to be secured through unions then depends on different factors that relate to the institutionalizations of each social cause. In this study, I used media coverage and legal provision as proxies for measuring this institutionalization of activist claims.

This research also uncovers some consequences of the structural inequalities in the current anti-discrimination universalist legislation in France. By studying the extent to which different categories of activists can claim rights through unions, I show how the French state produces structural inequalities between minorities in the workplace. Unions allow some opportunity windows to secure rights for minorities. Yet, these rights are unequal in nature according to the minorities (collective agreement for planning employment of disability workers on the one hand, add of one provision for LGBT parents on the gender equality agreement on the other, nothing found in my data for securing rights for religious minorities). These differences depend both on the State's orientation (favorable to women, age group, and disabled workers), and on the political orientation and the expertise of the unions in identity issues. Although unions are often described as class-based and incompatible with identity politics, they do defend some minorities better than others.

My research thus emphasizes that we need to study insider activists not in a monolithic way. Different activist groups have different agendas, but also different status and resources to meet their goals. This work is a first attempt at studying the alliance and collaboration between insider activist groups with unequal resources and power. LGBT and disability rights activists coopted or collaborated with unions, but these collaborations were most of the time instrumental (to obtain a policy, regulation or agreement) and temporary (they left the unions after obtaining their claim). They oftentimes criticized unions for lacking commitment to their issues and lacking the expertise and knowledge necessary to design, enforce or monitor new regulations for them.

ACKNOWLEDGMENTS

I would like to thank Jérôme Pélisse, Sophie Dubuisson-Quellier, Brayden King, Sébastien Billows, and Joshua Basseches for their generous comments and suggestions on previous versions of this paper.

NOTES

1. As I will develop later, this quota, passed as a law in 1986, had little initial impact on corporations because the agency in charge of enforcing it was toothless, and the fees for non-compliance rather low. A 2005 law drastically increased the fine, but we can actually trace the impact of disability rights activists in firms from earlier, as some developed disability programs before this law (late 1990s and early 2000s). The 2005 law that increased the fine for non-compliance was yet another argument that helped these activists advocate for internal programs for workers with disabilities within corporations.

2. I draw this distinction from Edelman and Stryker (2005), who argue that the first "involves production and widespread acceptance of particular construction of law and

compliance," while the second "shape which constructions of law are produced and became institutionalized" (Edelman & Stryker, 2005).

3. See the section below "Bringing Activist Back in" for a nuanced account of these distinctions.

4. This will be fleshed out in the following section ("Managerialization of the Law" as well as in the second case study of this chapter).

5. An example of these processes of managerialization of the law could be the development of training programs about diversity. They send an external signal that the company is doing something against discrimination – they are tangible, formal programs that external actors or courts could notice – but do not say much about how this changes the actual composition of the workforce (Edelman, 2016).

6. This research will present solely insider activists who belong to the minorities that they defend (e.g., LGBT workers who claim rights for LGBT inside their companies). By doing this, I do not claim that one needs to belong to a minority to defend minorities' rights. There are certainly allies to these causes who do not identify as belonging to these minorities. Yet, my research gave me primarily access to people who were advocating for their minorities (because they might have been the most visible and vocal advocates). It would be enlightening to explore – in future research – how the position of these non-minority allies (who might benefit from a different status or be less stigmatized than discriminated minorities) had different opportunities structures when defending minorities' rights. Similarly, I do not claim that belonging to a minority is enough to be perceived as being an insider activist: to identify insider activists, I looked at whether they were claiming rights and accommodation, had a critical view of their company's action, and articulated a politicized discourse with taking steps to change corporate practices.

7. See the case 3 for an example of the challenges with joining a union for some identity-based activists.

8. McDonnell et al. summarizes impression management as defensive "strategies that evade, rather than address, activists' concerns" (2015: 656). Similarly, she defines social management devices as "structures or practices meant to assist a firm in managing its social strategy and demonstrating an enhanced commitment to socially responsible values." (ibid. 658).

9. Scholars identify different mechanisms through which social movements develop dynamic response to firms' impression management to increase firms' responsiveness and accountability (McDonnell et al., 2015), such as the development of monitoring practices (Aguilera & Jackson, 2003), and potential subsequent shaming (Bartley, 2007).

10. Both the assumption that unions are representative and their legal power is discussed in Pélisse: "Indeed, beyond the assumption that they are representative, the judicial framework provides union an exceptional place in the judiciary order" (translation from the author) (Pélisse, 2007, p. 178).

11. Article L. 2251-1 du Code du travail français. This principle was true at the time of my fieldwork (up to 2015), but is challenged since 2016 with changes in the Labor Code.

12. Some unions in France were historically attached to religious belongings – mainly Christian – but they went through a process of de-confessionalization.

13. These references are American but reflect a current trend in the French system. Most of this section is otherwise based on French scholars or American scholars studying France.

14. The accommodations and policies claimed by the feminist movement are numerous: measures to fight the glass ceiling effect, to monitor wage differences and compensate them, to allow more flexible schedules for parents, to provide paid maternity leave, and develop women networks and affinity groups to promote women leadership and raise awareness against sexism, etc (Bereni & Lépinard, 2004, Blanchard, 2013; Scott, 1997).

15. For instance, throughout history, different societies have framed homosexuality as something innate or acquired, as visible or invisible, as a source of shame or of pride, and as an illegitimate or legitimate source for political mobilization and right claims. Similarly, the understanding and visibility of disabilities varies across national context

and types of disabilities, and the current pushback against the mobilization around Muslim identity in France should be looked at through a similar lens.

16. Respectively: 17 disability rights activists, 11 LGBT rights activists, four Muslim rights activists, and nine union representatives.

17. Both Technormas (company) and Tech-Homos (the LGBT affinity group inside of the said company) are pseudonyms, but I tried to keep the pun with the name of the company, which is a common tactic of LGBT affinity group inside French companies to stress their connection with the corporation in which they are doing advocacy work.

18. The CGT (General Confederation of Labor – Confédération Générale du Travail in French), is one of the two largest union organizations in France.

19. All the names are pseudonyms. All translation from French are from me.

20. Conscious of the still prominent disregard of the quota by most companies – Maggi Germain claims than more than 50% of the companies did not take any action for disability before 2005 (Maggi-Germain, 2010) – this new law made sure to include a provision that companies that would not have pursue any effort to comply with the quota within four years (by 2010) would have to pay a sharply increased fine. The fine would be worth 1500 times the hourly minimum wage for each missing worker with disability. Virtually, it meant that companies with no disability policies had to roughly pay a 10-month minimum wage fee for every worker with disability they did not hire into their company.

21. Even if we might question the reliability of Annie's claim that her company was not at all aware of the possibility of this collective agreement to avoid paying the quota fine, this still shows how she played a role in moving her firm from paying the fine to negotiation of a collective agreement. This also highlights the centrality of legal knowledge and legal expertise to negotiate rights here.

22. By "safer," I imply that activists attempt to alter the firm's perception of the different risks pending on non-compliant or non-optimally compliant firms. By "more beneficial," my point is to show how these activists frame their discourse so as to make their own compliance strategy sound rewarding for the firms, notably by adopting "business case" types of arguments (Noon, 2007).

23. Previous studies showed how unions were not highly involved in the defense of disabled workers' rights in France (Barel & Frémeaux, 2010, p. 213).

24. I conducted 28 interviews with disability managers, and 17 of them fit this mode of being disability rights activists, themselves disabled, and who worked as institutional entrepreneurs to promote the development of disability policies in their companies (e.g., signing a collective agreement, setting recruitment targets, or initiating disability departments in companies). The nine who did not fit this description got appointed to this position often after it was created already.

25. In my fieldwork, the social movement organizations I studied outside of corporation similarly rebranded their action under the category of "underprivileged areas" when trying to develop collaborations with French companies, and attempts of securing Muslim rights in French companies were dismissed as "communautarist" and against the French spirit of Laïcité.

26. Labor Code – Legislative Section (Article L1132-1): "No one can be denied from a hiring process, the access to an internship, a training program, no employee can be penalized, fired, or be subjected to a discriminatory measure – direct or indirect – […] on the grounds of their origin, their sex, their mores, their sexual orientation, their gender identity, their age, their family situation or their pregnancy, their genetical characteristics, their specific vulnerability pertaining to their economic situation – visible or unknown – their belonging or non-belonging – assumed or real – to an ethnicity, a nation, or a so-called race, of their political views, their union activities, to their religious beliefs, their physical appearance, their family name, their place of residence, their bank domiciliation, their health status, their loss of autonomy or disability, their ability to talk in another language than French."

27. Respectively: LOI n° 2004-228 du 15 mars 2004; Rapport du Défenseur des droits. L'égal accès des enfants à la cantine de l'école primaire, 28 mars 2013; LOI no 2016-1088 du 8 août 2016; Affaire C-157/15, G4S Secure Solutions, 2017, Court of Justice of the European Union.

28. I interviewed four people in later fieldwork, that is early 2018.

29. My final material was a set of 30 articles from mainstream newspapers directly dealing with French corporations. The initial result showed much more references, but I restricted my research to the articles specifically talking about the rights of Muslim workers in French companies through qualitatively sorting these references. These articles come from journals all across the political spectrum: Les Echos, Liberation, L'Express, Nouvel Obs, France TV Info, le Figaro, le Parisien, Opinion, Slate, France 24, Marianne, Le Point, La Croix. I conducted a qualitative content analysis of these articles through Nvivo in order to explore them. The following section summarizes my results.

30. This includes the CFDT guide for managing religious claims in the workplace "Le fait religieux en entreprise, guide CFDT" and press releases from other unions. For Muslim rights' literature, I reviewed the archives from *Les Indigenes de la République*, a movement and then party defending the rights of people originating in French former colonies, and that created as a platform for collecting claims from different activists working against racism and Islamophobia.

31. Two unions: the French Democratic Confederation of Labour and the French Confederation of Christian Workers.

32. The initial words in French conveyed the idea of speaking up for one's idea but used a medieval warfare metaphor ("monter au créneau").

33. Indeed, the official declaration of the Union States that the union decided on the halal option for the kebab and grill because the advantageous cost of the meat, while other organizers claimed they did not know anything about the halal of the meat altogether.

34. This cultural reframing shows well the challenges to sustain a discourse on defending claims that specifically relate to Muslims. The emphasis on *Laïcité* is interesting as well, since this concept relates to the public sector, but is often misleadingly expanded to the private sector. The way these claims are framed as a threat to French identity seems also to play a role – as people felt obliged to reiterate their faith in Republic and Laïcité, but also to justify the decreased consumption of pork.

35. These articles also enabled me to identify some of the reasons why these claims did not receive as much attention by the unions as the previous ones. First, in the media descriptions, these claims are conflated with behaviors of Muslim individuals that are more directly controversial. Such behaviors include the refusal of mixed-gender work (shaking hands with women, driving a bus after a woman, etc.), boycott of the work requiring contact with alcohol, and practices of aggressive proselytism. While most of these articles describe these behaviors as being an extreme minority, they are still conflated in these articles with no clear reflexive distinction with claims that could be taken seriously and defended by unions. The same confusion appears around the idea of proselytism. Proselytism is indeed prohibited by French legislation, but its definition and comprehensiveness are often unclear to actors. Different sources, for instance, have felt the need to reiterate that wearing a headscarf, praying, or having a Muslim calendar in one's locker were not behaviors of proselytism (Défenseur des Droits, CFDT guidebook for union organizers).

BIBLIOGRAPHY

Aguilera, R. V., & Jackson, G. (2003). The cross-national diversity of corporate governance: Dimensions and determinants. *The Academy of Management Review*, *28*(3), 447–465.

Andolfatto, D., & Labbé, D. (2006). La Transformation des Syndicats Francais: Vers un nouveau "Modèle social"? *Revue Française de Science Politique*, *56*(2), 281–297.

Barel, Y., & Frémeaux, S. (2010). Quel Sens ont les Démarches d'Intégration des Salariés en Situation de Handicap pour les Parties prenantes? Le Sens donné par les DRH et Chargés de Mission. *Management & Avenir*, *33*, 204–222.

Barnay, T., Duguet, E., Clainche, C. L., & Videau, Y. (2016). *An evaluation of the 1987 French disabled workers act: Better paying than hiring*. St Louis, MO: Federal Reserve Bank of St Louis.

Baron, D. P. (2001). Private politics, corporate social responsibility, and integrated strategy. *Journal of Economics & Management Strategy*, *10*(1), 7–45.

Baron, D. P. (2003). Private politics. *Journal of Economics & Management Strategy*, *12*(1), 31–66.

Baron, D. P. (2005). Competing for the public through the news media. *Journal of Economics & Management Strategy*, *14*(2), 339–376.

Bartley, T. (2007). Institutional emergence in an era of globalization: The rise of transnational private regulation of labor and environmental conditions. *American Journal of Sociology*, *113*(2), 297–351.

Bartley, T. (2010). Transnational private regulation in practice: The limits of forest and labor standards certification in Indonesia. *Business and Politics*, *12*(3), 1–34..

Bartley, T., & Child, C. (2014). Shaming the corporation: The social production of targets and the anti-sweatshop movement. *American Sociological Review*, *79*(4), 653–679.

Bell, E. L. J. E., Meyerson, D., Nkomo, S., & Scully, M. (2003). Interpreting silence and voice in the workplace: A conversation about tempered radicalism among Black and White women researchers. *The Journal of Applied Behavioral Science*, *39*(4), 381–414.

Bereni, L. (2011). Le Discours de la Diversité en Entreprise: Genèse et Appropriations. *Sociologies pratiques*, *23*, 9–19.

Bereni, L., Debauche, A., Latour, E., & Revillard, A. (2010). Entre Contrainte et Ressource: les Mouvements Féministes Face au Droit. *Nouvelles Questions Féministes*, *29*(1), 6–15.

Bereni, L., & Lépinard, É. (2004). "Les Femmes ne sont pas une Catégorie": les Stratégies de Légitimation de la Parité en France. *Revue Française de Science Politique*, *54*, 71–98.

Bernstein, M. (2005). Identity politics. *Annual Review of Sociology*, *31*, 47–74.

Berrey, E. (2015). *The enigma of diversity*. Chicago, IL: University of Chicago Press.

Bethoux, E., Desage, G., Mias, A., & Pélisse, J. (2013). *Sociologie d'un syndicalisme catégoriel. La CFE-CGC ou la fin d'une exception*. Paris: Armand Colin.

Bevort, A. (2011). La réforme des règles de la représentativité syndicale (2008–2010). *Idées économiques et sociales*, *163*, 8–16. doi:10.3917/idee.163.0008

Blanchard, S. (2013). *De la Cause des Femmes au Marché de l'Egalité: l'Emergence de l'Espace de l'Accompagnement à l'Egalité Professionnelle en France (1965–2012) (Thèse de doctorat)*. France, Toulouse: Université Toulouse-Jean Jaurès.

Blatge, M. (2010). Le Handicap: Objet de Négociation Collective ou de Communication? *La Revue de l'Ires*, *67*(4), 123–136.

Briscoe, F., & Gupta, A. (2016). Social activism in and around organizations. *The Academy of Management Annals*, *10*(1), 671–727.

Brubaker, R. (2016). The dolezal affair: Race, gender, and the micropolitics of identity: Ethnic and racial studies. *Ethnic and Racial Studies*, *39*(3), 414–448.

Calvès, G. (2016). *La discrimination positive* (Vol. 4e éd.). Paris: Presses Universitaires de France.

Daly, K. (2007). *Qualitative methods for family studies and human development*. Thousand Oaks, CA: Sage.

Dobbin, F. (2009). *Inventing equal opportunity*. Princeton, NJ: Princeton University Press.

Dobbin, F., Kim, S., & Kalev, A. (2011). You can't always get what you need: organizational determinants of diversity programs. *American Sociological Review*, *76*(3), 386–411.

Dobbin, F., Kim, S., & Kalev, A. (2012). Progressive corporations at work: The case of diversity programs. Retrieved from https://dash.harvard.edu/handle/1/11315416

Dobbin, F., & Sutton, J. R. (1998). The strength of a weak state: The rights revolution and the rise of human resources management divisions 1. *American Journal of Sociology*, *104*(2), 441–476.

Doytcheva, M. (2009). Réinterprétations et Usages Sélectifs de la Diversité dans les Politiques des Entreprises. *Raisons politiques*, *35*, 107–123.

Edelman, L. B. (1991). *Legal ambiguity and symbolic structures: organizational mediation of civil rights law* (Rev. May 1991). Madison, WI: Institute for Legal Studies, University of Wisconsin–Madison Law School.

Edelman, L. B. (1992). Legal ambiguity and symbolic structures: Organizational mediation of civil rights law. *American Journal of Sociology*, *97*(6), 1531–1576.

Edelman, L. B. (2016). *Working law: Courts, corporations, and symbolic civil rights*. Chicago, IL: The University of Chicago Press.

Edelman, L. B., Fuller, S. R., & Mara-Drita, I. (2001). Diversity rhetoric and the managerialization of law. *American Journal of Sociology*, *106*(6), 1589–1641.

Edelman, L. B., Krieger, L. H., Eliason, S. R., Albiston, C. R., & Mellema, V. (2011). When organizations rule: Judicial deference to institutionalized employment structures. *American Journal of Sociology*, *117*(3), 888–954.

Edelman, L. B., Leachman, G., & McAdam, D. (2010). On law, organizations, and social movements. *Annual Review of Law and Social Science*, *6*, 653–685.

Edelman, L. B., & Stryker, R. (2005). A sociological approach to law and the economy. In N. J. Smelser & R. Swedberg (Eds.), *The Handbook of Economic Sociology* (pp. 527–551). Princeton, NJ: Princeton University Press.

Fraser, N. (2000). Rethinking recognition. *New Left Review*, *3*, 107–120.

Kalev, A., Kelly, E., & Dobbin, F. (2006). Best practices or best guesses? assessing the efficacy of corporate affirmative action and diversity policies. *American Sociological Review*, *71*(4), 589–617.

Kelly, E., & Dobbin, F. (1998). How affirmative action became diversity management. *The American Behavioral Scientist*, *41*(7), 960–984.

King, B. G. (2008). A political mediation model of corporate response to social movement activism. *Administrative Science Quarterly*, *53*(3), 395–421.

King, B. G., & Pearce, N. A. (2010). The contentiousness of markets: Politics, social movements, and institutional change in markets. *Annual Review of Sociology*, *36*(1), 249–267.

Luders, J. (2006). The economics of movement success: Business responses to civil rights mobilization. *American Journal of Sociology*, *111*(4), 963–998.

Maggi-Germain, N. (2010). Les Accords "Libératoires" sur l'Emploi des Travailleurs Handicapés. *La Revue de l'Ires*, *67*(4), 99–121.

McDonnell, M.-H., & King, B. G. (2013). Keeping up appearances: Reputational threat and impression management after social movement boycotts. *Administrative Science Quarterly*, *58*(3), 387–419.

McDonnell, M.-H., King, B. G., & Soule, S. A. (2015). A dynamic process model of private politics: Activist targeting and corporate receptivity to social challenges. *American Sociological Review*, *80*(3), 654–678.

Mena, S., & Waeger, D. (2014). Activism for corporate responsibility: Conceptualizing private regulation opportunity structures. *Journal of Management Studies*, *51*(7), 1091–1117.

Meyerson, D. E., & Scully, M. A. (1995). Tempered radicalism and the politics of ambivalence and change. *Organization Science*, *6*(5), 585–600.

Monchatre, S. (2014). Petits Arrangements avec la Diversité. Le Recrutement entre Marché et Mobilisation Salariale. *Revue française de sociologie*, *55*(1), 41–72.

Nadeau, D. (2012). Monopole de Representation Syndicale et Droits Individuels des Salaries: L'Incontournable Defi de la Diversite Colloque International – Les Systemes de Representation au Travail: A la Mesure des Realites Contemporaines. *Cahiers de Droit*, *53*, 139–160.

Noon, M. (2007). The fatal flaws of diversity and the business case for ethnic minorities. *Work, Employment and Society*, *21*(4), 773–784.

Pedriana, N., & Stryker, R. (2004). The strength of a weak agency: Enforcement of title VII of the 1964 civil rights act and the expansion of state capacity, 1965–1971. *American Journal of Sociology*, *110*(3), 709–760.

Pélisse, J. (2007). 7. Les Usages Syndicaux du Droit et de la Justice. In J. Commaille & M. Kaluszynski (Eds.), *La fonction politique de la justice* (pp. 165–189). Paris: La Découverte.

Pélisse, J. (2011). La Mise en êuvre des 35 Heures: d'une Managérialisation du Droit à une Internalisation de la Fonction de Justice. *Droit et société*, *77*(1), 39–65.

Piore, M. J., & Safford, S. (2006). Changing regimes of workplace governance, shifting axes of social mobilization, and the challenge to industrial relations theory. *Industrial Relations*, *45*(3), 299–325.

Sabbagh, D., & Peer, S. (2008). French color blindness in perspective: The controversy over "Statistiques Ethniques": Introduction. *French Politics, Culture & Society*, *26*(1), 1–6.

Scott, J. W. (1997). *Only paradoxes to offer: French feminists and the rights of man*. Cambridge, MA: Harvard University Press.

Scott, J. W. (2009). *The politics of the veil*. Princeton, NJ: Princeton University Press.

Scully, M., & Segal, A. (2002). Passion with an umbrella: Grassroots activists in the workplace. In M. Lounsbury & M. Ventresca (Eds.), *Social Structure and Organizations Revisited* (Research in the Sociology of Organizations, Vol. 19, pp. 125–168). Bingley: Emerald Publishing Limited.

Sénac, R. (2012). *L'invention de la diversité (Le lien social)*. Paris: Presses universitaires de France.

WHEN LEGAL INTERMEDIATION CREATES DISTRUST OF THE LAW: THE MARKET FOR TAX REBATES IN FRENCH REAL ESTATE

Camille Herlin-Giret and Alexis Spire

ABSTRACT

Since the 1990s, the French government has offered tax exemptions for people who buy property and rent it out for at least nine years. This legal framework, centered on incentives, can be considered a new kind of (de)regulation of housing policy, triggering a multiplication of private intermediaries devoted to finding clients for tax exemptions. Based on interviews with 28 investors who feel they have been abused (many of them have started legal proceedings against professionals from whom they bought a property), this study provides a new entry for analyzing legal intermediation, showing that it does not affect all laypeople in the same way, especially when looking at the latter's social and economic resources. We analyze how and with what devices professionals, whose commercial practices are not fully regulated by law, rely on the law for the success of their transactions, especially with taxpayers who have money to become investors but who are not rich enough to pay for the services of a tax professional. We argue that the ability to resist the appeal of putting money into investments that turned out risky depends on investors' social and economic resources. Finally, we analyze how the process of legal intermediation described in this chapter impacts investors' legal consciousness and creates distrust toward the law.

Keywords: Tax exemptions; investment; intermediation; financial skill; legal consciousness; distrust of the law

Legal Intermediation: A Processual Approach to Law and Economic Activity
Studies in Law, Politics, and Society, Volume 81, 45–67

ISSN: 1059-4337/doi:10.1108/S1059-433720190000081003

INTRODUCTION

The law regulating economic activities is based on relatively broad and general principles that leave firms and organizations some room for maneuver in complying with it while protecting their interests (Edelman, 1992). These are far from binary alternatives: legal compliance is a process through which institutions construct the meaning and limits they intend to give to the legal framework (Swedberg, 2003). This work of endogenization of law (Edelman, 2016) is entrusted to "compliance professionals" who may be legal professionals such as lawyers or legal advisors; private actors such as management consultants, executives working inside or outside of organizations; or public agents. Firms confronted with laws against discrimination in the workplace, for example, make use of "complaint handlers" who reframe and reformulate the legal principles in accordance with managerial criteria (Edelman, Erlanger, & Lande, 1993; Marshall, 2005). Compliance with new legal norms also affects understanding of the law (Pélisse, 2004), as shown by the example of hospital reforms in this issue (Vincent, 2019): middle managers may take advantage of it to increase their power within the organization (Kellogg, 2009). Firms make use of compliance professionals because they have an interest in complying with the law and they identify with the principles of justice laid down by the state (Edelman & Suchman, 1997). Legal intermediation is, however, not only used to display compliance with the law: economic actors may also make use of the law for commercial purposes, to make them more persuasive vis-à-vis consumers when seeking to sell them certain goods or services. The "managerialization of law" (Edelman, 2016) then becomes a weapon for economic agents to exercise domination over lay clients. Whereas, bureaucracies are in charge of the allocation of a certain number of rights and may favor or block access to these (Revillard, 2017, p. 459), private actors use the law differently, by infusing their own managerial logics into the legal field (Billows, 2019) and by taking part in the design of private regulation (Buchter, 2019).

This chapter is precisely concerned with the role of legal intermediaries when they impact the law's capacity to produce social change (Pélisse & Talesh, 2018). In the case of tax exemptions, an area that is particularly technical and legally dense, private legal intermediaries pursue economic goals and profit targets. In recent decades, use of these devices has become increasingly widespread among private actors, meaning that households now assume risks previously managed by associations or the state (Hacker, 2004). On both sides of the Atlantic, governments have offered small savers tax rebates to become "investors" (Aitken, 2007; Harmes, 2001, p. 103). For example, the policy which incentivized employees to organize their future pension through company savings schemes consisted in turning future retirees into individual investors on the markets (Carruthers & Kim, 2011; Dynan, 2009; Shuey & O'Rand, 2004). This conversion was accompanied in the United States by the emergence of investment clubs (Harrington, 2008). In France, the use of tax exemptions has developed on a similar scale, but the main beneficiaries have had less guidance in navigating the new financial and tax schemes at their disposal. Besides, the retirement system is based on social insurance, hence the majority of the population does not need to use the market to make provisions for future risks. As a consequence, the asymmetry between financial experts and laypeople is more salient than in other countries. The example of real-estate investment is particularly enlightening because it concerns a large number of taxpayers who want to save for the future but lack the necessary understanding of the legal schemes offered to them.

In France, since the late 1970s, successive governments have introduced many tax breaks[1] to draw taxpayers' savings into markets, especially in the housing sector. The Robien, Scellier, Censi-Bouvard and Pinel schemes – the main real-estate tax exemption arrangements, named after the ministers who promoted them – alone represent altogether more than €1.76 billion. Whereas for a long time the state invested in building social housing, this public policy has been progressively rechanneled toward a whole series of direct aids to tenants and tax incentives for would-be property owners (Pollard, 2009). By reducing the income tax of those who engage in "buy-to-rent" investments (with a mandatory period of nine years[2]), these schemes aim at stimulating the building of new rental properties.[3] These peculiar tools of government have not yet been studied, despite their weight in tax expenditures.

By focusing on tax exemptions in the French housing sector, we show that intermediation by private actors not only impacts organizations and economic behaviors, but also attitudes toward the law and the representations of legality: similar to the organizations described in the literature on legal endogeneity, the people who make such investments are "resocialized by law" (Edelman & Suchman, 1999, p. 981). In the case of households who sign up for real-estate investments, legality is shaped by how people perceive the domestic economy and risk: the decisions people make affect their private lives and their self-image. While most research on legal intermediation has focused on how organizations shape law, in this chapter we want to consider legal intermediation as a power relation (Dobbin, 2005, p. 27) between professionals representing large firms and laypeople who believe they are pursuing their own interest.

A first stage of our analysis aims to understand how private actors, in this case the sales representatives acting for big real-estate developers, take over and use the law for commercial purposes: through a comprehensive effort of persuasion, they succeed in selling properties to individuals by presenting tax exemption schemes set up by the state. We then show that the work of legal intermediation contributes to a power relation between professionals who thoroughly understand the possible uses of the law and the laypeople who are the public of these real-estate tax exemption policies. This power relation cannot, however, be reduced to a one-sided relation of domination: laypeople's capacities to resist depend on their economic resources and their ability to deal with financial matters. The commercial use of law impacts taxpayers' representations of law and justice, and also modifies these misled users' relation to the state.

Note: This text is part of the programme "The Ordinary Practices and Representations of the Governed in their Dealings with the State" (Profet), funded by the National Research Agency (ANR-15-CE28-0009).

Sources and Methods

While research on policy feedback (Mettler & Soss, 2004; Pierson, 1993) has not paid much attention to the social heterogeneity of the groups targeted by public policies, in this paper, we wish to focus on the social characteristics of the private individuals who invest in real estate, which raises several methodological difficulties. In the case of tax incentives negotiated at a distance, there is no physical place where the taxpayers who may benefit from these measures can be found. To meet them, we went through an association defending the victims of tax exempted rental investments. The interviewees who contacted us following the email sent to all the members have two particularities. First, they consider they have been cheated, mainly because they have discovered that the real value of the property they bought is actually much lower than what they paid for; their disappointment may also have to do with the characteristics of the property (location, neighborhood) or the difficulties they encounter in renting it. Second, many of these purchasers who consider themselves cheated are involved through the association in legal actions against the sales representatives who sold them these properties. We were able to carry out 28 interviews with people who had bought properties for tax exemption purposes. Focusing on disappointed investors makes it possible to reconstruct the sequence of events that led to the purchase of a property entailing a tax reduction and to pay attention to the actors who are blamed for the investors' unfortunate situation. By then, following these misled investors in their legal proceedings, this chapter helps to understand the relationships between laypeople and various legal intermediaries: sales representatives who promote tax exempt properties as well as lawyers who encourage misled investors to initiate legal proceedings. This qualitative material was complemented by a survey on a sample of 2,676 individuals, collected thanks to the Elipss panel (Longitudinal Internet Studies for Social Sciences), an online panel that is representative of the population living in metropolitan France.[4] The combination of quantitative and qualitative data enables understanding the impact of the lower-than-expected yields on the domestic economy and the future plans of the people who invested in it.

THE COMMERCIAL USE OF LAW

The particularity of France compared with many other countries is that for a long time, the agents of the state occupied a central place in the work of legal intermediation. But since the early 1980s, as in other countries (Salamon, 1995), successive governments have set up a growing number of partnerships with non-state actors to implement public policies (see in this book, Pélisse, 2019). The example of the tax exemption schemes favoring investments in real estate perfectly illustrate this new form of regulation that privileges intervention by the "hidden welfare state" (Howard, 1997). Far from standing apart from the state authorities, private agents seek to instrumentalize it as effectively as possible in order to achieve their aims. Due to its reliance on private actors, the implementation of tax exemptions in the housing sector has drifted away from its initial goals (Pollard, 2011).

Committing Decisions

Tax rebates in the housing sector, in particular, have strong repercussions on the activities of real-estate developers and consequently on the rate of housing construction. Beyond the developers, these repercussions more generally affect the whole landscape of financial intermediation: bankers, notaries and realtors, who specialize on the sale of tax-break properties, have been able to adapt to the changes in the regulations and have thus massively contributed to the "success" of real-estate tax exemption. Banks, for example, have expanded their tax-advice departments. Beyond them, a whole network of firms and sales representatives have played an active part in the sale of these various tax devices.

The main objective is to convince taxpayers of the possibility of turning flows – even small sums, regularly set aside – into a valued, visible asset generating future income – capital, in other words. The logos devised by the firms specializing in tax exemption highlight the security of investment in brick and mortar, and are used as a certificate of quality (Stanziani, 2004).

All our interviewees bought their properties after having been approached by a sales representative, who had expounded on the benefits of tax exemptions and real-estate investment. Some were contacted by telephone, some through an acquaintance, others through a bank employee. In all cases, they were persuaded to buy small apartments for which they paid between €100,000 and €200,000, entirely through loans. The properties in which they invested were all located in medium-sized towns, hundreds of miles from their own homes. Many expected to keep the property for the time required to qualify for tax exemption (often nine years) and then sell it, making a handsome capital gain ("plus value immobilière") on the sale. But after a few years, they realized that their investment had turned into a financial loss: the ancillary costs had increased, the property was in an area where tenants were difficult to find, and when they had their property appraised, they found out the real value was generally half what they had paid for (a figure the legal intermediary had persuaded them was an excellent deal).

Despite being a risky, long-term commitment, the decision to embark on the purchase of a property, on credit, for tax exemption purposes is, in most cases, taken fairly quickly. One interviewee described the conditions in which he was led to take this decision. Aged 61, he was living alone in a small town near the Swiss border, where he had worked as a technician (annual income €33,000) until he was made redundant and set himself up as a self-employed vendor of alternative medicines. He was approached at home in September 2006, just after the death of his father, which left him "emotionally fragile." In September and October, he had several meetings with a salesman, who described in glowing terms the performance of real-estate investments and handed him a brochure explaining the profits he could expect from his own investment:

> You can build up a final sum of €181,216, yielding additional annual income and pension of €8,889, with just €76,946 capital invested. With this sum of €181,216 that you will have built

> up with the aid of guaranteed rental income, you will have made a significant gain of €23,871 over 10 years or €28,354 over 20 years, ensuring you a profitable financial operation, with an internal annual yield, after tax, of 9.48%. With just €76,947 capital invested, you will have made a net gain of €104,270, and all this for an average monthly outlay of €321 over a period of 20 years.

In mid-October, he signed a preliminary contract, and in early November, he had an appointment at the bank to set the conditions of the loan, the investment being financed entirely on credit. The advisor at the bank who met him with the salesman persuaded him to take out a loan in Swiss francs. The loan application was rapidly approved by the bank at the end of December, and on February 8, he signed the purchase agreement in the notary's office. So, in a few months, he had become the owner of a new property bought on credit for tax exemption purposes. The rental started one year later (in 2008), once the property was built. In 2010, because of difficulties in renting, the increased service charges, and the financial problems he ran into when he was made redundant, he considered selling the property, accepting the loss of the tax exemption – in fact he eventually had to repay €9,000 to the tax authorities. He had several valuations made and then discovered that the apartment was valued at €70,000, less than half the price he had paid for it. To pay off his loan, which had grown considerably because of the dramatic rise in the value of the Swiss franc, he was forced to sell his main residence in March 2014.

How do taxpayers with little knowledge of financial or tax matters end up very promptly signing up to investments that commit them for several years? How do legal intermediaries persuade them to engage in such investments, which later prove to have been disastrous? Commitment, in this sense, refers to situations "where a person finds that his involvement in social organization has, in effect, made side bets for him and thus constrained his future activity" (Becker, 1960, p. 36).

Behind the Trust in Legal Intermediaries: the Shadow of the State

The first particularity of private legal intermediaries is that they work for large real-estate developers. They introduce themselves to their clients using vague terms: as asset managers, real-estate or investment experts, or tax specialists. In fact, they have no training in law or finance and only know about the tax break that will enable their client to reduce their tax bill. A job description for a seller of this type of scheme states, for example: "Beginner accepted, training provided, motivating salary, no ceiling." No previous experience in the area is required, but the candidate must have "a taste for challenges, an appetite for results and a determination to exceed your goals." One interviewee, approached by a salesman and impressed by the scheme, was himself invited to join the sales network. Having no previous knowledge of taxation or real estate, he relates his surprise at the content of the training courses he attended:

> Living in a small town a few miles from the Swiss border, he had first worked as a nurse before becoming a manager in a Swiss hospital. The property was bought on his initiative when he was still married. He has since divorced and has to deal with the consequences of this momentous purchase.

> 'In these meetings, they explain that there is a lot of money to be made. And then I told myself; but where is the social dimension in all this? Because they sell it to you saying: "Yes, socially it's excellent." And then in fact what you find is that it's only the financial benefits that lie behind the operation: for you, and for the advisors. We were told to present ourselves as specialists in asset management, despite having no skills in that area. When I asked the question, they told me I could talk to my neighbors about it and get them to sign up [...]. And at that point I said: "Enough!"'

His disappointment was first triggered by the absence of a "social dimension": helping alleviate the housing shortage, increasing the supply while offering affordable rents, were arguments that had persuaded him to sign up for such an investment. Moreover, the training he attended was extremely rudimentary and contained none of the technical aspects he expected. Finally, the undisguised emphasis on the profitability of the operation alerted him to the nature of the contract he had signed a few months earlier.

These sales representatives play the role of intermediaries between the taxpayers and the law, while advancing their own interests: they get a 10% commission (or more) on the value of each property they manage to sell. Rather than just implementing the law, they orient and adapt the application of the law in line with the interests of the firms for which they work. The properties they offer are located in areas where it is advantageous to build and where they have agreements with several building firms that take part in the project. They just not sell a property but a package including the notary's fee and the bank loan. Their whole aim is to build up a relation of "trust" (Bradach & Eccles, 1989; Shapiro, 1987) so that the client will decide to buy a property even in cases where he or she has not the means or the need to do so. To achieve this, they rely on other professionals with whom they work in partnership and who are directly and financially interested in the conclusion of the transaction. The foremost of these is the representative of the bank that grants the loan and then the notary who oversees the transaction. To produce this trust, the sales representatives use various persuasion strategies, which mingle commercial and non-commercial considerations (Granovetter, 1985).

The advisors first exploit networks of mutual acquaintance linked to the personal sphere. Several interviewees were approached in an informal context: a dinner with friends, a phone call in which the advisor emphasized mutual acquaintances: he was the "friend of a friend," a student who graduated the same year as the interviewee's spouse, etc. The recommendations that arise from interpersonal networks facilitate commercial exchanges (Baker, 1984; Chan, 2012; Uzzi, 1996; White, 2002) and become the nucleus of an expanding clientele. As with access to the labor market (Granovetter, 1973), it is not the close family circle who is mobilized but rather contacts with individuals whom the purchaser knows at a distance – either through his or her occupational activity, or as a client, or through networks of friendship. Potential clients who are approached in this way give more credence to the salesman's word because they are already trustful. In the first stage, the sales representatives may benefit from the positive effect of reputation linked to the satisfaction of clients who, in the early years, mainly see the benefits in their tax bills. The sizeable gap between the decision to invest and awareness of the harm suffered works in their favor. Thus, legal intermediation sets up a power relation that initially works in the mode of mutual acquaintance – in many cases, the commercial relationship is embedded in more personal connections.

The relation of trust that is built through this commercial relationship is also based on a sacralized representation of the law and of the agents who produce it. The sales representatives emphasize the legal dimension – that is to say, the institutional and state-sponsored dimension of the contracts they offer their clients. The possibility of tax exemption is not just a motivating argument in financial terms: it is also a powerful vector of symbolic legitimacy in the sense that this is a device set up and organized by the state. The social and symbolic power of the law (Bourdieu, 1986) is a crucial element in the legitimization of these contracts. The security of bricks and mortar is associated with the state, which appears as the guarantor of the enforcement of the commercial relationship (North, 1991, p. 99). In dealings with private intermediaries, the label of a scheme organized and overseen by the state constitutes a reassuring element, a factor of trust. Sales representatives do indeed make extensive use of this official and institutional dimension. The logos used to sell these schemes systematically highlight the term "law" (see Fig. 1), so as to benefit from the legitimacy associated with the legal process. As a further part of this marketing work, many sales brochures feature the logo of the state – the French flag and the motto *Liberté, égalité, fraternité* over the words *République française* – which appears in all administrative documents. All this symbolism generates trust, as this interviewee explains:

> A former police officer, he is now a high ranking civil servant. He owns property in Paris and is married with no children. He is the one who manages the household budget, paperwork, and taxes. In 2007 and again in 2009, he bought two apartments under real-estate tax exemption schemes.
>
> "I didn't worry much about where I was buying because we were dealing with schemes organized and guaranteed by the state. […] The state puts its seal on it. So there's no risk. What risk would there be? There is the mayor as guarantor, representing the state at town level, authorizing the construction of a building where there is big demand. So I didn't ask myself existential questions in terms of price and so on. […] I didn't check, I took it trustfully. It was Pinel, Borloo, Scellier, the state, in other words. We need to build, they tell you, there is not enough housing in France. So you don't ask questions."

This interviewee listed a whole series of actors who explain how the state appeared to him as a guarantor: from the mayor who authorized the development, to the definition of the construction zones in the texts that define the tax exemption, and the recital of the names of the various ministers who initiated each of them. The trust placed in the state is a constant background guaranteeing the solidity of these operations, even for interviewees who work in the private sector.

The production of trust in legal intermediation is finally based on a relational effort (Cochoy, 2007), which consists in stressing the technical dimension of the product so that the client readily places his faith in the competence of the intermediary. The interviewees describe many graphs and figures handled with ease by the sales representatives, from the first meeting: "He showed me his statistics in the form of graphs, I couldn't make head or tail of it. I never liked math"; "He seemed like a very professional salesman, quite restrained, very technical"; "She showed us impressive graphs of capital growth; she made calculations"; "He showed you with a diagram, a curve, how you could pay less tax; he used lots of technical terms that I didn't understand." These brief remarks indicate that the interviewees were *impressed* by these salespeople, in both senses: they were both intimidated and won over by their apparent mastery of financial data and techniques. The prospective clients are overwhelmed by a seller who seems to master a subject of which they know little. In the present case, the commercial relationship does not lead to a transfer of knowledge that would enable the consumer to acquire competences and proceed without the prescriber (Hatchuel, 1995); the social relationship that is formed around tax exemption makes the buyer dependent on the seller. The intertwining of legal intermediation and trust sets up an asymmetrical relationship: it is an exchange relationship based on inequality inasmuch as the layperson must put himself in the hands of a professional who is both interpreter and seller. It is this confusion of roles that opens the way to abuses in the work of intermediation.

The construction of the relation of trust by the sales representatives is based on a combination of social and commercial considerations (Zelizer, 1979), but it does not affect all taxpayers in the same way. Those who are most inclined to entrust themselves completely to the advisors and consider themselves duped also have particular social characteristics.

LEGAL INTERMEDIATION AS A POWER RELATION: UNEQUALLY ENDOWED LAYPEOPLE

If sales representatives make every effort to build a relation of trust with potential investors, these efforts do not always pay off. Legal intermediation becomes a power relation especially when potential clients leave it up to sales representatives. To understand that, one has to take into account the various ressources of households concerned. The tax exemption schemes have also to be replaced in the range of tax incentives offered to them.

Tax Exemptions and Their Public

Tax exemption schemes are officially targeted at a public of executives with high incomes and strong savings capacity, but in practice the sales representatives address a much broader population. The survey gives an insight into the social characteristics of the taxpayers who decided to make tax exempt real-estate investments. On the basis of this survey, it is possible, in particular, to compare two types of practices giving rise to a tax reduction: donations to charities or associations and the main investments subject to tax reductions (investment in rental property, investment in the capital of a small company or in overseas French territories).

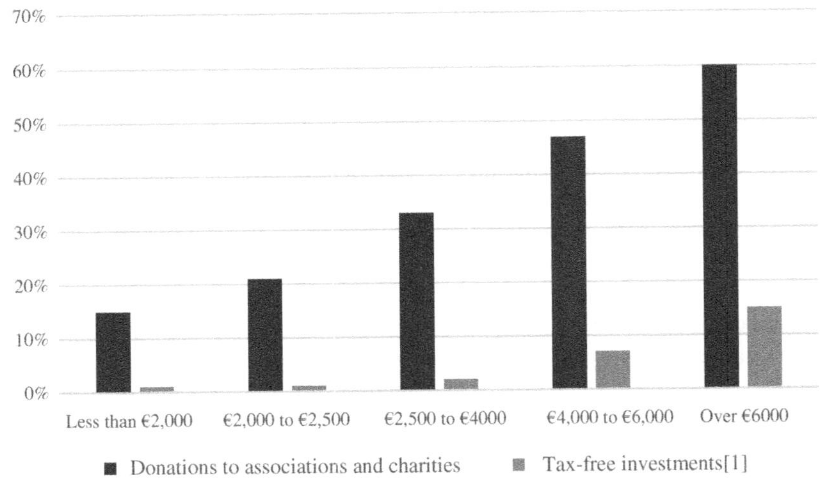

Fig. 1. Proportion of Households Benefiting from a Tax Exemption by Monthly Income. *Source*: *Pratiques and représentations face à l'État* (February 2017), Équipes PREFACE/ELIPSS, Fondation Nationale des Sciences Politiques (FNSP), Centre de Données Socio-Politiques (CDSP). *Note*: Population: Interviewees who answered the questions on income and tax exemptions ($N = 2411$). How to read: 15% of taxpayers living in a household with a monthly income over €6,000 benefited from a tax reduction for tax exempt investments.

These two practices are correlated with income: the percentage of taxpayers who say they have made donations or tax exempt investments rises with the amount of available resources (Fig. 1). Moreover, only 23% of households with monthly resources over €6,000 benefit from no tax exemption, whereas this is the case for 55% of households with monthly resources between €2,000 and €2,500. However, the distribution of making donations or tax exempt investments is very different. In the case of donations, income sensitivity does not mean the practice is reserved to an elite: even among households with less than €2,000 monthly income, 15% state that they have made donations. Tax exempt investments, by contrast, are a practice that seems to be less widespread: no more than 2% of households with monthly resources less than €4,000 make use of them. This practice is thus much more frequent in households with substantial resources. While households with monthly resources over €6,000 are four times more to make donations than households with monthly resources under €2,000, the ratio rises to 15 times more for tax exempt investments. This is no doubt explained by the heterogeneity of the amounts in question: they may be very low for donations (€100), whereas tax exempt investments often require a capital of €10,000.

When one considers all taxpayers who made a tax exempt investment (Table 1), it can be seen that a large proportion of them are in white-collar occupations (they make up almost 40% of the taxpayers using them), whereas

Table 1. Distribution of Taxpayers Benefiting from a Tax Exemption by Socio-occupational Category.

	Donations to Associations and Charities (%)	Tax-exempt Investments (%)	Whole Population (%)
Farmers	1.6	3.8	1.6
Self-employed craftsmen and traders and heads of businesses	4.5	14.4	5.8
Executives and higher mental occupations	28.8	38.7	16.9
Intermediate occupations	31.2	26.7	26
Clerical employees	23.3	12.8	30.2
Manual workers	10.7	3.6	19.4
All	100	100	100

Source: *Pratiques et représentations face à l'État* (February 2017), Équipes PREFACE/ELIPSS, Fondation Nationale des Sciences Politiques (FNSP), Centre de Données Socio-Politiques (CDSP).
Notes: Population: All persons who answered the question on occupation ($N = 2411$; fourth column) and who made either donations ($N = 898$; second column) or tax-exempt investments ($N = 121$; third column). How to read: Of the taxpayers who benefited from a tax reduction for a tax exempt investment, 38.7% are executives.

manual and clerical workers make up almost 50% of the whole population and more than 30% of the taxpayers making donations account for only 16.4% of the people who made a tax exempt investment (Table 1). Taxpayers getting tax exemptions by virtue of investments are thus mainly recruited among the executives and the intermediate occupations. It can thus be stated that the investor population is over-represented in the higher classes. Tax exempt investments stand out by the length of the commitment they entail, which may explain why those who make use of them are higher-up in the social hierarchy.

While we have identified the social characteristics of the households which made tax exempt investments, the persons we interviewed are harder to situate precisely. When they made their investment, they were financially relatively stable: they all owned their main residence and the great majority no longer owed money on it. Some are in intermediate occupations, or were independent craftsmen or clerical workers, but most are private-sector executives (11 interviewees out of 28), heads of small businesses or professionals. The financial loss resulting from the investment affects them very differently, depending on the stability of their situation. For the majority, the investment primarily affects previous savings rather than the income used for current expenditures. The interviewees with the smallest incomes are the hardest hit; some found themselves over-indebted and were sometimes forced to sell their main residence. Others had to moderate their lifestyle because of the additional costs entailed by the investment:

> This auxiliary nurse in a private clinic, married to an independent craftsman, lives with her husband and two children near a large city. While her husband makes the financial decisions, she deals with all the paperwork and is in charge of the day-to-day spending.

> "Every month, I liked to buy myself something; if I wanted to, I would spend €150. I don't do that any more, that's for sure. And I say to myself, too bad, we have to […] I don't '*need*' it, but all the same you need to treat yourself. When you reach the age of 50, you think you ought to be able to, but I can tell you I have reduced the budget."

Thus, the investment that was made for accumulation purposes – or even to attain a higher social status – brings about *déclassement*. How can one explain that these taxpayers, who are relatively strongly endowed economically and socially, place their faith in salespeople extolling the merits of these investments? To understand it, we have to examine the relationship formed with the intermediaries who market such investments.

Laypeople Ill-equipped to Stand Up to "Professionals"

Taxpayers who lack the skills to embark alone in complex schemes are the preferred targets for the salespeople, as shown by the account of this retired speech therapist.

> Having first worked as a self-employed speech therapist and then as an employee, this taxpayer is now retired, like her husband, a former salesman in a small electrical goods business. In the household, she deals with administrative matters, handles the budget, and deals with tax matters. She relates how they had had a tax reduction of €3,000 for loan interest when they bought their house and, some years later, launched into a much bigger operation:

- "In 2007, my husband was already thinking of a tax exempt investment, whereas I chiefly wanted our children to be able to house themselves properly. We talked about it with our advisor at the bank, who recommended us to another person who sold apartments under a tax exemption scheme. What I liked about it was that it was two-way."
- "What do you mean?"
- "He explained to us that there was a housing shortage and this scheme produced affordable rented accommodation. We were naïve. He told us it was a well-located apartment, in an expanding town where there would soon be schools, shops – a very desirable area. We trusted him implicitly. We were so trusting that we didn't look at property prices in the area. We bought it on a credit plan for €145,000, without knowing the prices in the town […]. When it was finished we had a look, and we saw how we had been duped: it's next to a highway which makes terrible noise. But it was too late. Now it is valued at €55,000."

Like many taxpayers of her age, this young retiree, who had paid off her main residence, wondered how to make use of her savings, without having skills in investment matters. Having already benefited from tax reductions for her main residence, she was immediately won over by her bank advisor's suggestion that she invest in a new property and be exempted from income tax on the corresponding sums. With a layperson's relation to taxation, she therefore let herself be referred ("trusting implicitly") to a salesman who offered the couple the opportunity to buy on credit an apartment subject to tax exemption: by committing themselves to rent it for nine years, they could expect a tax reduction equivalent to the installments on the loan over the whole period. Having no initial capital, the couple abandoned the (wife's) idea of buying an apartment that could be used immediately by their children and embarked on the tax exemption project preferred by the husband, which meant not being able to choose the location and having to wait several years before using it themselves. This change of direction accepted by the household was based on three main arguments. Having already benefited from several tax exemption schemes, the couple thought they were taking a decision in line with the previous ones, whereas it was in fact a real investment decision committing them over a longer period. Next, the tax reduction mechanism was encouraged by the state, which lent it an intrinsic legitimacy: for taxpayers unused to investing, the choice of putting one's savings into real estate is rather reassuring, especially under a scheme backed by the authorities. Finally, the measure was presented as a way of facilitating access to housing for students or families living in "expanding areas" where accommodation is in short supply. This opportunity to combine an individual advantage via tax exemption with a contribution to a good cause constitutes a third, more symbolic argument: for many middle-class households, this form of property ownership is also a way of demarcating themselves from the working classes by adopting the optimization practices of the upper classes. Like many others, the couple did not take the time to visit the site or inform themselves about local property prices. Lacking the means to hire the services of an accountant or an asset manager, they put themselves in the hands of these sales representatives who offered them a ready-made purchase for which they had to make no administrative effort. Having been persuaded that they could thereby reduce their tax bill and at the same time build up capital for their retirement, they indebted themselves for several years to purchase an over-valued, poorly located apartment. A year or two later, the apartment bought on credit turned out to be hard to rent and over-priced. This account illustrates the attractiveness of tax exemption schemes for middle-class households seeking to reduce their tax bills and, at the same time, derive advantages for the future. Lacking the expertise to handle housing loans and the tax exemption rules, they are more likely to lose their way than more experienced taxpayers or those better guided in this area.

The aggrieved taxpayers often mention their incompetence in financial and tax matters to explain their gullibility and the trust they placed in the salesman. An engineer, married to a teacher with whom he had just bought a house on credit when signed up to buy a tax investment property, recalls the painful memory of this investment, which led to financial losses.

> They created a lot of small investors, who had just about enough to invest but knew nothing about investment, and they presented things to them in a hyper-simplistic way, when they weren't simple at all. But really I'm not an investor, I just wanted to set aside a bit of money for my retirement, build up a nest for my children, that's all [..]. I really wanted to do it for the sake of security.

In this extract, the engineer counterposes a logic of investment, specific to experienced operators, and a logic of savings, that of the laypeople among whom he classifies himself. The tax exemption schemes set up by the state lead to confusion between saver and investor, and this ambiguity gives rise to disappointment. Unlike buyers who can and know they should consult one or more advisors to weigh the risks of each decision, they found themselves in a "forced channeling" (Trompette, 2007, p. 5). They were approached about a construction project which might not even have started and which involved capital that was largely fictitious at the moment of signing: most of the investments require no initial input and are therefore based on monthly installments in the years to come. The risk is therefore less perceptible than when the capital at stake is already assembled.

Another engineer worked in an executive role in an aeronautics firm in southern France. Having divorced, he found himself handling the administrative and tax matters that his wife used to address. He relates:

> They were the ones who came looking for me. I didn't even know you could get tax exemption, I tell you, I knew nothing about all that. If you ask me to fix your computer or make a drone fly, or how a mechanical watch works, then I can draw you diagrams, explain everything to you, but if you ask me how tax exemption works, anything administrative, there I know absolutely nothing. So, these people came looking for me, I didn't ask anyone for anything.

While he has a significant income from his executive status and modest liquid savings which he wants to use to pay for his daughter's higher education, this interviewee had never thought about ways of investing this money. He placed himself in a logic of accumulation oriented more toward capital build-up than yield. The salesman indeed invited him to invest without drawing on his savings, envisaging an entirely loan-based scheme. He encouraged him to commit himself for money he did not yet have. The terms of the discussion remained very abstract: the capital involved was not visible, the money to be borrowed did not yet exist, and the apartment was virtual because it was not yet built.

Lack of financial expertise, mentioned by the interviewees to explain their misfortunes, does not suffice to explain the relation of domination established by the salespeople. Indeed, some respondents diverge from the image of the layperson in financial and tax matters that is found in most of the interviews. For example, a microelectronics engineer with a PhD, working in a start-up, described at length the set of precautions he took before embarking on a purchase of real estate: he "reworked all the calculations" to check the outline plan he had been given, considered that he had "quite quickly understood how it worked," and stressed that he had refused a loan in Swiss francs as "too dangerous" and himself negotiated a loan from his bank. In this case, as in some others, his signing up to a risky investment did not stem from a lack of competence in financial and tax matters, but from a relation of deference towards the law and the intermediaries who claim to work for it.

The technical nature of law and taxation is conducive to the development of a relationship of delegation, favored by sales representatives who offer to take charge of everything, from management of the property to help with the tax declaration, including negotiating a loan from a bank and finding a notary. This delegation is initially seen as positive, for people who want to invest their money without investing too much time. This is why the interviewees agreed to buy apartments sometimes very far from their own homes, imagining they would never need to go there because everything was taken care of. The relation of delegation is also induced by numerous reassuring signals that the salesman gives from the first encounter, by visiting the clients at home and promising to assist them throughout the process. The interviewees describe them as affable experts, precise, generous with their time: "The gentleman made a very good impression"; "The man was very […] yes, very nice. And he really knew how to talk to people at their level"; "But very charming, you know. Charming, good-looking, and everything." This mechanism of delegation to a figure perceived as competent is reminiscent of the relation of deference toward the educational system among populations deprived of cultural capital (Bourdieu & Passeron, 1979). As in the case of the educational institution, someone who follows the rules has less chance of making the most of it than someone who has learned to play with the rules, without following them to the letter. Legal intermediation functions like any institution possessing a legitimate knowledge: the technical character of tax matters makes it possible to distinguish those who have learned to be wary of intermediaries and keep them under control and those who entrust themselves completely to them. The difference may be fine, but it seems essential for understanding the impression of having been duped through lack of awareness of the risks associated with these investments.

The taxpayers endowed with the most economic capital do not necessarily have a greater grasp of financial matters; they may even find administrative documents and tax forms repellent (Sherman, 2017). Unlike small savers who see tax reduction as an end in itself, they have sufficient resources to optimize their investment decisions by targeting yield and not being locked in a tax-based logic:

> As regards tax on individuals, there are many ways of optimizing your tax bill. Personally, I have already made two tax-exempt investments, under the Scellier scheme, taking care that they were in areas where you could easily be rented out. I didn't do it in a development of 500 dwellings built next to a village with 1,000 habitants. I took advice from my advisor at the bank and from a friend who is an asset manager. It's an investment, after all, and not a decision to be taken lightly […]. I've never had unpleasant surprises with tax exemption. (Interview with finance manager of a fashion business, Paris)

The former head of an IT firm who specializes in management takes a close interest in all the ways of optimizing the tax bills of his various clients and is also careful to minimize his own contributions. He sees these schemes as investment-leverage devices and chooses them on economic and accounting criteria, taking advantage of the windfall effect of these opportunities. His way of using tax exemption schemes is very different from that of the taxpayers we encountered, who, enchanted by the idea of reducing their taxes, entrust themselves to the expertise of salespeople working on behalf of real-estate firms.

Laypeople are unequally equipped to stand up to sales representatives. What distinguishes them from other purchasers is not so much their economic, financial, and taxation competences as their deference toward legal intermediaries, the place of investment in the household finances, and also the captive configuration in which they find themselves. Legal intermediation is thus the source of a division between users who entrust themselves completely to intermediaries and others who can afford to face possible financial setbacks and/or are concerned to keep full control of the capital at stake.

THE PRODUCTION OF DISTRUST OF THE LEGAL SYSTEM

The interesting aspect of the cases of the taxpayers misled by tax exemption salespeople also lie in the experience that many of them had with the legal system. When they realized the losses they had incurred, some tried to secure redress and contacted an association for the defense of investors.[5] They very quickly had an interview with the chairwoman, who encouraged them to mobilize the other purchasers of the building where they had bought their property, so to engage a collective action. They were then brought into contact with a second type of legal intermediaries: lawyers specializing the legal representation of duped investors. With these legal professionals, intermediation was again a source of domination for laypeople who did not always understand legal procedures and most of whom were encountering the legal system for the first time. As the long and expensive procedure went on, their positive view of lawyers, justice, and the state progressively turned into a deep sense of mistrust.

Starting an Action: A Prospect of Redress

For many of these cheated taxpayers, engaging a legal action offered a prospect of securing redress, on the condition that were aware of the wrong done to them ("naming") and could identify those responsible ("blaming") (Felstiner, Abel, & Sarat, 1980). For example, a teacher in a public conservatory describes how she understood the cause of her misfortunes while listening to a radio program in which a Paris-based lawyer described the plight of people who, like her, had lost money on a property investment:

> There were lawyers and the testimony of people who had done the same operation as me. They described what had happened to them, and it was exactly the scenario I had gone through. I could see myself in it. [...] And then I said to myself, 'That's it, now I understand, it's a great fraud.' Somehow that was a relief, because I had been cheated and somehow I knew I was not responsible. I had been stupid, of course, but it wasn't bad management on my part. At last I understood the situation.

Struggling with debt after becoming unable to repay her mortgage, she describes this radio broadcast as a turning point at which she became aware for the first time that other people had also been misled and that she could put herself in the hands of a specialist to seek redress through the legal system ("claiming"). For her, akin to the other cheated savers, the prospect of undertaking a legal action was a way of retaking control and giving legal and political meaning to their sense of victimization. Because the cost of a consultation was not very high, many asked the lawyer for an opinion on their individual case in order to know their chances of winning. Those who engaged an action were often neither the richest nor the poorest, but rather those who had been hit hard enough financially to have to change their lifestyle but who could still find the resources to take legal action. The harm done to them was seen as an insult; it was also a matter of "keeping face" (Goffman, 1959) and obtaining legal recognition of their status as victims. Many of them thus started legal proceedings with a view to obtaining redress and avoiding the role of passive victim. This interviewee, living in the Paris metropolitan area, trained as an engineer but now working as a sales executive for a car company, had invested in a tax exempt property and explains the reasons that led to start the proceedings:

> I didn't intend to leave it at that. Even if the lawyer cost me still more money and even if I did not get redress. At least, I would have tried what it takes to be compensated. For me it was a way of showing the people who made me buy this property that I wouldn't let them get away with it, that they couldn't just ring doorbells and rip off everyone like that, that some people would stand up for themselves.

The legal action ("claiming") thus took on a symbolic significance: it enabled the misled investors to reverse the stigma of the confidence trick and show that their story was not the product of individual but of an organized deception by professionals who should be punished and sanctioned. The association strengthened them in this idea by encouraging them to fight a battle in the name of small savers against the banks and the tax exemption marketers. But while presenting itself as a legal intermediary alongside the victims, it maintained an ambivalent attitude toward the courts: the legal system was presented both as a tribunal from which one could obtain redress and as a wheel in a system that protects the powerful and crushes the weakest. Thus, one reads in the book published by the chairwoman that "the embryonic revolt of some investors suffered unfairly from the ignorance of the authorities and the judges."[6] The association engaged them in a legal battle which it explained in advance it might not necessarily win, implicitly suggesting that the judges and the developers would protect each other. This was also a way of excusing itself in advance of a trial in which the investors lost.

The whole work of the association consisted in hearing and grouping the complaints of the cheated savers: it asked each claimant to mobilize all the other purchasers of the estate so as to organize a collective action which could be brought before the courts. It then referred them to two lawyers who presented themselves as specialists in commercial contracts and who reformulated an individual and singular wrong into an injustice perpetrated against savers. They could thus play the role of "cause lawyers" (Sarat & Scheingold, 1998). A former senior manager in a publicly owned enterprise, now retired, relates first meeting with these legal professionals:

> When we heard the lawyers talk on the subject, we thought they were people committed to a certain justice. They were not seeking gain but helping people who had been cheated. It isn't right that people are cheated. We thought they were on the side of social justice.

Far from stressing the legal dimension of tax exemption schemes, the lawyers, like the association that recommended them, emphasized their commitment to secure justice for people cheated by a coalition of the powerful – developers, banks, notaries, and insurance companies. It was this image that subsequently began to fade away, when the complainants' case entered the judicial arena.

The Production of Distrust

The relationship that formed between the lawyers and their lay clients progressively revealed a relation of domination at the expense of laypeople who did not master legal proceedings and were forced to entrust themselves to experts. As they waited and saw their requests for advice ignored, the clients of these lawyers began to distrust these professionals. Many of them felt they received little support and shared with others their sense of abandonment. One of them was this hospital manager:

> I think all the same the worst thing is feeling alone. Now, I have the impression of having written checks and just having to wait for justice. [...] The only recourse you have is to pay a lawyer, who gives you very little information. You see, you have the impression of being shut out [...]. The lawyer tells me nothing. Not a word. And I have the impression that I'm disturbing him when I telephone or send an email.

As the proceedings wore on, there was growing tension in his relations with the lawyer, whom he thought treated him disdainfully. Other interviewees highlight their incomprehension of the legal process. In the first meeting, the lawyers had used a language of moral redress that they found convincing, but the confrontation with the technical character of the law gave rise to great incomprehension and the sense of not being listened to. This interviewee, an executive in an aeronautics firm who, as has been seen, had already declared himself incompetent in financial and tax matters, likewise says of the case:

> When I read the documents from the lawyers, I don't understand half of what they are saying. They go off into details I can't see the point of. I ask myself, why is he telling me that? [...] He goes into aspects that make no sense to me but facts that seem fundamental to me, he doesn't even mention.

The discrepancy between the wrong done to them as seen by the plaintiffs and the legal definition of it as formulated by their lawyer was a source of disappointment. There followed from it a sense of dispossession regarding a case in which they were nonetheless actively involved in bringing together other savers for a collective action. One was surprised that the bank was attacked, another that the grounds for the complaint were reformulated, or was concerned about the vocabulary used. This senior civil servant who followed the procedure closely was critical of the vocabulary used by the lawyer in his conclusions:

> At first it was 'victim of a calamitous investment, sir', and so on. Then later he replaces that with 'considering himself misled and in any case having been ill-informed.' That's a big difference. [...] It's staggering. You start out with the status of victim and then in his conclusions, he's talking about impressions by writing 'considering himself misled.' That's unacceptable.

The often negative outcome of the hearings and the cost of the procedure completed the reversal of the view taken of the lawyers. For one building financed by tax exemption schemes, a single lawyer could take on the cases of ten or so clients brought together by the first plaintiff. For each individual case, the lawyer charged almost €5,000 and could double this sum in the event of an appeal. He could then handle a large number of cases heard in the same sessions and for which the arguments and procedures were identical. This collaboration between actors of the association and legal professionals gave a considerable scale to the judicialization of these disputes: the more the two lawyers dealt with similar cases, the more they could present themselves as specialists in these matters.

For the plaintiffs, the financial cost of the legal action could turn out to be considerable. This new experience compounded the earlier grievances and gave rise to a feeling of distrust of the legal system, as the same complainant explained:

> I regret it now. I regret having invested €10,000 only to end up in the same situation as at the start of the business [...]. We had no idea where we were going, we were stumbling from stage to stage [...]. My lawyer never gave me any indication [...] No support from the state, from the legal system, in fact not from anyone. We were abandoned by everyone!

As the judicial proceedings went on, there was a growing sense of having been duped a second time. The accumulation of lawyers' and court fees helped intensify a sense of incomprehension of a legal system that had seemed to offer the hope of redress. The expression "a justice that feeds itself" (*la justice se nourrit elle-même*) illustrates the suspicions that lurked about the probity of judges and lawyers, who often are accused of earning money whatever the outcome of the trial. At the end of a session in which the claim was denied, another interviewee, who manages a small construction firm, also declared:

> The lawyer doesn't give a damn whether you win or lose. If you end up homeless, that's not his problem. [...] One contact with the legal system and you learn straight away. You learn that, in the end, the lawyer is there to run his business.

The sense of distrust is thus first expressed towards the lawyer and then progressively expands to the whole profession, the legal system, and also to the state. The plaintiffs' defeat in the courts confirmed a sense of alienation from judicial institutions. The interviewees describe their indignation at an outcome that seems to them profoundly unjust.

Legal intermediation thus reveals itself to be a paradoxical process: it was just when the plaintiffs had the sense of retaking control, thanks to their legal battle that their sense of injustice was doubled by the decisions of the courts, who often awarded them neither financial compensation nor recognition of their status as victims. Through the trial, they had the sense of reliving the wrong they had already suffered. In the interviews, the similarity in the vocabulary used to describe the dishonesty of the salespeople and the ineffectiveness of the lawyers is striking. Having failed to win their case, both symbolically and materially, the plaintiffs have the sense of having been obliged into legal action despite themselves. Altogether, their indignation and sense of being abused are directed to the courts and the judges: "We wouldn't wish it on anyone to have to deal with the French justice system"; "I think the legal system is rotten." Ultimately, it is the state that is called into question, both because of its role as guarantor in the tax exemption scheme and because of the impunity the judges guaranteed for the commercial organizations responsible for the wrongs committed. Many consider that the judges' decision is explained by their wish to protect the state: "An unfavorable judgement would amount to admitting the responsibility of the state." Another interviewee interpreted the refusal of the tribunal to recognize the wrong done to him as the sign of an implicit alliance between the government, real-estate developers, and judges.

After their defeat in the courts, the plaintiffs thus felt they had doubly lost face. The misdeeds of the legal intermediaries had the effect of supporting or even increasing their distrust of judges, justice, and the state.

CONCLUSION

The case of tax exempt rental properties makes it possible to confirm that the law can be a resource instrumentalized by economic actors (Stryker, 2003). In the case of the real-estate tax exemption schemes in France, commercial intermediaries were able to persuade savers to indebt themselves so as to buy over-valued apartments in areas where it is difficult to find tenants. In a second stage, lawyers as legal intermediaries were able to persuade the plaintiffs to undertake legal actions, whereas these people often do not see their problem as connected to law or rights (Yngvesson, 1993). These legal actions were often bound to fail or gave rise to compensation rarely covering the legal costs. Thus, the work of legal intermediation between these professionals and their lay clients is a power relation enabling one side to take full advantage of the law and leading, for the other side, to disappointment and disagreeable consequences. The state plays a central role in these complex power relations. On the one hand, it is the guarantor of legitimacy in the sale of tax exempt real estate. It also appears, through the legal system, as the last-instance arbiter of disputes between misled clients and property developers. In the same way that Granovetter (1985) showed that the relationships that generate trust can also favor malfeasance, so too can legal intermediation contain the same ambivalence. To measure the scale of this difference, it is indispensable to adopt a sociological reading that takes account of the individuals'social position, resources, and capacity to defend their interests. These differentiated uses of the law also have powerful effects on the actors' legal consciousness, as in the case of sexual harassment (Marshall, 2005). We, again, find here the idea of a "managerialization" of understanding the law (Edelman, 2005), which stems from people's experiences of the law's application but takes different forms depending on the social position of the individuals concerned. It is then possible to show that representations of law and justice vary according to social positions of the actors involved and are closely correlated with their everyday experiences of these institutions.

NOTES

1. Depending on the year, they were equivalent to between a quarter and a third of all tax revenue; in 2016, there were still 451 such exemptions, amounting to €89.9 billion.

2. The conditions regarding the length of the rental, the reality of the rental, the location of the property, and the rent may then change according to the laws.

3. These schemes incentivizing investment in rental property, a French specificity, have had some degree of success. Two-thirds of the sales of new housing sales were made in the framework of the "Scellier" and "Robien" laws when these schemes were set up.

4. For more details, see http://quanti.dime-shs.sciences-po.fr/en/

5. The association was created in 2008 by a former saleswoman who had worked for a firm specializing the sale of tax devices encouraging investment. In her book (Giroz, 2012), she describes how for several years she sold such investments to clients and a network of acquaintances until she realized the recurrent risks and poor yields of these investments.

6. Giroz (2012).

BIBLIOGRAPHY

Aitken, R. (2007). *Performing capital: Toward a cultural economy of popular and global finance*. New York, NY: Palgrave Macmillan.

Baker, W. E. (1984). The social structure of a national securities market. *American Journal of Sociology*, *89*(4), 775–811.

Becker, H. S. (1960). Notes on the concept of commitment. *American Journal of Sociology*, *66*, 32–40.

Billows, S. (2019). Contracts as compliance mechanisms. Legal intermediation and the failure of French Retail Regulation. In A. Sarat (Ed.), *Studies in law, politics and society* (Vol. 81, pp. 151–174). Bingley: Emerald Publishing Limited.

Bourdieu, P. (1986). The force of law: Toward a sociology of the juridical field. *Hastings Law Journal*, *38*, 814–855.

Bourdieu, P., & Passeron, J.-C. (1979). *The inheritors: French students and their relation to culture*. Chicago, IL: University of Chicago Press.

Bradach, J. L., & Eccles, R. G. (1989). Price, authority, and trust: From ideal types to plural forms. *Annual Review of Sociology*, *15*(1), 97–118.

Buchter, L. (2019). "Companies can do better than the law": Securing rights for minorities as an insider activist in French corporations. In A. Sarat (Ed.), *Studies in law, politics and society* (Vol. 81, pp. 11–44). Bingley: Emerald Publishing Limited.

Carruthers, B. G., & Kim, J.-C. (2011). The sociology of finance. *Annual Review of Sociology*, *37*, 239–259.

Chan, C. (2012). *Marketing death: Culture and the making of a life insurance market in China*. Oxford: Oxford University Press.

Cochoy, F. (2007). A brief theory of the 'Captation' of publics: Understanding the market with little red riding hood. *Theory, Culture & Society*, *24*(7–8), 203–223.

Dobbin, F. (2005). Comparative and historical approaches to economic sociology. In N. J. Smelser & R. Swedberg (Eds.), *The handbook of economic sociology* (Vol. 2, pp. 26–48). Princeton, NJ: Princeton University Press.

Dynan, K. E. (2009). Changing household financial opportunities and economic security. *The Journal of Economic Perspectives*, *23*(4), 49–68.

Edelman, L. B. (1992). Legal ambiguity and symbolic structures: Organizational mediation of civil rights law. *American Journal of Sociology*, *97*(6), 1531–1576.

Edelman, L. B. (2005). Law at work: The endogenous construction of civil rights. In L. B. Nielsen & R. L. Nelson (Eds.), *Handbook of employment discrimination research* (pp. 337–352). New York, NY: Springer.

Edelman, L. B. (2016). *Working law: Courts, corporations, and symbolic civil rights*. Chicago, IL: University of Chicago Press.

Edelman, L. B., Erlanger, H. S., & Lande, J. (1993). Internal dispute resolution: The transformation of civil rights in the workplace. *Law and Society Review*, *27*(3), 497–534.

Edelman, L. B., & Suchman, M. C. (1997). The legal environments of organizations. *Annual Review of Sociology*, *23*(1), 479–515.

Edelman, L. B., & Suchman, M. C. (1999). When the "Haves" hold court: Speculations on the Organizational Internalization of Law. *Law and Society Review*, *33*(4), 941–991.

Felstiner, W., Abel, R. L., & Sarat, A. (1980). The emergence and transformation of disputes: Naming, blaming, claiming. *Law & Society Review*, *15*(3/4), 631–654.

Giroz, C. (2012). *Défiscalisation ou défricalisation*. Marignier: Éditions Le Porte-Voix.

Goffman, E. (1959). *The presentation of self in everyday life*. Garden City, NY: Doubleday Anchor.

Granovetter, M. (1973). The strength of weak ties. *American Journal of Sociology*, *78*(6), 1360–1380.

Granovetter, M. (1985). Economic action and social structure: The problem of embeddedness. *American Journal of Sociology*, *91*(3), 481–510.

Hacker, J. S. (2004). Privatizing risk without privatizing the welfare state: The hidden politics of social retrenchment in the United States. *American Political Science Review*, *98*(2), 243–260.

Harmes, A. (2001). Mass investment culture. *New Left Review*, *9*, 103–124.

Harrington, B. (2008). *Pop finance: Investment clubs and stock market populism*. Princeton, NJ: Princeton University Press.

Hatchuel, A. (1995). Les marchés à prescripteurs. In Jacob, Warin (ed.). *L'inscription sociale du marché, Paris, L'Harmattan*, 203–224.

Howard, C. (1997). *The hidden welfare state: Tax expenditures and social policy in the United States*. Princeton, NJ: Princeton University Press.

Kellogg, K. C. (2009). Operating room: Relational spaces and microinstitutional change in surgery. *American Journal of Sociology*, *115*(3), 657–711.

Marshall, A.-M. (2005). Idle rights: Employees' rights consciousness and the construction of sexual harassment policies. *Law & Society Review*, *39*(1), 83–124.

Mettler, S., & Soss, J. (2004). The consequences of public policy for democratic citizenship: Bridging policy studies and mass politics. *Perspectives on Politics*, *2*(1), 55–73.

North, D. C. (1991). Institutions. *Journal of Economic Perspectives*, *5*(1), 97–112.

Pélisse, J. (2004). From negotiation to implementation. A study of the reduction of working time in France (1998–2000). *Time and Society*, *13*(2–3), 221–244.

Pélisse, J., & Talesh, S. (2019). How legal intermediaries facilitate or inhibit social change. In L. Holden & A. Sarat (Eds.), *Studies in law, politics and society* (Vol. 78, pp. 111–145). Bingley: Emerald Publishing Limited.

Pélisse, J. (2019). Varieties of legal intermediaries. When non-legal professionals act as legal intermediaries. In A. Sarat (Ed.), *Studies in law, politics and society* (Vol. 81, pp. 101–128). Bingley: Emerald Publishing Limited.

Pierson, P. (1993). When effect becomes cause: Policy feedback and political change. *World Politics*, *45*(4), 595–628.

Pollard, J. (2009). Political framing in national housing systems: Lessons from real estate developers in France and Spain. In H. Schwartz (Ed.), *The politics of housing booms and busts* (pp. 170–187). New York/Basingstoke: Palgrave Macmillan.

Pollard, J. (2011). Les groupes d'intérêt vus du local. Les promoteurs immobiliers dans le secteur du logement en France. *Revue française de science politique*, *61*, 681–705.

Revillard, A. (2017). Social movements and the politics of bureaucratic rights enforcement: insights from the allocation of disability rights in France. *Law & Social Inquiry*, *42*(2), 450–478.

Salamon, L. M. (1995). *Partners in public service: Government-nonprofit relations in the modern welfare state*. Baltimore, MD: Johns Hopkins University Press.

Sarat, A., & Scheingold, S. A. (Eds.). (1998). *Cause lawyering: Political commitments and professional responsibilities*. Oxford: Oxford University Press.

Shapiro, S. P. (1987). The social control of impersonal trust. *American Journal of Sociology*, *93*(3), 623–658.

Sherman, R. (2017). *Uneasy street: The anxieties of affluence*. Princeton, NJ: Princeton University Press.

Shuey, K. M., & O'Rand, A. M. (2004). New risks for workers: Pensions, labor markets, and gender. *Annual Review of Sociology*, *30*, 453–477.

Stanziani, A. (2004). Wine reputation and quality controls: The origin of the AOCs in 19th century France. *European Journal of Law and Economics*, *18*(2), 149–167.

Stryker, R. (2003). Mind the gap: law, institutional analysis and socioeconomics. *Socio-Economic Review*, *1*(3), 335–367.

Swedberg, R. (2003). The case for an economic sociology of law. *Theory and Society*, *32*(1), 1–37.

Trompette, P. (2007). Customer channeling arrangements in market organization: Competition dynamics in the funeral business in France. *Revue française de sociologie*, *48*(5), 3–33.

Uzzi, B. (1996). The sources and consequences of embeddedness for the economic performance of organizations: The network effect. *American Sociological Review*, *61*(4), 674–698.

Vincent, F. (2019). A multi-level approach to 1 legal intermediation: The case of the 12-hour work derogation in French Public Hospitals. In A. Sarat (Ed.), *Studies in law, politics and society* (Vol. 81, pp. 69–100). Bingley: Emerald Publishing Limited.

White, H. C. (2002). *Markets from networks: Socioeconomic models of production*. Princeton, NJ: Princeton University Press.

Yngvesson, B. (1993). *Virtuous citizens, disruptive subjects*. New York, NY, Routledge.

Zelizer, V. (1979). *Morals and markets: The development of life insurance in the United States*. New York, NY: Columbia University Press.

A MULTI-LEVEL APPROACH TO LEGAL INTERMEDIATION: THE CASE OF THE 12-HOUR WORK DEROGATION IN FRENCH PUBLIC HOSPITALS

Fanny Vincent

ABSTRACT

Adopting an intra-organizational viewpoint is essential to grasp legal intermediation. To deepen our understanding of such phenomena, this chapter proposes a qualitative and "multi-level" approach drawing on insights from the neo-institutional literature, policy ethnography analysis and the research on legal intermediaries. Such a perspective is particularly suited to capture the complexity and the depth of institutional change. Using the 12-hour work legal mechanism of derogation in the context of French public hospitals as an example, this chapter highlights how both macro-level actors (actors of a "reform network"), and micro-level ones (hospital directors) contribute to the shaping and framing of legality in French public hospitals. Results show that variation in how those actors use law depends on the local configuration. Second, results demonstrate that the legal games they play are not merely based on symbolic and superficial compliance with the law, but also on outright manipulations and conscious rule-breaking.

Keywords: Legal intermediaries; French public hospitals; managerialization of law; working time law; multi-level approach; 12-hour work derogation

Legal Intermediation: A Processual Approach to Law and Economic Activity
Studies in Law, Politics, and Society, Volume 81, 69–99

ISSN: 1059-4337/doi:10.1108/S1059-433720190000081004

INTRODUCTION

Hospital managerialization is a well-documented process in both the United States and Europe (see Scott, Ruef, Mendel, & Caronna, 2000 for the US; McNulty & Ferlie, 2004 for different European countries; and see Belorgey, 2010; Juven, 2016; Pierru, 2007, 2013 for France specifically). Beyond national specificities, reforms in the organization and management of Western health systems are inspired by the principles of the New Public Management "doctrinal puzzle" (Bezes, 2009; Hood, 1995; Pollitt & Bouckaert, 2004; Pollitt, van Thiel, & Homburg, 2007). They are also based on certain convergences in institutional logics (Friedland & Alford, 1991), in particular on the increasing importance of management, control and evaluation tools aimed at streamlining the hospital, making it more "efficient" and less costly (Juven, 2016; Ruggie, 1992). It has also consisted in a process of rationalization, normalization, and protocolization of professional work (Castel & Robelet, 2009; Timmermans & Berg, 1997, 2003). In addition, the introduction of "new governance" has reorganized relations between health system actors and transformed the internal hierarchical structure of hospitals. This has challenged the position of the medical profession (Light, 2004; Quadagno, 2004; Starr, 1982) and consolidated the place of a results-based management centered on achieving objectives, while being submitted to performance evaluation (Domin, 2011). This logic has resulted in a "managerial *aggiornamento*" of the hospital (Divay & Gadéa, 2015), which has transformed the work of directors and how they interpret and use labor law. In this configuration, legal rules regulating working time have undergone a process of managerialization (Vincent, 2016). The position and role of directors has also been reconfigured (Schweyer, 2006). While, in the 1980s, this professional group was still strongly structured around the idea of public service, during the 1990s its development was ultimately influenced by the management-based approach, with a strengthening of State control over public hospitals, and tended to make them follow the standards of private-sector executives (Pierru, 1999). They now viewed themselves as business leaders responsible for managing the hospital as a company by balancing revenue and expenditure, defining the hospital's working time policy and being held accountable for it. All these different dynamics led to *a managerialization of the hospital*. In other words, it means the introduction and diffusion of market-oriented ways of thinking and acting, practices, and instruments within the public sector.

In this chapter, I study the general phenomenon of managerialization of the hospital in the light of the concept of *legal intermediaries*. These actors interpret and implement the law, appropriate and transform legal norms without necessarily being legal professionals, according to the definition made by Jérôme Pélisse (2014). They thus play an important role in shaping and framing legality. I propose to illustrate the relevance of this analytical approach through a study of the French empirical case. More especially, the main thrust of the chapter is to analyze the role hospital directors and hospital's reformers play in the hospital managerialization process and the rise of derogation in French labor law. To achieve this, I investigate three examples of legal strategies that hospital directors pursue to justify their use of a specifical derogation: *the 12-hour derogatory shifts*. I also study the discourse of the members of a wider "reform network" at the national level because it supports a conception of law that legitimizes the managerial uses of the derogation made by directors.

I therefore identify these actors as different types of legal intermediaries. First, I consider hospital directors, who work inside hospitals, that is at the micro-level. Neither street-level bureaucrats (Lipsky, 1980) nor frontline workers (Maynard-Moody & Musheno, 2004), they may be considered intermediaries in two ways: because of their position between the State and caregivers – they are the privileged spokespeople of the State authorities to whom they are accountable – and for their role in applying the law to hospitals. They establish, guarantee and authorize a specific use of the rules, transposing and adopting their own standards and "[sometimes] giving themselves rights while applying the law" (Pélisse, 2011b). Hospital's reformers are the second type of legal intermediaries I consider. They act on the national level (i.e., at the macro-level) and, in this respect, can be considered to be institutional entrepreneurs. They belong to the Health Ministry, the Finance Ministry, the Regional healthcare agencies, consulting firms, the French Hospital Federation (FHF – a lobby group representing public hospitals in dealings with the public authorities), the Court of Auditors, etc. They pinpoint the uncontrolled rise in medical spending and blame hospitals' internal organizational problems as the chief source of their difficulties. They exert managerial pressure on hospital directors and constitute a "reform network" (Topalov, 1999) of the French public hospital.

Through the way they reconfigure, circumvent, and abuse the law to serve hospitals' economic interests and managerial logics, all these actors play a structural role in constructing the meaning of working time law and compliance. They contribute to the framing of legality within organizations and thus become actors of social change (Talesh & Pélisse, 2019).

Then, in this chapter, I describe more especially how hospitals grapple with 12-hour derogatory shifts. The term "derogation" refers to a legal tool that organizes and allows exceptions to certain regulatory provisions. Technically, it means that one norm is allowed to replace another norm. In France, this technique is almost as old as labor law. Whether derogations change rules in favor of workers or employers has varied over time. Historically, per the "principle of favour" (*principe de faveur*), derogations improved the condition of workers. However, since the 1980s, this principle of favor has faded away: now, a new local rule can replace another one, even if it is less favorable to workers. This new type of derogations is increasingly used by organizations (Pélisse, 2004). The 12-hour shifts in public hospitals should be understood in this context. The growing trend toward derogatory work schedules is part of a broader pattern – already described by sociologists and economists – of destabilization of working time standards (Bouffartigue & Bouteiller, 2003; Devetter, 2002) and a "rise of illegalisms regarding the law" (Pélisse, 2004) in a context of economic crisis.

The 12-hour derogation mechanism is stipulated in Article 7 of the decree of January 4, 2002, which regulates the working time of French public hospital workers.[1] This chapter authorizes hospital directors to extend the working time of non-medical staff beyond the legal limit of nine consecutive hours for day shifts and 10 consecutive hours for night shifts (while fixing a new limit of 12 hours). Over the last 15 years, 12-hour shifts work has increased among nurses and assistant nurses in French public hospitals. Faced with controversy over the increase of these schedules, the Health Ministry decided to include the question in its 2013 annual social review of public health institutions. In 2015, it emerged that around 11% of staff did 12-hour shifts on a regular basis and that almost 80% of hospitals established these working hours for at least one section of their staff (ATIH, 2016). However, this figure hides significant disparities between hospitals and professional groups. While less than 10% of staff work 12-hour shifts in some hospitals, in others the ratio increases to over 50% of staff. These schedules also mainly concern caregivers: nurses, specialist nurses[2] and assistant nurses. Shifts divided into two teams working 12 hours each tend thus to settle down as a norm as the traditional organization in shifts of 7.5 or 8 hours for morning and afternoon teams and 10 hours for night teams. For reformers and hospital directors, the 2 × 12 pattern is a useful tool for managing human resources and saving money (Figs. 1 and 2).

This type of non-standard work schedule appears overall to have a harmful effect on employees' health (Weibel, Herbrecht, Imboden, Junker-Mois, & Bannerot, 2014). It is particularly true in terms of fatigue, sleep, safety, risk of industrial accidents (Geiger-Brown et al., 2012; Knauth, 2007; Salminen, 2010; Smith, Folkard, Tucker, & Macdonald, 1998) and high-risk behaviors (Bushnell, Colombi, Caruso, & Tak, 2010). All of which increase under poor working conditions (Bourdouxhe et al., 1997; Folkard & Tucker, 2003). Despite this, 12-hour work shifts are paradoxically accepted and even requested by a high proportion of caregivers primarily because of the lower number of working days that result from the longer shifts (Vincent, 2017). Indeed, in France, the number of hours spent at work is counted and limited on a weekly and yearly basis. Compared to the traditional 8 or 10-hour work organization, working a 12-hour shift allows caregivers to fulfill their contractual obligations by working only 12 days per month, or around 128 days per year. In a context of deteriorating working conditions in hospitals (Algava, Davie, Loquet, & Vinck, 2014) and growing dissatisfaction (Dejours, 2015; Estryn-Behar, 1997; Sainsaulieu, 2003),

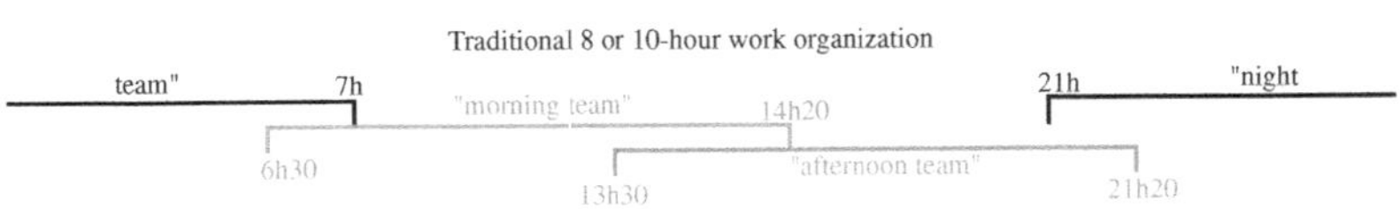

Fig. 1. Traditional 8 and 10-hour Shifts in French Public Hospitals.

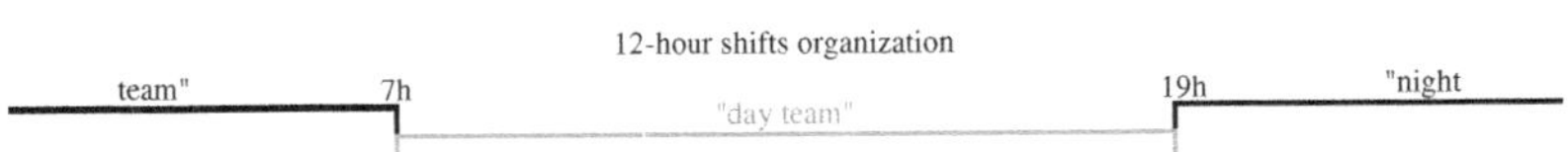

Fig. 2. 12-hour Shifts.

working 12-hour shifts allows nurses and assistant nurses to reduce the place of work in their lives. They say they have more time at home for their private lives and can better organize themselves (Vincent, 2014).

THEORETICAL FRAMEWORK: HOW THE LITERATURE ADDRESSES THE ROLE OF LEGAL INTERMEDIARIES IN THE MANAGERIALIZATION OF THE LAW

To analyze the role that legal intermediaries play in French public hospitals, I rely on three main frameworks: (1) the neo-institutional approach; (2) policy ethnography analysis; and (3) legal intermediation studies. Each of them highlights different aspects of the legal intermediation process I try to understand and explain. Following Kellogg (2011), I claim that to achieve a fine-grained analysis of legal games, the multi-level approach is the most relevant one.

The neo-institutional approach provides insight into the macro-level processes of institutional change. They allow to explain how the legal intermediaries who operate at the macro-level act: it helps to analyze who they are, specify and detail their practices, interests, discourses and worldviews. In other words, it helps to understand their impact on hospital organizations: that is, the way they disseminate practices across organizations by enacting and shaping new regulations, circulating new norms and developing new ideologies (Baron, Dobbin, & Jennings, 1986; Edelman, Uggen, & Erlanger, 1999; Tolbert & Zucker, 1983). But while these scholars with a macro-level approach help to understand the institutional framing of legality, they cannot explain how it is shaped within organizations. For example, some other neo-institutional scholars who have conducted empirical studies inside organizations have described that low-level actors (frontline actors) are critical to wielding ideas and accomplishing change in institutionalized practices (Barley, 1986, 2008; Hallett & Ventresca, 2006). Some medical sociologists have also shown through ethnographic studies that groups of actors inside hospitals support reform and implement regulations depending on their professional interests, beliefs, definitions of the situation and resources (Heimer, 1999; Heimer & Staffen, 1998). To explain the potential difference in outcomes between organizations, Katherine Kellogg demonstrated also that it is important to examine collective and individual actors inside organizations, their properties, organization members' capacity to resist or press for change, or micropolitical resources available in the local context (Kellogg, 2011). All these scholars show that a microsociological approach supplements the macro-institutional one.

Policy ethnography analysis developed by Vincent Dubois (2009, 1999) and others (Abdelnour, 2012; Belorgey, 2010; Spire, 2005) offers interesting perspectives to analyze the relationships between macro- and micro-levels. This sociology of public action breaks away from the top-down approach to public policy that is marked by a certain normativity and which seeks to evaluate the effectiveness of public policy (analysis based on decision-makers' initial objectives and discourses). Instead, it takes lower-level actors as its starting point, seeking to identify the chains of interdependence they form (Elias, 2004 [1981]) and the way in which they contribute to public policy. From this perspective, regulation cannot be summarized in terms of "public authorities" as the sole actors, nor be detached from social organization or the functioning of society of which it is a part. On the contrary, actors have different statuses and occupy a variety of positions. In fact, the macro-rationalization process of French public hospital affects the way directors consider legality, and how they build compliance, use, interpret, manipulate, apply or not the law and especially the 12-hour work derogation inside hospitals. But to understand how it occurs, we must pay attention to the local context, the intra-organizational resources they have and mobilize, the constraints they face, their properties, professional identities, beliefs, in addition to their material or symbolic interests.

But while this perspective encourages us to take the role of intermediary actors seriously, few researches take into account their role vis-à-vis the law (Spire, 2005, 2008). On that point, *legal intermediaries' studies* provide an interesting perspective on the work and role of these actors (Pélisse, 2014; Talesh & Pélisse, 2019). Indeed, besides variation in their resources and practices, these legal intermediaries act in a way that is comparable to legal professionals, appropriating and transforming legal norms, contributing to mediate laws in the book and legality, as Jérôme Pélisse suggests (Pélisse, 2016; see Pélisses contribution in this edited issue). These legal intermediaries may be part of the State, private organizations, or the civil society (Talesh, 2015a). Examples include members of human resources departments (Edelman, 1992, 2016), insurers (Talesh, 2015b), regulators (Abbott, Levi-Faur, & Snidal, 2017), job counselors, union representatives (Pélisse, 2014), safety officers in scientific laboratories (Pélisse, 2017), immigration office bureaucrats (Spire, 2008; Spire & Alpes, 2014), national tax center workers (Spire, 2012). More especially, many legal intermediaries' studies observe that these actors act in a managerial sense and refer to the legal endogeneity theory and more precisely to the theory of legal managerialization (Dobbin & Kelly, 1998; Edelman, 1992; Edelman, 2016; Edelman, Fuller, & Mara-Drita, 2001; Pélisse, 2014). Located at the intersection of the sociology of law and the sociology of organizations, the managerialization of law is "the process by which conceptions of law may become progressively infused with managerial values as legal ideas" and thus "move into managerial and organizational arenas" (Edelman et al., 2001, p. 1592). It sheds light on the way organizations take advantage of the ambiguity of regulations, develop a variety of visible symbols of compliance which help to reconfigure and reorient law towards their own economic interests and logic. As a result, the managerialization of law leads to an internalization (or even endogenization) of law by organizations, thus transforming the latter into legalized settings. While the theory of legal managerialization was developed to analyze Civil Rights in the United States, many studies show that it is also relevant to study other organizational contexts and countries (Bereni, 2009; Bereni & Chappe, 2011; Bessy, Delpeuch, & Pélisse, 2011; Billows, 2016; Chappe, Guillaume, & Pochic, 2016; Pélisse, 2004, 2011a, 2014; Vincent, 2016). As we will see, such managerialization occurs in the French public hospital, where key actors must meet managerial priorities such as efficiency, productivity or cost-saving, while complying with a tight framework regulating working time.

In order to highlight the work of these different legal intermediaries and their role vis-à-vis the law in the French public hospital, following Kellogg (2011, 2009) and Dubois (2009, 1999), I rely on *a multi-level approach of legal intermediations.* As exemplified by the case study presented in this chapter, such a multi-level approach is critical to understand who legal intermediaries are, both at the institutional/macro and "intra-organizational"/micro- level, and to explain how they contribute to the managerialization of law. Focusing on their interactions, the trade-offs they make, the justifications they give, this method allows capturing the complexity and the depth of institutional change. For that, I study three examples of legal games that directors play inside hospitals. The three cases show multiple dimensions of the managerialization of law and allow understanding the different uses or misuses of the law in the French public hospitals. Several elements allow analyzing these differences: the importance of local context, the interactions between actors at the micro-level, that is, directors, trade unions, care unit managers, but also the role played by actors at the national level by diffusing managerial norms inside hospitals. Paying attention to the interactions and practices of both macro- and micro-level actors shows how these actors make institutional change occur (Kellogg, 2011). All of them contribute to shaping regulations and framing legality, in different ways: either by influencing practices of hospital directors (at the macro-level) or using the law in managerial or illegal ways in order to comply with demands made by the French State. Their roles deserve thus to be analyzed together. Such a multi-situated approach brings to light the chains of interdependence that link these actors at different levels.

In what follows, I present the methods I used and then I describe how the intermediation processes led to a managerialization of labor law in French public hospitals, and what were the factors underpinning this dynamic. I show first that to understand practices and discourses of those legal intermediaries, it is necessary to review the way the law on working time was phrased in the first place. The ambiguity of the law helps to understand how actors used it strategically to justify their managerial practices. Based on the three different hospitals I studied, I then demonstrate that the way directors justified their uses of the 12-hour derogation depended on the context and social climate of the hospital. Finally, I underline that behind these differences lied a deep transformation of the function and the representation of labor law. This very managerial and manipulative conception of the law was developed by the actors of the "reform network" at the national level, who viewed the 12-hour shifts work as an "efficient" way of running hospitals.

METHODS

Ethnographic Data Collection

This chapter is based on a four-year qualitative and microsociological study. It centers here on a series of around 30 interviews conducted with institutional actors at the national level and with directors in three different French hospitals:

North Hospital, East Hospital and West Hospital. Then, I analyzed some trade union archives about the negotiations on the 35-hour week reform (which led to the decree on January 4, 2002 about the working time of French public hospital workers). I also analyzed documents from the archive of the Health Ministry about the working time issues since 1960s. My aim was to understand why the 12-hour work limit emerged as derogation and how it was negotiated. Moreover, I observed related events such as meetings about hospital management and trade union meetings. Finally, I relied more broadly on the ethnography that I conducted with caregivers over a four-month period in the care units of these three hospitals.

Those data provide a multi-situated approach of the 12-hour derogation, which allows getting at the political and social substance of this legal device. This approach avoids the trap of a sociology that is too singular, because exclusively based on the analysis of micro-level data, or disembodied, because only focused on macro-level phenomena with no concrete examples.

Three Case Studies

The three hospitals I studied are all of similar size, with a staff between 2,500 and 3,000, and at least two of them are in same financial situation, that is, have a balanced budget (I don't have that information for East Hospital). In each of them, I conducted interviews with the directors.

For West Hospital and North Hospital, I also read and analyzed the minutes of the meetings of the employee representative bodies – the committee on hygiene, safety and working conditions (CHSCT) and the establishment's technical committee (CTE) – for the last years (3 years for West Hospital and 12 years for North Hospital). I was particularly interested in the minutes of discussions held between hospital directors and trade union representatives regarding the introduction of 12-hour work shifts in new units. The objective was to identify their positions, the discourses they develop on the 12 hours in a context of increased rationalization of work organization and working time, and the way in which power relations take shape.

The analysis depends on the limitations of the material itself, which varies in size according to the session and the hospital in question, sometimes lacks information or details that may be of interest to sociologists and is potentially biased in the transcribing of each speech and the reliability of the content. But the documents are nevertheless useful for understanding the issues related to the 12 hours and law enforcement in hospitals.

THE LONGSTANDING AMBIGUITY OF THE LAW ON WORKING TIME: AN IMPORTANT SPACE OF INTERPRETATION THAT FAVORS MANAGERIAL USES OF THE LAW

A commonly held view of French government is that of a strong, centralized state with a well-developed welfare state and public infrastructure serving the general interest (Castel, 1995; Supiot, 2014). Depictions of this mode of government often refer to the Weberian ideal-type of rational bureaucracy and insist on how the French state ensures even and homogenous enforcement of decisions made at the top through centralized administrative management (Dobbin, 2009, p. 7). However, this view overlooks the heterogeneity and influence of local dynamics in the French political and administrative system (Frinault, 2012; Worms, 1966). In a survey of immigration policies, Alexis Spire shows, for example, how immigration officers working for the central state have maintained a monopoly over immigration control (Spire, 2005, 2008). Back-office managers have considerable leeway in deciding how to apply the law, regulations and procedures and in defining bureaucratic practices, while senior officials working as counter staff implement these practices in a socially situated way. He shows how the interpretation of these legal intermediaries and the mediation between legal texts and practices result in differential treatment of foreigners' requests.

In the French hospital system, history also shows that the laws established at national level have been implemented in multiple ways (Chevandier, 2009). On working time and shift supervision, hospitals have interpreted and applied the law unevenly depending on local power relations, despite administrative control by the State. Historically, hospitals and their directors, healthcare executives and trade unions have played a key role in constructing the legislative and normative framework for working time (Vincent, 2016). The result is a broad heterogeneity of work practices and shift systems in French hospitals. It is partly to remedy this situation and to homogenize practices that the 35-hour working week reform in 2002 sought to clarify the law (Ruhl & Katz, 2015). The reform led to increasingly dense, technical, and complex regulations on working time. It also intensified the workload of staff responsible for their implementation, particularly healthcare executives and hospital directors. However, behind the French government's desire to supervise hospitals' practices, the rules have sometimes remained ambiguous. It is the case with Article 7 of the implementation decree enacted in 2002, which provides for the possibility of derogating from the maximum legal working time within the limit of 12 consecutive hours. Such ambiguity is not an accidental outcome. To understand this, it is useful to look back at the time when this derogation was established in 2001, in the mid of the negotiations surrounding the 35-hour week reform.

The drafting of the derogation is primarily the *result of a compromise* between the trade unions and the Health Ministry. From 1982, the minimum period of uninterrupted rest between two jobs was 12 hours for public hospital workers. This mechanism already went further than the 1993 European directive imposing a compulsory rest period of 11 hours. Yet in the heavy-duty technical units of some hospitals where work does not follow a set schedule and the emergency factor plays an important role, midwives and specialist nurses work 12, 16, 24 and sometimes even 48 consecutive hours (including time spent on duty). It is mainly the case in intensive care units, gynecology-obstetrics departments, operating theaters and emergency units. Regarding occupational safety and safety of care issues, in 2001 the trade unions requested a better framework for working hours in these departments as well as clarification of the grounds for derogation and the staff concerned. The CFDT (French Democratic Confederation of Labor, a major trade union confederation) demanded a ministerial list of departments authorized to derogate from the 12-hour limit. Moreover, the CGT (General Confederation of Labor – another large trade union[3]) requested the maximum working time to be reduced to less than 12 hours. At the end of these negotiations, a compromise was finally reached with the ministry based on the following wording, which was transposed into Article 7 of the decree of January 4, 2002:

> Where the constraints of continued public service require so on a permanent basis, the head of the establishment may, having consulted the establishment's technical committee or joint technical committee, derogate from the daily working hours established for employees in continuous employment, although the working time may not exceed 12 hours.

The legal wording remains ambiguous. First of all, no definition is given for key terms such as "constraints of continued public service." While the term "continued public service" is traditionally understood as the need to guarantee continuity and safety of care 24 hours a day by providing an adequate supply of care, there is no mention of the nature of those constraints: does it refer to any type of organizational demands (level of staff needed, occurrence of an exceptional incident, the nature of the work carried out)? Does it include financial constraints? Second, the meaning of the verb "require" and the "permanence" of these constraints remain particularly ambiguous, opening up the possibility of multiple interpretations.

Article 7 was immediately condemned by the trade unions. The CGT expressed concerned about the ease with which directors could use the derogation by simply stating vague grounds. Moreover, the trade union pointed out the weakness of safeguards against directors' managerial use of the derogation when seeking to "respond to a need to put fewer people to work (particularly at weekends)" (a mere opinion from the establishment's technical committee would in fact suffice). It condemned the "institutionalization of the 12-hour work shift" that could result. For its part, the CFDT stressed the need to "remain vigilant" with regard to the 12-hour limit. According to the former general secretary of the UNSA (the National Union of Independent Trade Unions, another trade union, particularly present at hospitals) who had taken part in the negotiations, "all the unions were opposed to this notion of 12-hour working time" but the agreement was finally reached "tacitly with the government in order to let it go through for mid-wives. Only mid-wives." The content of the agreement thus remained implicit between the trade unions and the government, and the derogation was worded generally with no specific references to the cases concerned. While trade unions cited safety as a justification for supervising hospital practices, the Health Ministry emphasized the organizational aspect, as explained by the former director of Health Ministry hospitals who led the negotiations: "That's how it was viewed, as an organizational method. It was included in the national agreement so that the local [hospital] agreements would not oppose it." Far from regulating abusive practices in labor law, the Ministry considered the law as a means of protecting hospital organizations from a legal standpoint. The derogation led unions to believe they were providing a better framework for working time, while in fact the ambiguity it created allowed hospitals to maintain their 12-hour work practices in those units that were already using them, or even to derogate further for other units because of the many possible interpretations of the law. As Edelman clearly showed, ambiguity in the wording of laws and their vagueness are to blame for their weakness, as they "give organizations wide latitude to construct the meaning of compliance" (Edelman, 1992, p. 1532).

As a result, there is now a proliferation of hospital units and staff working permanent 12-hour shifts even though the derogation did not initially concern them: surgery, internal medicine, geriatrics, etc., as well as assistant nurses, hospital porters, ambulance technicians or fire safety officers. Moreover, there is usually no reference to the legal grounds for derogation.

(IL)LEGAL GAMES AND PRACTICES INSIDE HOSPITALS: THE IMPORTANCE OF LOCAL CONTEXT AND SOCIAL CLIMATE

What working time practices take place inside hospitals? The aim of this part is to analyze in concrete terms how hospitals' directors use and interpret the law. The examples I studied are drawn from the case of three hospitals: North Hospital, East Hospital and West Hospital. These three hospitals vary across key dimensions: financial status, social climate, proportion of staff on 12-hour work, when 12-hour work was introduced [...]. As I demonstrate below, these variables explain why hospitals behave differently vis-à-vis the law (Table 1).

West Hospital: Symbolic Compliance with the Law Based on a Strong Local Participatory Management Policy and Non-contesting Unions

At West Hospital, the number of 12-hour work shifts has skyrocketed since 2010. The issue clearly emerged in CHSCT debates from mid-2011 and was on the agenda in every meeting held in 2013 and 2014. The human resources director (HRD) and the director of care units continually claim that they are not responsible for this shift, which they cannot control: caregivers would voluntarily request them and under no circumstances would 12-hour shifts be used for workforce reduction purposes. In order to prove their goodwill and to rationalize the development of 12-hour work schedules, they ask caregivers to request those shifts through a well-argued written proposal. Requests should be collective and be supported by an entire team of caregivers.

The longest debates on the matter primarily concerned the move to 12-hour schedules among caregivers in geriatric units. They have systematically drawn criticism and concern from trade unions, due to the strenuous nature of the work performed in these units and the impact these new schedules may have on employees' health. The directors also expressed their reservations on the matter but they accepted faced with what they claim to be the team's overall

Table 1. Differences Between the Three Hospitals.

	West Hospital	North Hospital	East Hospital
Hospital size	Around 2,100 workers and 1,100 hospitalization's beds	2,200 workers and around 500 hospitalization's beds	2,900 workers and around 600 hospitalization's beds
Financial situation of the hospital	Surplus financial position	Surplus financial position	Unknown
Elements about directors' policy and position	Strong local tradition of participatory management and a key role of the director of care units and the human resources director	Succession of different general directors strongly concerned with developing the hospital activity and revenues, in particular in order to strategically position the hospital	Directors strongly convinced of the advantages of the 12-hour shifts in terms of healthcare organization and for team management
Part of staffs and/or caregivers in 12-hour work	21% of its staff but 65% of care units and around 40% of caregivers	40% of staff and almost 70% of caregivers	Around 5% of caregivers (only in the few highly technical units of the hospital: intensive care unit, constant cares unit […])
Year of introduction of the 12-hour shifts and development	First implementation in the 1980s in few units, but strong growth from the 2010s	First implementation in the 1980s, but strong growth in the early 2000s	2000s
Context of the implementations of the 12-hour shifts	*From the 2010s:* recruitment difficulties due to the competition from several private hospitals in the territory	*In the 1980s:* years of the hospital's creation: need to attract caregivers and will to implement a so-called "modern policy" of flexible working hours *In the 2000s:* recruitment difficulties; financial difficulties (big deficit); competitive environment for hospital Yet, only still two units without 12-hour shifts	Merger of two intensive care units with different schedules; many caregivers leaving following the merger and the introduction of the 12-hour
Justifications put forward for the introduction of the 12-hour shifts	*From the 2010s:* a way to attract and retain caregivers; an answer to the request of the caregivers; a way to develop "the quality of life at work"	A way to develop the attractiveness of the hospital to attract young caregivers, and to develop activity And also an answer to the request of the caregivers from the 2000s	A way to facilitate recruitment and team management in the merged intensive care unit; schedules considered more suitable for highly technical work with physicians (from the point of view of care organization)

Social climate	Peaceful relations between unions and directors. Unions non-contesting but questioning about long-term health effects of 12-hour shifts	Strained relations between unions and management Unions denounce that units with traditional working hours are decreasing alarmingly (concerned about long-term health effects), and denounce the non-accounting of handovers time	Strained relations between unions and management Unions contesting and bring the matter to court: they denounce the departure of caregivers due to the imposition of 12-hour work and the long-term health effects of this kind of shifts

commitment to trying the 12-hour schedule. They reassured the CHSCT that it was the staff themselves who had chosen this organization. The directors also justified their position by the flexibility they claimed to show, regardless of whether it takes them away from the legal grounds allowing the derogation: "Why would we refuse if caregivers generally request it?," said the HRD.

As 12-hour schedules were progressing to new units, directors wanted to protect themselves from trade unions opposing the move. To achieve this, they asked managers of units to submit all proposals to the CHSCT and CTE, and to establish a trial period. They also guaranteed the possibility to return to the previous work schedules, should the teams wish so. Gradually, union intervention became limited to organizational and procedural elements. Discussions were getting poorer and occupying less and less space in the debates. These schedules also raised less apprehension in other units than in geriatrics (in terms of physical pressure and risks for health). For these other units, the move to a 12-hour work schedules was perceived as a formality, considering how well-established the proposals procedure is. The proposals that care units' managers submit to the CHSCT were presented as based mostly on consensus, both in terms of the impact of 12-hour shifts on working conditions and support among caregivers. Concretely, these proposals were a nondescript document that left little room for criticism from unions. The issue of work reorganization was a central part of them. When a team requested to move to a 12-hour schedule, one manager she asked explained that the planned schedule followed three rules, which she presented to caregivers as follows:

> The institution needs to be happy with it [the 12-hour shifts], you [the caregivers] need to be happy with it, but the patient must be the one that benefits. I don't want to be given proposals for work schedules that mean we have to delay meal times and care times. Once I've made that clear I want to hear every side, but I want the patient to be happy and everyone else to be happy.

For caregivers, the idea that "everyone needs to be happy with it" meant proving that the 12-hour schedules they were requesting were more "rational" in terms of work organization than a traditional schedule based on three teams, regardless of whether or not they were a derogation. First, these work schedules had to be geared towards satisfying "users" (patients and families). This objective went hand in hand with performance: a well-performing organization was better able to meet its users' expectations. By focusing on users and optimized care units, that is on improving quality of care, the organization of work would become more "efficient." Backed by participatory management, this approach tended to encourage caregivers to support and commit to this process of seeking a rationalized organization of work. Mobilized as actors of change and supported by their manager, caregivers took responsibility for overhauling that organization. They defined and debated the priority objectives adapted to the unit in question and their work and proposed a method that was consistent with the policies of quality and "performance" advocated by the management. Managers could therefore assert that caregivers "felt they were more efficient" at work, thanks to the 12-hour work shift (greater autonomy, better organization of care, better continuity of care, better patient follow-up, etc.) and more satisfied with their work.

All these arguments were repeated ad infinitum in managers' discourse and proposals submitted to the CHSCT to supposedly "prove" the suitability of the 12-hour shift for the unit and caregivers. These documents were striking in their similarity. They were all drafted in the same style – with identical font, presentation and phrases used, giving the impression of having been passed on by managers – and follow the same pattern. They were based on an acknowledgment of staff dissatisfaction with the current organization and explain they had "reflected" on the relevance of a 12-hour shifts organization. Then, they clarified the advantages and disadvantages of such a change and finally highlighted the fact that "the entire team confirms its wish to try a 12-hour work schedule." The disadvantages were always fewer in number than the advantages and centered primarily on the risk of fatigue and sometimes the difficulties experienced during handovers. All the requests submitted focused on the optimization of care, patient follow-up, distribution of care throughout the day, staff numbers, pair work, increased rest days, better work-life balance for staff, reduction in fatigue, etc.

At West Hospital, the system organized by directors and managers appeared therefore as a device designed to maintain peaceful relations with unions by demonstrating compliance with the procedure and that the uses of the 12-hour schedules were justified. This device enabled directors to strengthen their right "to give themselves the right" (Pélisse, 2011b), while paradoxically allowing them not to mention the legal grounds required to authorize the derogation. The directors were clearly outside the legal framework but accepted and justified it. This case was thus representative of both violations or circumvention of the law, as well as the managerialization of law in French public hospitals: the attempt to prove that the hospital was complying with the law was based more on its adherence to established procedures and its desire to show that a 12-hour schedule was appropriate in managerial and organizational terms than on any actual respect for the content of the law. It was even more revealing of the role played by the unions. Compliance with a procedure established by the directors, even when that procedure disregarded some of the legal grounds required, seemed to be enough to disarm and neutralize any social critique traditionally made by trade unions and to impose, usually with their blessing, a managerial use of labor law or even a bypass of it.

North Hospital: Using the Law as a Resource to Justify Illegal Practices in the Face of Contesting Unions

Unlike West Hospital, at North Hospital 12-hour schedules are as old as the hospital. In fact, North Hospital was built in the late 1980s and was created with the ambition of being a modern and attractive hospital in terms of working time policy, with flexible and personalized schedules. 12-hour work was part of this policy. As a result, the unions consider that their resistance capacity on that issue is limited. For them, the balance of power is unfavorable to them because theses schedules existed from the beginning. However, the growth of 12-hour schedules happened in the 2000s. They have been mainly debated in CHSCT and CTE meetings. During meetings, unions and occupational physicians condemned the gradual move towards 12-hour shifts in all units of the hospitals (currently only two care units have not implemented 12-hour shifts) and questioned the impact on caregivers' health. The unions' criticism focused more especially on one particular point: accounting for handoffs times over the 12-hour limit. They claimed that the daily working time of caregivers was closer to 12.5 hours than 12 because teams overlapped to pass on information on each patient's situation – which was confirmed by my own observations in hospitals. Successive directors showed themselves uncompromising, arguing that working time cannot legally be counted beyond 12 hours because it was illegal. Officially, teams were staggered in the caregivers' arrivals, departures and handovers so as to avoid exceeding the 12-hour limit. In fact, directors were aware that their staff organize things differently and that the caregivers in one team all arrive and leave at the same time. It was making it easier for staff to pass on instructions, rather than having to repeat them to colleagues who arrive 30 minutes later. This practice nevertheless meant that they went over the 12-hour limit. As one former hospital director interviewed admited, "we modestly looked the other way."

Faced with pressure from union representatives to record the time actually worked, one executive director made an attempt to justify the legality of her choice. She commissioned one of the hospital's healthcare executives to make an audit of handover times in departments that used 12-hour shifts. The report highlighted considerable disparities between units, mostly for nurses (with times ranging from 10 to 50 minutes) and estimated that 15 minutes was the minimum time required for handovers. Based on these findings, the hospital director decided that the handover time would officially be set at 15 minutes twice a day (in order to cover morning and evening handovers). Some time later, she commissioned another review with the aim of quantifying handover times and the total breaks taken in a day. Based on a vague and debatable definition of what constituted a break time, both in terms of the law and the reality of the job, the director concluded that some of the breaks taken by caregivers exceeded 20 minutes per 6 hours of work provided by the law. As a result, she argued that they did not need to be paid. By allowing 15 minutes per team for handovers and withdrawing "non-regulatory" break times, the hospital's management thereby concluded that caregivers were not "actually" working for more than 12 hours and that the shift pattern was therefore legal.

The dissociation created between the time during which staff are present at work and the time they are actually working casts doubt on the legality of her decision. But the director insisted that the system used was compliant with the law. She based her justification on the audits she had commissioned, which she held up as evidence of her compliance with the legal framework. She thus used the law in two ways. On the one hand, she used it to support her decision not to count handover times, while on the other hand she bent the rules for calculating working time in an effort to prove the legality of 12-hour work schedules. However, she made only partial use of the legal repertoire, because the legal grounds of "constraints of continued public service" imposed by the 2002 decree were neither verified nor asserted in this case. Nor did the director seek to prove the legal compliance of the (clearly illegal) 60-hour working week in the hospital's units working 12-hour shifts. The legal standard was therefore used as a tool to legitimize the way directors protected the hospital's management interests: thanks to the 12-hour work schedule a part of the caregivers' labor costs was economized.

East Hospital: Using the Law as a Weapon against Unions

Much like North Hospital, East Hospital's directors make extensive use of procedures and the law in order to prove that the organization is compliant. The 12-hour work shift is not widely used in this hospital, but the caregivers in the intensive care unit (ICU) are among those who work with these derogatory schedules. According to the HRD at East Hospital:

> The 12-hour shift was chosen for reasons relating to the organization of care, because it turned out to be a classic shift pattern. 98% or 95% of intensive care units [in Parisian hospitals] work in 12-hour shifts. So it's a typical shift pattern. It's better adapted to the care and needs of patients. Also, we were still having real difficulties recruiting staff at the time. There was a logic of care organization and recruitment needs that led us to choose the 12-hour schedule.

This director clearly indicates that their transition to a 12-hour shift pattern was undertaken primarily for organizational reasons. The context is also important. In fact, the ICU is the result of the merger of two ICU, one operating with 12-hour shifts, the other with 8-hour shifts. In order to facilitate the management of the new big team, healthcare manager and directors decided to implement the 12-hour work for all the units, arguing furthermore that these schedules were the most appropriate for intensive care work, for the organizational reasons described above. But the ICU's healthcare manager decided to implement these work schedules before this change was presented to the union representatives in the CHSCT. Moreover, many departures of caregivers followed the merger. Considering that these schedules had been enforced without any respect for the procedure and the caregivers' will, the hospital's CGT representatives filed an appeal with the administrative court. Several months later, the court ordered the cancellation of the 12-hour schedule in the ICU, on the grounds of a procedural defect and non-compliance with the provisions of the 2002 decree, namely, the absence of "constraints of continuity of public service," which are normally needed to authorize a derogation from the legal working time. Meanwhile, most caregivers who had been subjected to these work schedules had left the hospital and the caregivers who had been recruited as substitutes were largely in favor of their continuation. Therefore, when the court ruled that the 12-hour work schedule must be cancelled, the caregivers' teams mobilized to maintain it and criticized the union's actions. The hospital's directors and the unit's managers supported the caregivers and came together to develop an organization based on 12-hour schedules that complied with the legal framework. The new organization was submitted to the union representatives in the CHSCT. However, the main argument put forward by directors, managers and caregivers remained focused on the organizational benefits of 12-hour shift patterns. Supported by data, they identified reduced need for weekend substitutions, lower levels of absenteeism, better caregiver training, better coordination with physicians, more efficient organization of care, fewer cases of lost information, improved patient follow-up, increased attractiveness for job, and the risk that the potential cancellation of the 12-hour shift pattern could lead to recruitment difficulties.

As management failed to enforce the court order and continued to use the 12-hour work schedule, the CGT filed a second appeal, which the directors countered by repeating what it had submitted to the CHSCT. All these factors were cited as evidence that "the constraints of continued public service specific to the intensive care unit require permanent use of this schedule." The directors used this argument in order to demonstrate the legality of the 12-hour schedule. They also relied on the many medical and managerial recommendations, which they used as evidence of their compliance with the law (the 12-hour shift pattern was recommended for the intensive care unit by doctors and the National Support Agency for the Performance of Hospitals alike). For the second time, the administrative court ruled in favor of the union, believing that the hospital had "not justified, with such arguments, the need to organize its working time into 12-hour shifts in the name of continuity of public service." The directors of East Hospital were furious and appealed the decision.

- The human resources director: "We have appealed in order for a legal position to be given. The text explicitly states that this is possible. [...] The judge's position is paradoxical."
- The director of care units: "The judge is trying to do our job for us. We cannot reasonably be expected to drop this appeal. [...]."
- The HRD: "And not just for our sake but for others' sakes too. It's madness that the judge has said [...]."
- The general director: "The issue of job attraction means that there could be a break in continuity of care if we are unable to recruit. [...]."
- The HRD: "As he can't issue a ruling by law he's issued one at his own discretion. [...] We oppose his decision. We have therefore appealed to the Administrative Court Appeal in the hope that they will rule in our favor. [...] The idea is not to save time but to show that we have the right to implement this kind of organization. If it has to go to the Council of State then so be it. Because this isn't just about us; it's about France as a whole."

The directors questioned the judges' legitimacy in ruling on the validity of the unit's work organization. They referred to another administrative court decision in which the judge had stated that it was not his job to replace the administration in evaluating the unit constraints and had therefore considered the chronic staff shortage to be valid grounds for a derogation. In that particular case, it is interesting to note that the court ruled in favor of the hospital's economic demands. This illustrates that directors were able to use an ambiguous rule to their own advantage. However, the court decision was different for East Hospital. Convinced of their rights, the directors criticized the judges' interpretation of the law, claiming they were more "ideological" than lawyers, and called for the rules to be changed: "the notion [of constraints of continued public service] is too imprecise, constricting and rigid. [...] If the court has once again ruled against us, then it means the decree needs to be modified; the text should be written from a management perspective," insisted the HRD. His comment clearly shows the directors' desire to legalize a work schedule that had nonetheless been judged illegal twice in court.

Far from ignoring the legal grounds for the derogation, managers of East Hospital referred to them and used them as evidence of their compliance with the law. Just as the executive director of North Hospital had done with handover times, they took advantage of legal ambiguity to bend the law in favor to them.

Following Kellogg (2009), we can say that the cases of these three hospitals reveal the importance of taking account *the local configuration and characteristics* to understand the different outcomes observed. They reveal that games with the law depend above all on local context, social climate and relationship with trade unions.

At West Hospital, unions appear to be muzzled by directors, which seems to want to preserve the social peace of the hospital. Directors argue their right to deviate from the law insisting on the request of the caregivers shown through the proposals drafted by managers and plead their innocence in the face of a bottom-up pressure. They also rely on a participative and delegated management policy. They thus avoid conflicts with unions.

At North Hospital, in consideration of the hospital's history, unions focus their demands on the preservation of classic schedules, the respect of the will of caregivers and the respect of the law on the accounting of handoffs times. Facing their claim, directors adapt their discourses and strategies. They try to justify not taking into account handoffs time by the same reference to the law as unions, seeking to prove that their interpretation is legal.

At East Hospital, the merger between units (which has led to the departure of many caregivers) and the forced passage of 12 hours by managers and directors drove unions to take action in court. Convinced of their right and the relevance of these schedules for organizational reasons, directors argued for a change in judges' interpretation of the law.

Finally, *severals factors allow to explain the directors's different justifications of their managerial uses of the law*. First, the time and contextual dimensions are central. The local configuration is not only defined by the interactions and positions defended by directors (supported by care managers) and unions at a specific time. It is also explained by "the interpenetration of the experiences and actions" of these actors (Elias & Dunning, 1994), depending on past and present circumstances. Depending on the context, directors use the law as a framework (West Hospital), as a resource (North Hospital) or as a weapon (East Hospital). Second, this perspective highlights that the role of unions is critical. It is when directors do not respect the rules of the game (organizational or economic justifications, non-compliance with the law, the procedures or the will of caregivers, etc.) that union action is transformed into a sanction and leads directors to justify the rights they give themselves vis-à-vis the law. This leads paradoxically to a double process of managerialization of law and legalization of organizations.

BEHIND DIFFERENT PRACTICES AND JUSTIFICATIONS, A MANAGERIAL CONCEPTION OF THE LAW, ENCOURAGED BY NATIONAL ACTORS

Games with the Law that Go beyond Symbolic and Superficial Compliance to the Law

The other finding that can be drawn from the case studies is the way hospital directors *claim legitimacy*.

In the same way as in Edelman's work (Edelman, 2016), these three cases reveal a juridicialization of hospitals (i.e., the "extension of the law as a model and practical reference for actions"; see Pélisse, 2009) based on a symbolic intermediation of law. Indeed, directors develop mechanisms and formalized procedures (audits, collective agreements, votes, legal actions, etc.) in order to prove that they are paying attention to and complying with the law. One of the formalized procedures most commonly used by hospital directors is the approval of 12-hour shifts in new care units by unions and particularly by those who sit on CHSCT. While the law specifies that the use of 12-hour shifts can be decided on by the director following a consultation with CTE, the practice now extends far beyond what is mandated by the law. It requires directors to present any proposed 12-hour shift first to the hospital's CHSCT union meetings and then submit it to the CTE. Indeed, changes to working schedules are known to affect working conditions and therefore the unions expect to be consulted on the issue. However, in many hospitals the procedure for discussing the move toward 12-hour shifts is largely symbolic. First and foremost, trade unions do not have voting rights and cannot veto the director's decision to establish derogatory working times. Second, the plans to implement 12-hour shifts, often defended by the managers of the affected units, tend to be portrayed as beneficial for the unit and as having been the subject of in-depth discussions with the care teams. Finally, through this procedure directors pretend to show that they are complying with the law – by demonstrating they submit 12-hour shifts to committees – but in reality they avoid a large part of legal obligations on the application of the working time law.

Furthermore, by contrast with the neo-institutional approach to legal intermediation, symbolic and superficial implementation is not the only approach to law. Manipulative intermediation is also central in the way directors use the law and try to prove their practices are compliant with it. They demonstrate the importance of 12-hour schedules for the care units' organization, for patients and caregivers, and use these arguments as evidence of their compliance. North Hospital and East Hospital provide further examples of how directors play with the law.

Finally, I also find clear circumventions and violations of the law. Some directors openly call for a work organization that exceeds the maximum of

12 hours, others "turn a blind eye" to staff working over the 12-hour or 60-hour limits, while most of them implement 12-hour shifts without any regard for the legal criteria of the constraints of continued public service allowing the derogation. These arrangements *with the law* (Ewick & Silbey, 1998) sometimes also lead to resistances *against the law* (Pélisse, 2003): the case of East Hospital is the most illustrative. In order to prove they are right, they advocate realism against dogmatism, argue that the law conflicts with the changing aspirations of caregivers and campaign for the law to be brought into line with practices.

All these games with the law show that directors are most of the time outside the legal framework but try to legitimize it or change its interpretation. They attempt to prove that a 12-hour shifts schedule is an appropriate and practical organization on a managerial point of view even if it is a derogation. The way directors play with the law has thus symbolic dimensions *as well as* manipulative and constitutive ones. Compliance with the law and legitimacy are not only symbolic or superficial. Hospital's directors interpret the law in the name of a superior managerial norm tied to utilitarian goals. It appears that the law is only valid when consistent with organizational practices, needs and aspirations. More broadly, the extensive use of this derogation has helped it to become established as a rule. In so doing, they contribute to frame legality in a deeper way: they participate also to the neutralization and the obsolescence of the working time law. Far from condemning it, the Health Ministry contributes to the legitimation of this trend.

A Passive Health Ministry and State: Between Justification and Excuse of Illegal Hospital Practices

In spring 2014, facing the insistence of the national unions sitting on the national Committee for Health, Safety and Working Conditions of the Higher Council of the public hospital unit about the growth of 12-hour schedules inside hospitals, the Health Ministry set up a working group to investigate the issue of 12-hour shifts patterns. While the issue gained a public and political attention, thanks to the Ministry's decision, it is nevertheless difficult to see it as a public problem in the traditional sense of public policy analysis (Felstiner, Abel, & Sarat, 1980–1981). Indeed, the way the Ministry chose to approach and deal with the issue seems more like an attempt to defuse conflict with trade unions than any real political desire to offer solutions. For the authorities, the chief aim of this working group was to "document the organization of the 12-hour work schedule," using existing studies in ergonomics, occupational medicine, chronobiology, sociology, and hospitals' experiences in order to "move towards strengthening, monitoring and observation of staff, and raising hospitals' awareness about best practices, both in terms of staff monitoring and social dialogue," as explains the director of the Department of Social Relations and Social Policy at the Ministry. For their part, the unions rejected the idea of a "best practice guide" and instead asked the Ministry to amend the law to better regulate hospital practices. This is summarized as follows by a nationally elected representative I interviewed from the Force Ouvrière trade union (a minority union, but which played a role in negotiations):

> The law provided for the 12-hour working time within a derogation framework. When we negotiated the text on the 35-hour week in 2002, the problem of the 12-hour shift was raised, in the sense that – and also for extraordinary reasons, i.e. that cannot not be foreseen – staff were required to stay at work in order to guarantee continuity of public services. They could work for up to 12 hours. In other words, between the 7 or 8 hours a day [which was the standard working time] and the 12-hour shift, hospital administrations had time to turn the situation around and guarantee the replacement of people who had to increase the length of their shift. So there was that aspect of the 12-hour shift which was a derogation of the standard working time, and that hasn't changed. Management, solely for financial reasons, by watching and observing, realized that 12-hour shifts saved them between 4% and 6% of their budget for the staff involved. In the short term, I mean. Without taking into account the possible absenteeism it could cause. So they looked at it and said, 'That's a good solution to the problems of budgetary discipline we're encountering: being able to reduce the payroll. So that was the management's sole interest. The regulatory side for us was unavoidable. It had to remain a derogation.

In addition to the regulatory aspect, the unions also wanted to draw attention to the harmful effects of this type of organization on caregivers' health and on the risk of professional errors. They asked the Health Ministry for a moratorium while the group finalized its findings, but the request was rejected. In January 2015, the Ministry reiterated the content of the law and the derogatory nature of the 12-hour work shifts in an order – mainly informative – addressed to hospitals' directors, announcing that a working group would be set up to examine the issue (eight months after the group's first meeting). Considering this response to be insufficient, several unions wrote an open letter to the Health Ministry in July 2015 demanding a suspension of the 12-hour proposal in hospitals and calling for protective measures for the staff concerned. However, the letter was flatly rebuffed by the minister, who insisted that a "best practice guide" would be drawn up. As the Ministry's representative to the unions recalled during a working group meeting in November 2014:

> This is not about saying there is no impact on people's health. It is about saying that in hospitals, on account of the constraints of continuity of care, there are a number of non-standard work schedules. And we need to find out which kind of 12-hour organization is worse in terms of its impact on staff's health in comparison with other forms of organization in three teams, etc., and [which] forms of organizations cause no changes to the health of hospital staff [...] What is it like in comparison with all the other types of organization, and what are the most harmful effects of the 12-hour work shift? Secondly, are all the 12-hour shift patterns equally harmful?

So the aim is not to know whether or not 12-hour work shifts are "harmful" but rather to identify the cases in which they are so and to highlight the cases in which they are not, or are less so than for other forms of organization. While the derogatory nature of the 12-hour work shift is reaffirmed, under no circumstances does the Ministry establish the working group in order to condemn the reinterpretations or the non-applications that are made of the law inside hospitals. At best, it tries to explain and rationalize them. At worst, it justifies or excuses illegal practices. The association of trade union organizations within a working group serves to legitimize an approach that aim to calm the debate and reassure hospitals' directors over their use of the 12-hour work shifts. Behind what appears to be increased attention from the authorities and a desire to "open a dialogue" on a controversial issue, the working group helps to assert the organizational and managerial nature of this legal provision.

The Role of the "Reform Network": A Managerial Pressure on Hospital's Directors

This erasure of the State's role and its refusal to condemn the increased use of the derogation mechanism is in fact symptomatic of its relative withdrawal from hospital management, which it has subcontracted or outsourced to the Regional Health Agencies and seemingly independent public agencies such as the National Support Agency for the Performance of Hospitals (ANAP), working in conjunction with consulting firms (Belorgey, 2010; Pierru, 2010, 2012). Together with the Court of Auditors and its regional chambers, the French Federation of Hospitals and some professional associations of hospital directors are part of the same "reform network" (Topalov, 1999). They play the role of financial watchdog and promote managerial logics in hospitals. They framed the organizational life of hospitals based on "objective" economic and social laws, the use of a single "management logos" (Boussard, 2008), and a common set of goals. These include establishing working time as a variable for adjusting and optimizing work organization. In recent years, there has been an increasing number of references to – and even recommendations of – 12-hour work shifts in public reports and in the positions taken by these reformers. Considering the 12-hour shift as a source of flexibility that enables "efficiency," some regional audit chambers regret the fact that these schedules are still not widely used. At the same time, the Regional Health Agencies sometimes recommend 12-hour shifts as part of the "return to balance plans" that they are imposing on hospitals in financial difficulty in order to save money on a small number of caregivers' jobs. Behind these arguments is their belief that 12-hour shifts would reduce handoffs time between teams: "in terms of efficiency and optimizing staff presence, you only have two handoffs instead of three [in any 24-hour period]. That means you save money," explains one ANAP official (see Fig. 3).

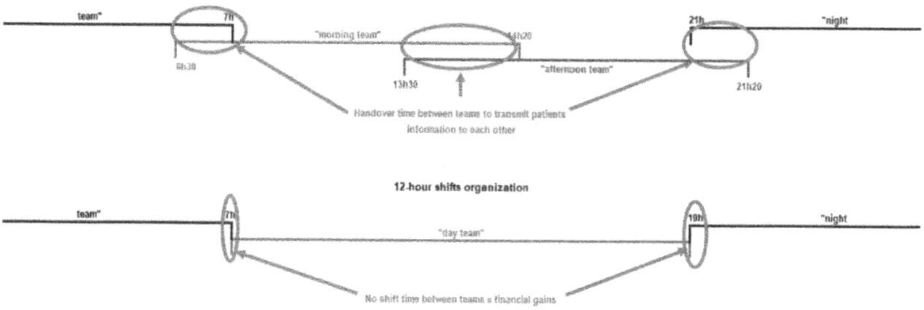

Fig. 3. The Financial Gains of a 12-hour Shifts Organization.

However, the hand-off between two caregivers teams requires at least one of the two to stay longer than 12 hours, that is, longer than the time allowed by the derogation. This is the point at which the debate crystallizes: a work schedule organized into two 12-hour shifts is mostly incompatible with the law. For the network reformers, it is evidence that the method is appropriate for departments such as emergency rooms or operating rooms where the hand-off is done more quickly (given the speed with which patients come and leave). In these cases, there are almost no instances in which the shift exceeds 12 hours due to handovers. This method appears to be more appropriate for day hospitals or dialysis units that operate only during the day and where one handover between morning and afternoon shifts could be economized.

This economic advantage is also justified on public health grounds. Indeed, from the reformers' point of view, one shift rotation between just two teams in a 24-hour period brings a guarantee of better quality and better safety of care. This would mean higher reliability of information exchanged and a limited risk of any details going missing. By this logic, increasing the number of handoffs means increasing the opportunities for forgetting to pass on information. The 12-hour shifts would also improve continuity of care, help to synchronize physicians and caregivers shifts, and fit into "a context of high financial constraints and more efficient management of staff resources" (AdRHess and AFDS, 2014). The 12-hour work shift therefore appears as a solution to the conflict between "social performance" and "economic performance," which were initially thought to be incompatible. These actors contribute to spread the idea that a derogation mechanism is just another form of organization and a useful tool for hospitals. The 12-hour work is never criticized for its original purpose as a derogation provision. Instead, it is always related to the current financial situation and the continuous search for "efficiency." Thus, even if it is a derogation, the 12-hour work pattern is useful for adapting to the reality emphasized by reformers. Their arguments reflect the low importance given to the rules in managerial rationality when compared with economic demands.

More broadly, the discourse used by actors of this "reform network" aims to instill in hospital's directors a particular notion of working time: the one that converts the hospital's macro-budgetary issues to the micro-level. From this perspective, hospitals' managers should invest in working time, given its "performance potential." This encourages directors to make a managerial application of the law, legitimized by the passivity of the tutelary authority of the Health Ministry (Fig. 4).

CONCLUSION

The chapter sought to study the role of macro- and micro-legal intermediaries in the light of hospital managerialization and the rise of derogation in French labor law: who are they? How do they act? What work do they do? How do they contribute to the framing of legality and in which sense? I argued that the articulation of neo-institutional approach and more especially the legal managerialization framework, policy ethnography analysis, and legal intermediation studies helped

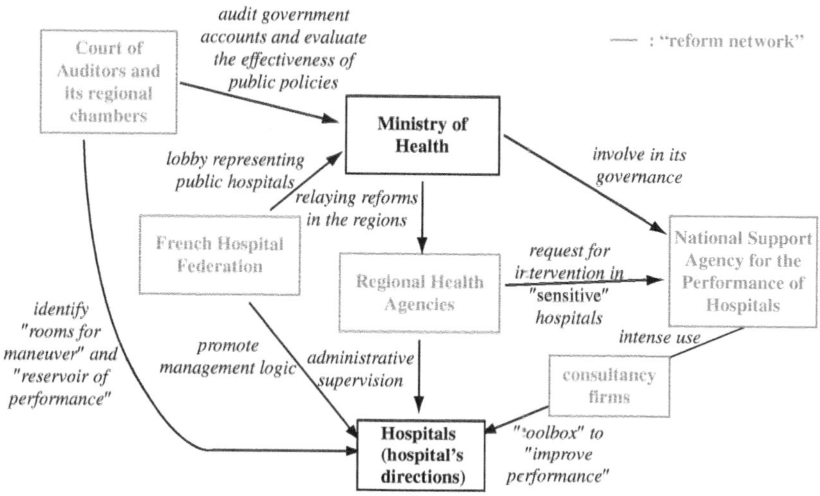

Fig. 4. Managerial Pressure on Hospital's Directors.

to analyze this particular case of the 12-hour shifts work in the French public hospital. More especially, I claimed that a multi-level approach was the most relevant one to achieve a fine-grained analysis of legal games.

The chapter has highlighted four core findings.

First, the position of intermediaries is mostly characterized by *games with the law*, using it contextually as a framework, as a resource or as a weapon – when they refer to it. The micro-analysis of three different hospitals brings to light a managerialization of law that is not only based on symbolic or superficial compliance with the law, as Edelman interprets it (Edelman, 1992, 2016), but also on manipulations (Lascoumes & Le Bourhis, 1996) and circumventions of the law. More broadly, I point out that the intermediation activity contributes to build an ambivalent and contextual legality in hospital: social norms (produced by the managerial rhetoric, by work, by reference to caregivers' private life) tend generally to fall back on legal normativity (Pélisse, 2014).

Second, *the unions' action* pushes directors to implement procedures, justify and defend their practices. It urges directors to take account law into account and modify their practices in some cases. From the three cases I studied, it appears that the law may become a constraint for management during confrontations with trade unions (see Fig. 5). Trade union action is thus the main variable in affirming the constitutive dimension of law in the practices of legal intermediaries. While they are mostly absent in the legal endogeneity theory and more particularly in Edelman's work, unions appear finally as central actors in intermediation processes and deserve thus to be included in the analysis. More generally, as Kellogg also shows, the chapter underlines the critical place of the local context and configuration in the explanation of social change (Kellogg, 2009).

Third, the *multi-level approach* allows to bring to light the chains of interdependence that link actors at different levels and helps to understand the work of

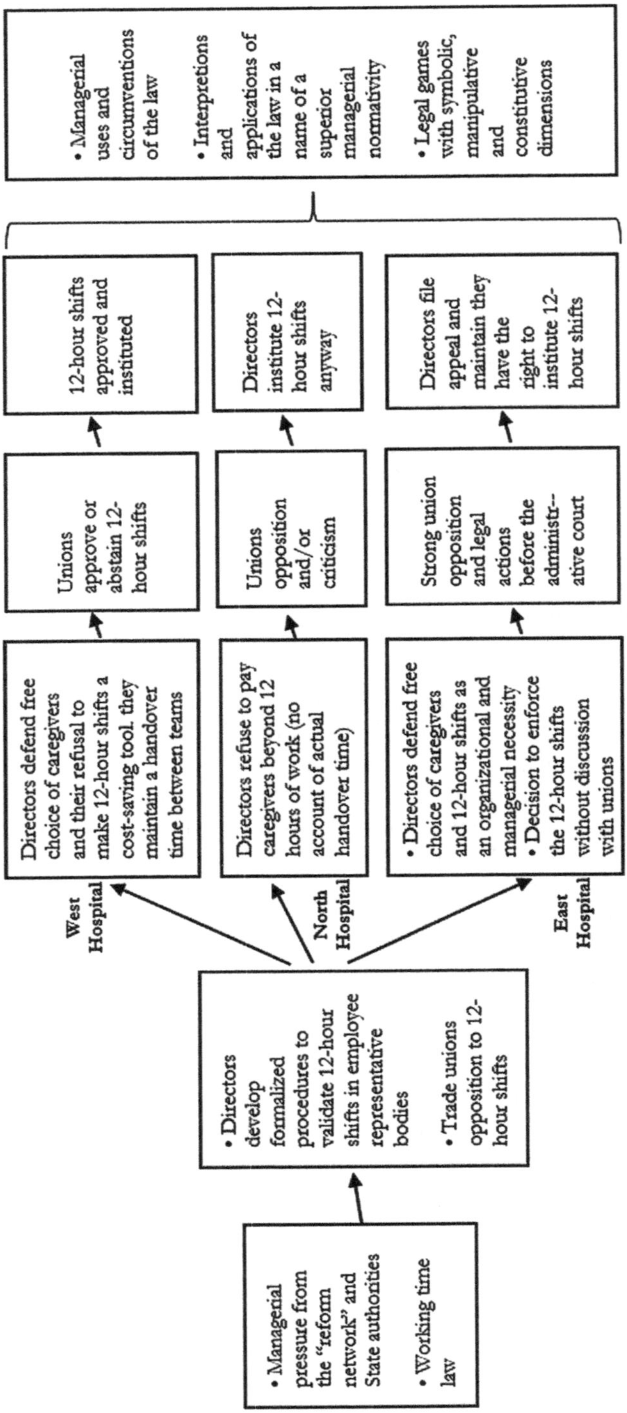

Fig. 5. How Intermediation Affects Legal Endogeneity.

each kind of legal intermediaries. It shows that both "the reform network" actors and hospital directors contribute to the framing of legality: the managerial rhetoric is spread by macro-level actors and is implemented inside hospitals, through increased use of the 12-hour work derogation. The way they behave vis-à-vis the law matches their managerial values and professional interests. Organizational factors, organizing processes, professional identities, beliefs and worldviews are significant. They affect compliance and shape the way all these legal intermediaries interpret and use or violate the law, often in a way that weakens employees' rights (Talesh & Pélisse, 2019).

Finally, the chapter describes the construction of a managerial and manipulative definition of law in French public hospitals that participates to the dismantling of social public order underway in France since the 1980s (Pélisse, 2004). Through the extension of violations, symbolic, manipulative and managerial uses of labor law in the regulation of hospital organization, certain worldviews acquire a social base (Kalberg, 1980, p. 1170). These uses are a vehicle for a manipulative and managerial normativity of law, which also progresses in the mindset of some caregivers. This dynamic raises a critical issue. On the one hand, it reveals an unusual alliance between managers and caregivers. On the other hand, it shows that unions are isolated in a position of archaic ideologues. This configuration is thus typical of the "managerial domination" (Boltanski, 2009), which succeeds to instill a managerial conception of labor law in the thoughts, feelings, and actions of the caregivers it is supposed to protect. It creates thus the right conditions for perpetuating the productive social order that exploits them.

NOTES

1. Decree n°2002–2009 of January 4, 2002 on working time and organization of work in institutions in the public hospital unit. This decree does not apply to non-staff hospital doctors. They are subject to their own specific text establishing their working hours at a maximum of 24 consecutive hours and 10 half-days per week (the duration of a half-day is not specified.) Unlike the 100-hour working week familiar to American surgeons (Kellogg, 2011), French hospital doctors are nonetheless considered to be an elastic workforce. Their working time can be extended and is subject to very weak and vague legal regulations (Vincent, 2018).
2. In France, there are three branches of specialization in nursing (each requiring a separate qualification): pediatric nurses, nurse anesthetists and operating room nurses.
3. The trade union division is indeed a French historical specificity.

ACKNOWLEDGMENTS

I would like to sincerely thank the anonymous reviewer of *Studies*, as well as the three editors of the issue, Sebastian Billows, Lisa Buchter and Jérôme Pélisse for their advice, comments and proofreading of the different versions of this chapter.

REFERENCES

Abbott, K., Levi-Faur, D., & Snidal, D. (2017). Theorizing regulatory intermediaries: The RIT model. *The Annals of the American Academy of Political and Social Science*, *670*(1), 13–35.

Abdelnour, S. (2012). L'auto-entrepreneur aux marges du salariat. De la genèse aux usages d'un régime dérogatoire de travail indépendant. PhD in sociology, EHESS.

AdRHess and AFDS. (2014). *Memorendum sur les horaires en 12 heures*, Paris.

Algava, E., Davie, E., Loquet, J., & Vinck, L. (2014). Conditions de travail. Reprise de l'intensification du travail chez les salariés. *Dares Analyses*, *49*, 1–11.

ATIH. (2016). Analyse des bilans sociaux des établissements publics de santé à fin 2014.

Barley, S. R. (1986). Technology as an occasion for structuring: Evidence from observations of CT scanners and the social order of radiology departments. *Administrative Science Quarterly*, *31*(1), 78–108.

Barley, S. R. (2008). Coalface institutionalism. In Greenwood, R., Oliver, C., Suddaby, R., & Sahlin-Andersson, K. (Eds.), *The SAGE handbook of organizational institutionalism* (pp. 491–518). Thousand Oaks, CA: Sage.

Baron, J., Dobbin, F., & Jennings, P. (1986). War and peace: The evolution of modern personnel administration in United State industry. *American Journal of Sociology*, *92*(2), 350–383.

Belorgey, N. (2010). *L'hôpital sous pression. Enquête sur le "nouveau management public" à l'hôpital.* Paris: La Découverte.

Bereni, L. (2009). "Faire de la diversité une richesse pour l'entreprise". La transformation d'une contrainte juridique en catégorie managériale. *Raisons politiques*, *35*, 87–106.

Bereni, L., & Chappe, V. A. (2011). La discrimination, de la qualification juridique à l'outil sociologique. *Politix*, *94*(2), 7–34.

Bessy, C., Delpeuch, T., & Pélisse, J. (Eds.) (2011). Droit et régulations des activités économiques. *Perspectives sociologiques et institutionnalistes*. Paris: LGDJ.

Bezes, P. (2009). *Réinventer l'État. Les réformes de l'administration française (1962–2008)*. Paris: PUF.

Billows, S. (2016). La politique de l'ambiguïté juridique. Quand l'État tente de réguler les échanges entre la grande distribution et ses fournisseurs. *Sociologie Du Travail*, *58*(1). 8–31.

Boltanski, L. (2009). De la critique. *Précis de sociologie de l'émancipation*. Paris: Gallimard.

Bouffartigue, P., & Bouteiller, J. (2003). À propos des normes du temps de travail. De l'érosion de la norme fordienne aux normes émergentes. *Revue de l'Ires*, *42*, 1–23.

Bourdouxhe, M., Quéinnec, Y., Granger, D., Baril, R., Guertin, S., & Massicotte, P. (1997). Effets de l'horaire rotatif de 12 heures sur la santé et la sécurité des opérateurs d'une raffinerie de produits pétroliers. Rapport de l'IRSST, Montréal.

Boussard, V. (2008). *Sociologie de la gestion. Les faiseurs de performance*. Paris: Belin.

Bushnell, P. T., Colombi, A., Caruso, C. C., & Tak, S. W. (2010). Work schedules and health behavior outcomes at a large manufacturer. *Industrial Health*, *48*, 395–405.

Castel, P., & Robelet, M. (2009). Comment rationaliser sans standardiser la médecine? Production et usages des recommandations de pratiques cliniques. *Journal d'économie médicale*, *27*(3), 98–115.

Castel, R. (1995). *Les métamorphoses de la question sociale*. Paris: Folio Essais.

Chappe, V. A., Guillaume, C., & Pochic, S. (2016). Négocier sur les carrières syndicales pour lutter contre la discrimination. *Travail et Emploi*, *145*, 121–146.

Chevandier, C. (2009). *L'hôpital dans la France du XXè siècle*. Paris: Perrin.

Dejours, C. (2015). *Le choix. Souffrir au travail n'est plus une fatalité*. Paris: Bayard.

Devetter, F. X. (2002). Vers une nouvelle norme des temps de travail ? Temps subis ou temps choisis? *Formation Emploi*, *78*, 53–68.

Divay, S., & Gadéa, C. (2015). Aggiornamento managérial des établissements publics et dynamiques professionnelles. Éléments d'analyse à partir de l'évolution des cadres de santé. *Gouvernement et action publique*, *4*(4), 81–99.

Dobbin, F. (2009). *Inventing equal opportunity*. Princeton, NJ: Princeton University Press.

Dobbin, F., & Kelly, E. (1998). How affirmative action became diversity management: Employer response to Antidiscrimination Law, 1961 to 1996. *American Behavioral Scientist*, *41*(7), 960–984.

Domin, J.-P. (2011). La "gouvernance" Canada dry ou la reprise en main de l'hôpital par une nouvelle bureaucratie gestionnaire. In Mas, B., Pierru, F., Smolski, N., & Torrielli, R. (Eds.), *L'hôpital en réanimation. Le sacrifice organisé d'un unit public emblématique* (pp. 103–112). Bellecombe-en-Bauges: Éditions du Croquant.

Dubois, V. (1999). La vie au guichet. *Administrer la misère*. Paris: Éditions du Seuil.

Dubois, V. (2009). Action publique. In Cohen, A., Lacroix, B., & Riutort, P. (Eds.), *Nouveau manuel de science politique* (pp. 311–325). Paris: La Découverte.

Edelman, L. B. (1992). Legal ambiguity and symbolic structures: Organizational mediation of Civil Rights Law. *American Journal of Sociology*, *97*(6), 1531–1576.

Edelman, L. B. (2016). *Working law: Courts, corporations, and symbolic civil rights*. Chicago, IL: The University of Chicago Press.

Edelman, L. B., Fuller, S. R., & Mara-Drita, I. (2001). Diversity rhetoric and the managerialization of law. *American Journal of Sociology*, *106*(6), 1589–1641.

Edelman, L. B., Uggen, C., & Erlanger, H. (1999). The endogeneity of legal regulation: Grievance procedures as rational myth. *American Journal of Sociology*, *105*(2), 406–454.

Elias, N. (2004 [1981]). *Qu'est-ce que la sociologie?* Paris: Pocket.

Elias, N., & Dunning, E. (1994). *Sport et civilisation. La violence maitrisée*. Paris: Fayard.

Estryn-Behar, M. (1997). *Stress et souffrance des soignants à l'hôpital: reconnaissance, analyse et prévention*. Paris: De Boeck Secundair.

Ewick, P., & Silbey, S. (1998). *The commonplace of law: Stories from everyday life*. Chicago, IL: University of Chicago Press.

Felstiner, W., Abel, R., & Sarat, A. (1980–1981). The emergence and transformation of disputes: Naming, blaming, claming. *Law and Society Review*, *15*(3–4), 631–654.

Folkard, S., & Tucker, P. (2003). Shift work, safety and productivity. *Occupational Medicine*, *53*(2), 95–101.

Friedland, R., & Alford, R. (1991). Bringing society back in: Symbols, practices, and institutional contradictions. In W. W., Powell & P. J., DiMaggio (Eds.), *The new institutionalism in organizational analysis* (pp. 232–263). Chicago, IL: University of Chicago Press.

Frinault, T. (2012). *Le pouvoir territorialisé en France*. Rennes: Presses Universitaires de Rennes.

Geiger-Brown, J., Rogers, V. E., Trinkoff, A. M., Kane, R. L., Bausell, R. B., & Scharf, S. M. (2012). Sleep, sleepiness, fatigue, and performance of 12-hour-shift nurses. *Chronobiology International*, *29*(2), 211–219.

Hallett, T., & Ventresca, M. (2006). Inhabited institutions: Social interactions and organizational forms in Gouldner's patterns of industrial bureaucraty. *Theory and Society*, *35*(2), 213–236.

Heimer, C. (1999). Competing institutions: Law, medicine, and family in neonatal intensive care. *Law and Society Review*, *33*(1), 17–66.

Heimer, C., & Staffen, L. (1998). *For the sake of the children: The social organization of responsibility in the hospital and the home*. Chicago, IL: Uniersity of Chicago Press.

Hood, C. (1995). The "New Public Management" in the 1980s: Variations on a theme. *Accounting, Organizations and Society*, *20*(2–3), 93–109.

Juven, P.-A. (2016). Une santé qui compte? *Les coûts et les tarifs controversés de l'hôpital public*. Paris: Presses Universitaires de France.

Kalberg, S. (1980). Max weber's types of rationality: Cornerstones for the analysis of rationalization processes in history. *American Journal of Sociology*, *85*(5), 1145–1179.

Kellogg, K. C. (2009). Operating room: Relational spaces and microinstitutional change in surgery. *American Journal of Sociology*, *115*(3), 657–711.

Kellogg, K. C. (2011). *Challenging operations: Medical reform and resistance in surgery*. Chicago, IL: University of Chicago Press.

Knauth, P. (2007). Extended eork periods. *Industrial Health*, *45*, 125–136.

Lascoumes, P., & Le Bourhis, J.-P. (1996). Des 'Passe-Droits' Aux Passes Du Droit. La Mise En Oeuvre Socio-Juridique de l'action Publique. *Droit et Société*, *32*(1), 51–73.

Light, D. W. (2004). Ironies of success: A new history of the American Healthcare "System". *Journal of Health and Social Behaviour*, *45*, 1–24.

Lipsky, M. (1980). *Street-level bureaucracy, dilemmas of the individual in public services*. New York, NY: Russell Sage Foundation.

Maynard-Moody, S., & Musheno, M. (2004). *Cops, teachers, counselors: Stories from the front lines of public service*. Ann Arbor, MI: University of Michigan Press.

McNulty, T., & Ferlie, E. (2004). *Reengineering health care: The complexities of organizational transformation*. Oxford: Oxford University Press.

Pélisse, J. (2003). Conscience du temps et conscience du droit chez des salariés à "35 heures". *Droit et Société, 53*, 163–186.

Pélisse, J. (2004). A la recherche du temps gagné. Sens et usages sociaux des règles autour des 35h. PhD in sociology, Centre d'Études de l'Emploi, Marne la Vallée University.

Pélisse, J. (2009). Judiciarisation Ou Juridicisation? Usages et Réappropriations Du Droit Dans Les Conflits Du Travail. *Politix, 86*, 73–96.

Pélisse, J. (2011a). La mise en úuvre des 35 heures: d'une managérialisation du droit à une internalisation de la fonction de justice. *Droit et société, 77*, 39–65.

Pélisse, J. (2011b). Dossier: Se donner le droit: la force des organisations face à la loi. *Droit et Société, 77*, 7–17.

Pélisse, J. (2014). Le travail du droit. Trois enquêtes sur la légalité ordinaire. Mémoire d'habilitation à diriger des recherches en sociologie, IEP de Paris.

Pélisse, J. (2016). Legal intermediaries as moral actors. SASE's Meeting, Berkeley.

Pélisse, J. (2017). Gérer les risques par le droit: articulation et intermédiation dans les laboratoires de nanosciences en France et aux Etats-Unis. *Droit et société, 96*(2), 321–336.

Pierru, F. (1999). 'L'hôpital entreprise'. Une self-fulfilling prophecy avortée. *Politix, 46*, 7–47.

Pierru, F. (2007). *Hippocrate malade de ses réformes*. Bellecombe en Bauges: Éditions du Croquant.

Pierru, F. (2012). Le mandarin, le gestionnaire et le consultant. Le tournant néolibéral de la politique hospitalière. *Actes de la recherche en sciences sociales, 194*(4), 32–51.

Pierru, F. (2013). Les mandarins à l'assaut de l'usine de soins. Bureaucratisation néolibérale de l'hôpital français et mobilisation de l'élite hospitalo-universitaire. In Hibou, B. (Eds.), *La bureaucratisation néolibérale* (pp. 203–230). Paris: La Découverte.

Pollitt, C., & Bouckaert, G. (2004). *Public management reform: A comparative analysis*. Oxford: Oxford University Press.

Pollitt, C., van Thiel, S., & Homburg, V. (2007). The new public management in Europe. Management Online Review.

Quadagno, J. (2004). Physician sovereignty and the purchaser's revolt. *Journal of Health Politics, Policy and Law, 29*(4–5), 815–834.

Ruggie, M. (1992). The paradox of liberal intervention: Health policy and the American Welfare State. *American Journal of Sociology, 97*(4), 919–944.

Ruhl, J. B., & Katz, D. M. (2015). Measuring, monitoring, and managing legal complexity. *Iowa Law Review, 100*, 191–244.

Sainsaulieu, I. (2003). *Malaise des soignants. Le travail sous pression à l'hôpital*. Paris: L'Harmattan.

Salminen, S. (2010). Shift work and extended working hours as risk factors for occupational injury. *The Ergonomics Open Journal, 3*, 14–18.

Schweyer, F.-X. (2006). Une profession de l'État providence, les directeurs d'hôpital. *Revue européenne des sciences sociales, XLIV, 135*, 45–60.

Scott, R., Ruef, M., Mendel, P., & Caronna, C. (2000). Institutional change and healthcare organizations. *From professional dominance to managed care*. Chicago, IL: Chicago University Press.

Smith, L., Folkard, S., Tucker, P., & Macdonald, I. (1998). Work shift duration: A review comparing eight hour and 12 hour shift systems. *Occupational and Environmental Medicine, 55*, 217–229.

Spire, A. (2005). Étrangers à la carte. *L'administration de l'immigration en France (1945–1975)*. Paris: Grasset.

Spire, A. (2008). Accueillir ou reconduire. *Enquête sur les guichets de l'immigration*. Paris: Raisons d'agir.

Spire, A. (2012). *Faibles et puissants face à l'impôt*. Paris: Raisons d'Agir.

Spire, A., & Alpes, M. J. (2014). Dealing with law in migration control: The powers of street-level bureaucrats at French consulates. *Social & Legal Studies, 23*(1), 261–274.

Starr, P. (1982). *The social transformation of American medicine*. New York, NY: Basic Books.

Supiot, A. (2014). *Grandeur et misère de l'État social*. Paris: Fayard.

Talesh, S. (2015a). Rule-intermediaries in action: How state and business stakeholders influence the meaning of consumer rights in regulatory governance arrangements. *Law & Policy, 37*, 1–31.

Talesh, S. (2015b). Legal intermediaries: How insurance companies construct the meaning of compliance with antidiscrimination laws. *Law & Policy, 37*, 209–239.

Talesh, S., & Pélisse, J. (2019). How legal intermediaries influence or inhibit social change. In Sarat, A. (Ed.), *Law and social change: Old questions, new answers, studies in law, politics and society* (pp. 111–145). Bingley: Emerald Publishing Limited.

Timmermans, S., & Berg, M. (1997). Standardization in action: Achieving local universality through medical protocols. *Social Studies of Science*, *27*(2), 273–305.

Timmermans, S., & Berg, M. (2003). *The gold standard: The challenge of evidence-based medicine and standardization in health care*. Philadelphia, PA: Temple University Press.

Tolbert, P. S., & Zucker, L G. (1983). Institutional sources of change in the formal structure of organizations: The diffusion of civil unit reform, 1880–1938. *Administrative Science Quarterly*, *28*(1), 22–39.

Topalov, C. (Eds.) (1999). Laboratoires du nouveau siècle. *La nebuleuse réformatrice et ses réseaux en France 1880–1914*. Paris: Éditions de l'EHESS.

Vincent, F. (2014). Travailler pour son "temps de repos" ? Sens et usages du temps hors travail des soignantes en 12 heures à l'hôpital public. Temporalités, 20.

Vincent, F. (2016). Un temps qui compte. Une sociologique ethnographique du travail "en 12 heures" à l'hôpital public. PhD in sociology, Paris-Dauphine University.

Vincent, F. (2017). Penser sa santé en travaillant en 12 heures. Les soignants de l'hôpital public entre acceptation et refus. PISTES. Perspectives interdisciplinaires sur le travail et la santé, 19(1).

Vincent, F. (2018). Tirer profit de l'hôpital public ? Effets de l'industrialisation et de l'extorsion du temps de travail des soignants. Communication au colloque Tant de capital, temps de travail ?.

Weibel, L., Herbrecht, D., Imboden, D., Junker-Mois, L., & Bannerot, B. (2014). Organisation du travail en 2 × 12h: les risques pour la santé et la sécurité des travailleurs. *Références en santé au travail, INRS*, *137*, 143–149.

Worms, J.-P. (1966). Le préfet et ses notables. *Sociologie du Travail*, *8*(3), 249–275.

VARIETIES OF LEGAL INTERMEDIARIES: WHEN NON-LEGAL PROFESSIONALS ACT AS LEGAL INTERMEDIARIES

Jérôme Pélisse

ABSTRACT

Legal intermediation is an emerging theoretical concept developed to grasp the importance of the process and actors who contribute to legal endogenization, in particular in the field of economic activities and work governed by various public regulations. This chapter proposes to extend the analytical category of legal intermediary to all actors who, even if they are not legal professionals, deal on a daily basis with legal categories and provisions. In order to deepen our understanding of these actors and their contribution to how organizations frame legality, this chapter investigates four examples of legal intermediaries who are not legal professionals. Based on field surveys conducted over the past 15 years in France on employment policy, industrial relations, occupational health and safety regulation, and forensic economics, I make three contributions. First, the cases show the diversity of legal intermediaries and their growing and increasingly reflexive roles in our complex economies. Second, while they are not legal professionals per se, *to different degrees, these legal intermediaries assume roles similar to those of legal professionals such as legislators, judges, lawyers, inspectors, cops, and even clerks. Finally, depending on their level of legitimacy and power, I show how legal intermediaries take part in the process of legal endogenization and how they more broadly frame ordinary legality.*

Keywords: Legal intermediaries; legal consciousness; professions; legal endogeneity; France; labor; economy

Legal Intermediation: A Processual Approach to Law and Economic Activity
Studies in Law, Politics, and Society, Volume 81, 101–128

ISSN: 1059-4337/doi:10.1108/S1059-433720190000081005

INTRODUCTION

Legal intermediation is an emergent theoretical notion developed to grasp the complexity of the process of legal endogenization and the diversity of actors who contribute to it, especially in the area of economic and labor activities that are targeted by diverse public regulations. This chapter proposes to extend the analytical category of legal intermediaries, not only to contexts like France, but to all the actors who, even if they are not legal professionals, deal on a daily basis with legal categories and provisions in their professional activities. To understand how legal registers and economic logics intertwine in different ways, if not the variety of capitalisms according to the countries and practices considered, it is indeed necessary to study how a great diversity of professionals act as legal intermediaries in their daily activities.

In order to deepen our understanding of these actors and of how they contribute to framing legality, this chapter compares different types of non-legal professionals who act as legal intermediaries. It is based on a broad overview of the literature on intermediaries and four field studies conducted by the author over the last decade on employment policy, industrial relations, occupational health and safety regulation, and forensic economics. Comparing the activities and roles of non-legal professionals in different contexts enables us to determine the main dimensions and variations of legal intermediaries and to develop a theoretical framework on this specific dimension of the legal intermediation process. While other contributions in the present special issue address other dimensions of the process of legal intermediation – such as the tools and instruments involved, like contracts, their temporality or their structural conditions – this chapter focuses on a specific set of actors who play a crucial role in this process.

This analytical account of the work performed by legal intermediaries is substantiated with results I collected on four sites of field research. The empirical cases include job counselors in French unemployment policy; human resources managers and union's activists in companies in France; safety officers in French and American scientific laboratories developing nanoparticles; and forensic economic experts working for French judges. Drawing on the sociology of professions and neo-institutionalist, organizational, and sociolegal perspectives, this chapter compares legal intermediaries with very different characteristics. This comparison seeks to understand how the legal environment frames economic and labor practices through the activities of professionals who act as legal intermediaries. It questions how rules are produced and implemented, supported and embodied by specific actors. These actors are not passive towards the law. They translate law-in-the-books into law-in-action, shape ordinary legality and what we take for granted as being "what the law says." By doing this, their action has a transformative effect on the law. Rights mobilization (McCann, 1994), legal consciousness studies (Ewick & Silbey, 1998), and legal endogeneity theory (Edelman, 2016) are the three main theoretical inspirations that I build on to craft the analytical category of "legal intermediaries." The chapter therefore returns to this notion, its origins and purposes, its definition and the issues that this category allows to address. By opening the notion of legal intermediaries to all the actors at the interface between the legal field and other fields (notably, but not only, organizational fields), who use law in their daily activities but are not legal professionals, their figures are empirically extended to many actors working in public institutions and agencies, companies and public interest associations or many other organizations. This empirical expansion yields convincing results, particularly in the four cases mentioned above. We show, for example, how crucial are the legal environments in which they navigate, the audiences with whom they interact, their ability and training to be reflexive when they handle legal rules. More or less close or far from the heart of the legal field, legal intermediaries play in moving and porous spaces. I, therefore, propose to compare them by using the power dimensions in which they find themselves, and which they mobilize when they broker between the legal field and other fields.

In the remainder of this chapter, the second part presents the theoretical issues and aims of a research agenda centered on legal intermediaries. The third part presents the different legal intermediaries that are analyzed in this chapter. This section lists the methods I used to collect and process data on legal intermediaries. It focuses then on the main power-oriented dimensions used to compare legal intermediaries. The fourth part proposes two main results. The first is related to the growing and increasingly reflexive roles of legal intermediaries in our complex economies. The second finding opens a paradox: these non-legal professionals who act as legal intermediaries assume often simultaneous roles similar to those of legal professionals, such as legislators, judges, lawyers, inspectors, police officers, and clerks. Finally, I discuss the conditions in which legal intermediaries influence and shape legality. I show that depending upon their level of power and legitimacy, legal intermediaries contribute to how organizations frame legality and take part in the process of legal endogenization in multiple ways. The conclusion proposes a very brief synthesis and opens future research perspectives.

THEORETICAL FRAMEWORK: THE ANALYTICAL CATEGORY OF LEGAL INTERMEDIARIES

Legal intermediary is a relatively novel category, which only a few scholars have used so far (see Edelman, 1992; Edelman, 2016; Stryker, 2011; Talesh, 2015a, 2015b; Talesh & Pélisse, 2019 in the United States; Bessy, 2014; Pélisse, 2014, 2018; Bessy, Delpeuch, & Pélisse, 2011; Spire & Weidenfeld, 2011 in France and also Guillaume, 2015 in Great-Britain or Gendreau, 2005 in Canada). Despite its novelty, this notion has a broad theoretical basis, which builds on three main approaches. I will discuss them and then propose my own conceptual definition of legal intermediaries.

Between Street-level Bureaucrats and Legal Professionals, the Centrality of Neo-institutionalist Approaches

A first origin of the idea to consider some actors as legal intermediaries is the research on street level bureaucrats and their administrative discretion. This line of research was initiated by Lipsky (1980) in the early 1980s and has subsequently expanded both in Great-Britain and in the United States (Hupe, Hill, & Buffat, 2015; Maynard-Moody & Musheno, 2004; Maynard-Moody & Portillo, 2010; Watkins-Hayes, 2009, for example). I claim indeed that legal intermediation is a key dimension of the work performed by street level bureaucrats; thanks to their inherent autonomy, when deciding how rules apply in practical situations, they are "ultimate policy-makers" (Portillo & Rudes, 2014, pp. 322–323). Street level bureaucrats contribute to the implementation of public policies by translating legal rules into provisions, administrative procedures, and many other documents. They represent the missing link between the State and the citizen, the administration and the public, or between policy-makers and policy-users. In France, this line of argument has been imported and reinterpreted by scholars who are interested in the interactions between low-level civil servants and their audiences – underprivileged people, foreigners, the unemployed, senior citizens, etc. This literature, known in French as *Sociologie du guichet* (sociology of the counter), typically insists on the way these interactions are structured by social determinants such as class, gender, or organizational characteristics (Dubois, 2010). In these various empirical contributions, the reliance of street level bureaucrats on rules is central to understand the various ways in which laws are implemented and interpreted. Front-line workers and street-level bureaucrats – and even more so the mid-level bureaucrats (Cavalcante & Lotta, 2015) or "back office" bureaucratic managers (Spire, 2008), who have more leeway to interpret and apply the rules – are thus considered as brokers between the formal and legal rules and the people who are targeted by those policies and regulations. A recent article even analyzed judges in family courts in both France and North America as street-level bureaucrats (Biland & Steimetz, 2017; who recalls that Lipsky himself had referred to judges as possible street-level bureaucrats). The job counselor helping the unemployed to find a new job, one of the actors considered in my own fieldwork, is a typical street level bureaucrat. However, the notion of legal intermediaries goes beyond the classical questions addressed in the literature on street level bureaucrats: rather than focusing on their discretion and on how they affect policy through implementation, the legal intermediation perspective draws attention to how they use and handle the legal rules, which helps understanding whether and how they influence the legality and legal consciousness of their audience.

In a broader perspective, intermediaries have generated empirical and theoretical works in many sub-fields of sociology such as sports and culture, political sociology, economic sociology, social studies of finance, labor market studies, or science and technology studies. Cultural intermediaries who stand between the market and the public like producers, theater owners, food reviewers, or founders of new magazines have been the object of well-known studies (Haveman, Habinek, & Goodman, 2012; Hennion, 1989: Karpik, 2000, 2010). Intermediaries like agents in professional sports are now analyzed at the intersection of the sociology of markets, professions and sports (Demazière & Jouvenet, 2013). In economic sociology, there is a sprawling literature on traders, brokers and other entrepreneurs, who use their intermediate positions to further entrepreneurial projects (Zalio, 2013). Human resources specialists and hiring departments (Marchal, 2015) became central figures in the analysis of professions and labor market trends. Finally, in social studies of science (Meyer, 2010) as well as in the sociology of controversies or power in public policy (for example, Lascoumes & Lorrain, 2007), brokers also became a central topic for many empirical researches.

This trend exists not only in France, but also in other academic spaces. In an American journal's publication, Stovel and Shaw (2012) have called for a development of sociological research on brokers and brokerage. The neo-institutional perspective has also furthered the understanding of brokerage. Ever since Di Maggio published his landmark article on this topic (1988), this neo-institutional literature has indeed discussed the role of institutional entrepreneurs, emphasizing their ability to broker between their various networks and to position themselves as intermediaries between different worlds (Battilana, Leca, & Boxenbaum, 2009; Bergeron & Castel, 2016; Lawrence & Suddaby, 2006; for instance). Thus, like a missing link between structure and agency, intermediaries have proliferated in the literature, especially since the early 2000s.

Two mechanisms explain this diffusion of intermediaries into various fields of sociology and eventually into sociolegal scholarship: the first one is grounded on a paradigm shift in the social sciences during these years, and the second is based on the transformation of governance, regulation, and the role of the state. At a theoretical level, intermediation processes are indeed considered more and more important: the Actor Network Theory developed by Callon, Latour, or Akrich in France during the 1990s and its international success gave a central role to go-betweens, mediators and intermediaries (see notably Callon, 1986 for one of the first impulsions of this approach). From a very different perspective, social network analysis – from the founding works of Granovetter and Burt to the current sophisticated developments (Lazega, 2014) – has also focused much on these key actors who open up cliques and gain social capital and power by filling structural gaps. The French school of organizational theory has also analyzed what Crozier (1977) and Friedberg (1993) defined as the "intersecting marginal," located between two or more systems of actions. And even Luhmann and Teubner and their systemic and autopoïetic theory based on autonomous spheres have showed interest for the actors and provisions (like "connected contracts" analyzed by Teubner, 2011), that couple and articulate spheres with each other, especially the economic and legal ones (see Delpeuch, 2011, who commented this point specifically by using the notion of legal intermediaries). Nevertheless, the notion of *legal* intermediaries remains confidential and recent, having curiously not spread as in other fields of social sciences.

A second reason for the rise of intermediaries in academic research is simply their growing role in the real world. Many arguments can be used to justify the empirical accuracy of the figure of the legal intermediary (Talesh & Pélisse, 2019), but I will only develop a few. Indeed, the location of lawmaking has shifted and the regulatory environment has gradually moved from a government to governance model. In the latter, state, business, and civil society actors act as "rule-intermediaries" that affect, control, or monitor relations between rule-makers and rule-takers (Abbott, Levi-Faur, & Snidal, 2017; Levi-Faur & Starobin, 2014). They verify, test, audit or certify legal rules, a process that provides a key insight into legal intermediation. Nevertheless, this approach remains a top-down one. By contrast, our perspective is more bottom-up and interactive. The concept of legal intermediation highlights not only the process by which rule-makers influence rule-takers, but also encompasses the tools, instruments, and hybrid categories used by these intermediaries and their participation in law in action, sometimes law in the books and often ordinary legality, as defined by legal consciousness studies.[1]

A Theoretical Strategy of Research: Borderline Professionals, Legal Endogenity, and Legal Consciousness

With this theoretical background in mind, I center my analysis on one specific type of legal intermediaries, namely *non-legal professionals*. Indeed, the few studies using this notion make no distinction between the legal intermediaries who are legal professionals and those who are not. In France, Spire (with Weidenfeld, 2009; with Alpes, 2014) evoked their role to understand the variation of what he calls "procedural capital" to understand the mobilization of administrative courts by citizens, assisted by NGOs or lawyers, who are all defined as "legal intermediaries." Lejeune and Orianne (2014) analyzed "the construction of workers' rights consciousness through legal intermediation in Belgium." But those are defined as:

> *legal professionals* active in a range of transactions as intermediaries, between citizens, governments agents, organizational members including employers and the law as a body of texts and set of processes and practices. (p. 225)

There are, however, a few exceptions, such as Vincent's and Buchter's contributions to this special issue (Buchter, 2019; Vincent, 2019), which analyze respectively the roles of hospital directors and nurse managers, and various activists working in companies and advocating different causes and related rights (disability, LGBT, and muslims).

In the American literature, non-legal professionals are mostly considered, especially in the work of Lauren Edelman. Most existing empirical works dedicated to legal intermediaries follow her approach, from her first contributions on Human Resources (Edelman, 1992; Edelman, Erlanger, & Lande, 1993; Edelman, Fuller, & Mara-Drita, 2001) to her latest book on the legal endogenization of US anti-discrimination law (Edelman, 2016). Yet similar to Dobbin (2009) or Talesh (2009, 2015a, 2015b, 2017) Edelman is more interested in compliance professionals than, more broadly, legal intermediaries. Despite the expansion of actors potentially considered as legal intermediaries (like judges or lawyers) to non-legal professionals such as HR members, consultants, managers or insurers, most of these works lump all types of legal intermediaries together. They insist rather on their roles into compliance process, more than in a broader perspective, on the way they articulate and manage conflicts between competing discourses of authority, including law, science, gender, economy, labor or health, depending on their professional field. The theory of legal intermediation is in this sense narrower and broader than the legal endogenity perspective. It is narrower because it does not directly address how judges parrot and defer to the claims, interpretations and means used by organizations to comply with the law. But it is also broader than the sole or main question of compliance, by exploring the articulation between the law and the various normative spheres. The questions are not how organizational internalization of law influences the judges, theirs decisions and the law in the book environment and not only if and how legal intermediaries contribute to the managerialization of the law, or the legalization of organizations, with more merely symbolic or substantive effects, as underlined by L. Edelman in her last book (Edelman, 2016). But more broadly, how do legal intermediaries – legal professionals as non-legal professionals – articulate and manage conflicts between competing discourses of authority, like gender, labor, and law (Albiston, 2010), medicine and law (Dodier, 1993; Juston, 2016), science and law (Huising & Silbey, 2011; Pélisse, 2017; Silbey, 2008; Stryker, 2011; Stryker, Docka, & Wald, 2012), and obviously, organizations, management and its values – efficiency, productivity, etc. – and law (Edelman, 2016; Pélisse, 2004a).

Expanding legal endogeneity theory toward legal intermediation perspective, as evoked in the introduction of this special issue, explains why I am focusing on a particular type of legal intermediaries: non-legal professionals. I thus propose theoretical contributions in two fields: (1) the sociology of legal professionals and its frontiers; and (2) the study of legal consciousness in organizations, and the limitations they encounter. Let me explain how I propose contributions in these two areas, to ground a theory of legal intermediation, which is not restricted to the question of compliance.

First, expanding the category of legal intermediaries toward actors who are not legal professionals appears to be interesting and challenging to the sociology of legal professions. I focus thus on legal intermediaries who are not at the core of the legal field (Delpeuch, 2011) and don't share two important characteristics: to be trained as lawyers and/or to be a member of an official legal institution. Obviously, the boundaries are porous, especially to distinguish between professional and laypeople (an activist can become a legal professional), people trained in law or not (one can learn law as a self-taught person), or even actors who belong to a legal institution or not. One can be a member of a formal legal institution on an occasional basis, like jurors or temporary labor or business judges in France. Or, one can work part-time for an institution with a different main occupation, like the French judicial experts who are physicians, architects, or accountants, for example, and are not allowed to become a part of a legal profession. In one word, legal intermediaries are situated on a continuum between the core of legal field, dominated by legal professionals, and its most distant borders populated by non-legal professionals. My empirical topic is thus about borderline cases with professionals who have little (or no) symbolic resources specific to the legal field, while participating in them, without officially being part of them. Moreover, I have two cases that are far from the core of the legal field, and two others closer, even if not formally into the legal field. Street bureaucrats contribute well to the implementation of laws and could be seen as working in a legal institution; but they generally have very few legal attributes and resources on which they can rely. The same applies to union activists and safety engineers, who work in private or public organizations, which are far from the legal field. Forensic economic experts, on the other hand, are closer to the heart of the legal field, since they are appointed by the judges and they work for them. But, as we will see, they cannot and should not rely on such legal resources to carry out their activities and they are not allowed to become legal professionals, by a full-time specialization in forensic economic expertise. The total or relative absence of legal and symbolic resources, as well as their distance from the core of the legal field, makes it fascinating to observe the work of legal intermediaries who are not legal professionals. We better highlight all the concrete operations of intermediation and construction of ordinary legality, at the border of the legal field and its interface with other fields. Finally, in relation to the works of Edelman, Stryker or Talesh, who also consider non-legal professionals, I broaden the category of legal intermediaries to include not only compliance activities and compliance actors, but more broadly, intermediaries who deal with legal rules without being legal professionals.

In addition, my approach is not only anchored into legal endogenity theory, but also into legal consciousness studies (Ewick & Silbey, 1998; McCann, 1994; Merry, 1990; Pélisse, 2005, 2006; Sarat, 1990). Tacking into account legal intermediaries who are not legal professionals is a means of overcoming certain criticisms made on this research perspective. Legal consciousness studies call to:

> go into small towns, rural and urban neighborhoods and observe how people in these places come to name, use or ignore the law as they build it in their own world. (Sarat & Kearns, 1995)

By overthrowing the law-first perspective, which was dominant in law and society studies, legal consciousness studies emphasized the construction of legality in the everyday life and by ordinary actors, like in the famous book written by Ewick and Silbey (1998). This perspective has been very fruitful, inspiring major research since more than 20 years, both in France and in the United States. Legal consciousness studies also faced tough challenges, which were raised by various scholars (Garcia-Villegas, 2003; McCann, 2006; Pélisse, 2005). One challenge was acknowledged by Silbey herself (Silbey, 2005). Popular conceptions of law are indeed framed by organizations and professionals, that is to say actors, who are not totally "ordinary," and processes, which are not totally "horizontal." On the contrary, intermediate actors and mediation processes participate in the construction of ordinary legality. McCann and Haltom (2004) have, for example, showed how media and active campaigns could frame popular consciousness on tort law and tort litigation in the US. In the field of organizational studies, Hoffman (2003) has shown how organizational forms of taxi companies (cooperative or conventionally hierarchical) influence legal consciousness and dispute resolution between workers and supervisors in the firms. To use the term coined by D. M. Engel (2012) and discussed by M. McCann (McCann, 2012), the "vertical approach" to legal consciousness has to be maintained, and the baby should not have been thrown away with the bath water when the "horizontal approach" came about. The McCann's comment on the necessity to keep both vertical and horizontal approaches, however, points three critical issues, which open new perspectives. McCann indeed insists, as a political scientist working on social movements, on the "importance of studying ordinary rights activists" (McCann, 2012, pp. 476–479). He calls also for "more sociology and power, please" (pp. 479–484) and to be attentive to "the variable content of rights consciousness" (pp. 484–486).

This program is exactly mine by focusing on legal intermediaries who are neither legal professionals nor compliance specialists. Indeed, most of ordinary people are not confronted with legal professionals in everyday life, in the United States as in France, neither to rights activists nor to compliance professionals. On the contrary, ordinary citizens often interact with actors who professionally use legal rules, manage them in their professional, associative or militant activities, even if they are not legal professionals, compliance actors, or activists. Through their non-legal professional activities, these intermediaries frame legality and rights consciousness; they shape power relations, because they are in power relations with their clients, patients, publics and they influence their conception of legality and law. As McCann suggests, we have to study these actors more sociologically, by comparing them and systematizing the analysis, by taking into account their characteristics and the contexts in which they work. Finally, by tackling various examples and comparing them with each other, this chapter aims at illustrating variations in the construction of legality, rights consciousness, and power relations between social actors. In other words, studying legal intermediaries is a solution to articulate theoretically the horizontal and vertical approaches to legal consciousness. We could thus explore what role legal intermediaries play in framing ordinary legality and the construction of one hegemonic reality.

My perspective, therefore, goes beyond the question of compliance: it proposes to study the ways in which the law and other forms of normativity are articulated, through intermediate actors who are on the boundaries of the legal field, as well as compliance functions. By paying attention to the nature of the legal environment in which these actors operate, the types of legal rules they deal with in their daily professional lives, even if they are not legal professionals, and the relationships they develop with their audiences – clients, users, patients, including potential legal professionals with whom they may interact – I propose to explore the ways in which legal intermediaries frame legality. In other words, how they integrate themselves into power relations, how they are constrained but also rely on the law, how they depend and also abstract themselves from the weight of the law and legal professionals to influence ordinary forms of legality.

AN EMPIRICAL OBJECT: NON-LEGAL PROFESSIONALS ACTING AS LEGAL INTERMEDIARIES

By revisiting four fieldworks involving legal intermediaries, the aim of this chapter is to analyze what they have in common and to what extent they differ.

The legal intermediaries I study are: job counselors working in an experimental organization funded by the French State and related to a public agency for vocational training (Agency for the vocational training of adults, AFPA in French); union activists and HR members in various companies in France; safety officers in scientific labs in France and in the United States; and forensic economic experts in France. I revisit these sites to specifically test the fruitfulness of the analytical category put forth in this chapter. Below, I will explain the methods I used to carry out data collection, the different research contexts I encountered and the main empirical characteristic of the legal intermediaries I analyzed. I, then, present the main dimensions used to compare them, which are problematized by the question of power.

Data, Methods, and Empirical Findings

A first study focused on job counselors working in one of France's many experimental employment programs, here the occupational transition contract (OTC) (Brun, Corteel, & Pelisse, 2012). Employees who had been dismissed for economic reasons by firms of less than 1,000 employees located in employment areas identified as "vulnerable," benefitted from a transition grant of up to one year that matched approximately their former net salary. They also had the right to work for short periods of time without losing their grant. As explained by one of its main designers, "The aim of the OTC is the return to sustainable employment, with the goal of updating and skills development, with personalized advice for people, particularly in terms of training." The law stated that each member was expected to "be active in their job search 'and' to meet his counselor and regularly communicate to him the results of his actions." The empirical research consisted of interviews ($n=37$) with job counselors and their managers, and numerous ethnographic observations ($n=70$) at two sites, especially the interactions between job counselors and unemployed people, as well as internal meetings between job counselors. The experimental nature of the program has been interesting for us, researchers, because it has served as a magnifying lens to understand the daily interactions that shape the lives of the unemployed in France – and there are many of them in this country – in particular with the job counselors in welfare job agencies. As legal intermediaries, job counselors frame the identity of the unemployed. They define what "looking for a job" or "building a career plan" means, what a "good" or a "bad" job is, as well as an "acceptable" or "unacceptable" job offer. In this sense, job counselors shape the meaning, the conventions and legality surrounding work, which in turn impacts how the unemployed feel about their rights.

The second source of data is grounded in several inquiries on collective bargaining and conflicts at the company level. At first, I studied agreements over working time reduction that resulted from two laws passed in the late 1990s (Pélisse, 2004a, 2004b). Then, I collected data on the subsequent evolution of conflicts and negotiations (during two studies in 2006–2008, then 2012–2014); thanks to a survey covering more than 3,000 French firms (Béroud et al., 2008; Giraud et al., 2014). During these years, I also conducted personally 15 in-depth studies of specific companies from various sectors (manufacturing, services, agriculture) and with different sizes (from 30 employees to 4,000). I combined interviews with employers, employees and union members, document analysis and made workplace visits. In France, unions are frequently present at the level of many firms (except for the smallest), which affects how companies endogenize labor law. Even though French industrial relations are not exclusively focused on the level of companies as in the United States, the trend since more than 30 years has been a decentralization of collective bargaining. As a result, HR managers and union's activists are more and more involved in the production of formal legal rules, contributing to the internalization of law by organizations. Their contribution is particularly salient in the negotiation of collective agreements, which concern not only wages, but all dimensions of the employment relationship (working time, working conditions, equal pay for men and women, dismissal conditions, etc.). This trend has also been strongly reinforced by the recent reforms of the Labor Code in 2016 and 2017, which considerably widened the autonomy of HR employees and union members in governing labor relations. These actors act thus as legal intermediaries between an evolving legal framework and practices on the workplace. They participate in the definition of the meaning of the laws, especially during phases of negotiation and conflict, giving substance increasingly procedural legal rules. Of course, as Edelman's work points out, other legal professionals, such as lawyers, in-house counselors and judges (one could add labor inspectors) play important roles in this process. But they rarely intervene on the workplace, and when they do, it is under very specific circumstances. Representing employers on the one hand, and employees on the other, HR members and union activists are therefore key players in the legal process of endogenization. They frame ordinary legality in the workplace, producing, negotiating and implementing intrinsically technical and organizational, socio-economic and legal rules.

A third study is grounded in an ongoing research on health and safety in nanoscience labs, which I started in 2014. Five nano-medicine and nano-chemistry laboratories in three prestigious universities in France and the United States are being studied through numerous observations and a wealth of ethnographic data, with two colleagues. I interviewed academics (PhD, postdoc and permanent scholars) and safety officers ($n = 70$) to understand the construction of legality in scientific contexts. I notably pay attention to the role of safety officers who take part in this process, both inside and outside the labs. Among other things, they indeed enforce an increasing body of regulations, acting as legal intermediaries. Trained and recognized for their technical skills and competences related to safety, chemicals or health risks, safety officers complete documents, authorize the experiments, monitor and ensure compliance in laboratories. They check the ability of laboratory workers to use any tool or equipment, and they check that they have their glasses, gloves, lab coat, etc. They play a crucial role between external regulations and internal practices in laboratories, developing a mediating role to ensure compliance of the labs and experimental practices. When they work in safety offices, as Environment Health and Safety (EHS) officers, they turn legal rules, good practices or recommendations from the

European Union (EU) or agencies such as INRS, SCENIHR, NIOSH, OSHA or EPA related to nano-risks into practical regulations.[2] When they work in laboratories, as safety representatives, they adapt these rules daily to the laboratory space, at the time of research (it can be Sunday or night), and to the passion and scientific spirit that characterize researchers (Pélisse, 2017). In every case, they act as legal intermediaries, even if they are far from the official legal field.

On the contrary, the last study was closer to the core of the legal field. Indeed, I met French forensic economic experts, who are called by the judges to help them in complex business cases (Charrier & Pélisse, 2012). The data I collected here are both quantitative and qualitative: I surveyed 135 experts using an in-depth questionnaire and interviewed 17 together with Emmanuel Charrier, himself accountant and who became a forensic expert after the study. Appointed by judges, rather than by the litigants as in the US, forensic economic experts are professionals who are very close to the judicial field. They are nevertheless expected to focus only on the technical dimensions of the facts and refrain from counseling the judge on legal or judicial dimensions of the case. Moreover, they are barred from becoming fully-fledged legal professionals, as rules prohibit them from practicing as forensic experts on a full-time basis. Moreover, they rarely interact with the judge: most of their communication is based on the initial task sent by the judge through written documents. Even if they are not legal professionals, they play an intermediary role between law in the books and law in action, legal rules and economic actors, helping to define what is legal and what is not, and how to comply with it. They greatly influence judges' decisions, the perception of the law for litigants and certain aspects of the legality of cases. During meetings and interactions with litigants (and their counsels and lawyers), experts exert influence, interpret rules and construct the technical, social, and intrinsically legal meaning of the business rules.

Three Power Dimensions for Comparing Legal Intermediaries

Beyond these successive identifications of legal intermediaries and their specific activities, the comparison between them yields variations. We can classify them along three dimensions that are closely related to power, in order to understand how and under what conditions legal intermediaries contribute to endogenizing the law and shaping ordinary legality.

The type of legal environment and legal rules handled, and manipulated by legal intermediaries is the first important dimension to be considered when drawing a comparison. Indeed, legal environments are not simple or unique, the rules can be very different, between facilitating, regulatory and constitutive dimensions, for example, to take the distinctions proposed by Edelman and Suchman (2007). One must distinguish between procedural and substantive rules, broad and ambiguous or precise and narrow rules, hard rules and other soft rules, in order to understand the context, the nature and the power that the legal intermediaries own and undergo.[3] These rules can be combined with various sanctions, ranging from exclusion from the program for employment counselors (e.g., when jobseekers do not come to the weekly meeting or do not seek employment) to refusal of an experiment by security officers. In one case in an American laboratory, they even excluded from the laboratory a PhD student considered too dangerous, and forced him, with his director, to change his dissertation topic to avoid experiments. However, sanctions are rarely as harsh and mostly combined with other means, like humor or mockery, but also strikes (for unions' activists), dismissal (for HR employees) or calls to the judge (for forensic economic experts) to implement, enforce or merely use the rules.

A second dimension is the audiences with whom legal intermediaries interact, and the different types of power relationships that they entail. Unions' activists are elected by their audience. Others legal intermediaries receive their mandate from the State or a university, or, like HR, received a private mandate to represent the interests of the firms (and mainly the stakeholder and managers). These mandates could be permanent like for the job counselors or EHS officers, or temporary like for the judicial experts or the union's activists. In all cases, these dimensions must be specified in order to grasp the power relationship that exists between the legal intermediaries and their clients, users, audiences, or supervisors. In this vein, to analyze the legal professionals with whom legal intermediaries interact, or who may be present in the practical and professional environment of legal intermediaries is important. For the French judicial experts in economics, it is not only the judge for whom they work and write a report but, more and more, also lawyers and "forensic counsels" appointed by the parties, with whom they must interact during the working meetings. For their part, unions' activists and HR members work more frequently with lawyers or in-house counsels, whereas job counselors can even be confronted with the judges, as in one of the studied centers. Even though a claim from jobseekers who sued the director of one of the studied two job centers, was dismissed. The job counselors became very cautious about the procedural aspects of their activities, in order to avoid possible legal proceedings.

These two dimensions are related to the institutional legal intermediaries' power and authority, which we have to take into account to understand their capacity to shape legality. This institutional power is strong for job counselors, for example, who may exclude unemployed workers from the program, even if they have to justify their decision in front of their colleagues and the director of the job center. From the other side, HR and union members have a great deal of bargaining power to elaborate rules, although framed by the Labor Code, legislation and judges. Even if they are not in the front line to implement them directly, they can often be enforcement agents and help shape day-to-day workplace practices and ordinary legality. Because, laboratory safety representatives share the daily lives of scientists (when they are not themselves scientists in training, such as safety representatives in American laboratories), they can intervene more directly in safety practices. But their power is weak because of their status (PhD students or technicians), their role (implementing external, bureaucratic and non-scientific rules in researchers' practices), and their lack of legitimacy compared to the authoritative discourse of science. Finally, for judicial experts in economics, because they own technical knowledge (inaccessible for judges), unrecognized but very important legal skills (notably to respect procedural

Table 1. Three Power-oriented Dimensions of Legal Intermediaries.

Figures of Legal Intermediaries	Job Counselors	Union Representatives and Human Resource Members	Health and Safety Officers (In and Outside the Labs)	Judicial Experts in Economy
Legal environment	Decree and legal instructions from the administration	European rules, Labor Code, judicial decisions, and legislations Collective agreements on various issues Internal rules issued by the employers	European and national rules and regulations; international recommendations, good practices reports from various agencies (NIOSH, EPA…), etc.	Procedural rules of expertise (due process, contradictory principle) and substantive rules of business (Commercial Code)
	Facilitative and regulative	*Facilitative, regulative and constitutive*	*Facilitative and regulative*	*Mostly procedural (facilitative) and constitutive*
Related audience (including legal professionals)	Unemployed, but also counselors' supervisors. Sometimes potential employers and funders for training program	*For HR members*: directions, employees	*Into the labs (safety reps)*: scientists, with various status and power	Primarily litigants, but also lawyers and more and more "forensic counsels" called and paid by the litigants
		For union's activists: employees, other union's activists	*Outside the labs (EHS officers)*: direction of their office and the university; PI and health and safety reps	The judges mission the experts but they rarely interact after the assignment letter.
	Possibly judges (in one case in my fieldwork).	*For both*: Labor inspectors and state bureaucrats; lawyers; in-house legal counsel and legal activists; judges	*For both*: Labor and environmental inspectors (like OSHA and EPA in US); possibly judges	
Power and authority of legal intermediaries	Strong vis-à-vis unemployed jobseeker but they have to justify their power in front of their colleagues and superiors in the job center	Power to negotiate and produce legal rules (notably to derogate to Labor Code), but less direct for the implementation and rules enforcement	*Inside safety reps*: lack of power vis-à-vis the scientists (they are PhD or technicians) *Outside EHS officers*: real but only formal power, considered as bureaucrats by the scientists	Their reports and opinions influence greatly the judges and their decisions
	Formally strong	*Variable, depending of the sectors and the firms*	*Often weak*	*Informally strong*

rules), and a judicial horizon (essential for drafting their reports in a form satisfactory for judges), they have real power to influence both judges' decisions and the legality of business relationships.

I map thus these variations in the Table 1, in order to show empirical details, but also synthetic points of comparison between the four types of legal intermediaries analyzed.

RESULTS: A TENDENCY AND A PARADOX

By contrasting these four different fieldworks and legal intermediaries along the main dimensions evoked above, I present two results. The first underlines the growing importance and reflexivity of legal intermediaries, and the second highlights a paradox showing how the comparison is useful in understanding the roles of legal intermediaries, the conditions under which they develop their intermediary positions and activities, and how they participate in the managerialization and legalization processes, shaping legality in workplaces or economic relationships.

Tendency: The Growing Role of Trained and Reflexive Legal Intermediaries

A first result is the growing, increasingly impactful and reflexive role of legal intermediaries in our complex societies and economies. In one word, it underlines their possible growing power in legal endogenization process. I suggest with Shauhin Talesh that three conditions have made intermediaries more likely to play a role in shaping legality: (1) the global shift from government to governance; (2) the inherent ambiguity in legal rules; and (3) the increasing complexity of legal rules (Talesh & Pélisse, 2019, p. 5). We argue that the interaction of these three elements have created greater space for non-traditional actors to emerge and influence law. In particular, a variety of legal and non-legal actors among and within organizations that come into contact with law have increasing discretion in their legal environments. If the hypothesis of a growing juridification and legalization of organizations is true, then legal intermediaries (legal and non-legal professionals) have to play a growing role in our economies and societies, gaining leeway and power to contribute to the endogenization process.

The four cases presented above show this growing role of legal intermediaries and notably of non-legal professionals, in various areas. It is really visible to each of them, even if it is for various reasons. The policies – and the legal forms they take, as in the experimental program studied – give more space to local agencies and job counselors in the process of implementing social assistance. For industrial actors, laws are now regarded as supplementary and are only implemented if collective bargaining fails: the role of industrial actors in the drafting and implementation of labor laws in companies increases considerably. For safety officers, there is a very perceptible trend toward the legalization of scientific laboratories, which contrasts with the past situation marked only by the domination of scientific logic. And for experts in legal economics, even if they don't have more activities in recent years, their role has become central in increasingly complex business cases, at least when the latter are judged by the courts. Finally, the diversity of the cases evoked above to nurture the idea that many professionals or occupational functions could be analyzed as a possible example of legal intermediaries. We need to take a fresh look at many actors, including workers, civil servants, street and middle bureaucrats in private and public organizations, but also activists and many intermediaries function between the law and different worlds (science, sport, art, and religion, etc.).

Secondly, although non-legal professionals, legal intermediaries are increasingly trained and called upon to be reflexive in their day-to-day management of legal rules. This is generally true, as in the fourth case mentioned above. One has to notice, for example, how master's degrees especially dedicated to non-legal students and professionals at various American and French universities are multiplying since a few years. At Northeastern, since 2014, one master of legal studies:

> is a distinctive program built from the ground up for the aspiring professional eager to enhance his or her understanding of the law and to help employers navigate complex regulatory terrain. The Master of Legal Studies is for non-lawyer professionals who work regularly with lawyers and legal issues. It was created specifically for those who do not wish to practice law, but would like to use the law as a means to achieve goals in environments where law is too often seen as an obstacle. (http://www.northeastern.edu/mls/program)

Mostly online and possibly at part-time, master of "science in law" at Northwestern and masters of "Legal studies" at Washington University, Pepperdine or University of Arizona – to take only a few examples – are designed in the same way and for the same audiences: non-legal professionals and non-lawyers. Most of the time, they are developed by law schools – but sometimes by business schools or under the screen of ethics and compliance, notably in France too. These training courses are an evidence of the possible diffusion of these legal intermediaries roles and actors, and the need for them to be trained, if not reflexive.

This growing reflexivity and training in the use of rules – different from classical legal training – is visible to most of the legal intermediaries I study. Although the job counselors have not received legal training, they are all very familiar with the decree creating the OCT program. We were also struck by the importance of the collective discussions they had among themselves, to decide on a case, interpret the rules and establish local jurisprudence enabling them to share common and effective ways of accompanying the unemployed. For HR members and union activists, it should be noted that the former are increasingly trained, particularly in law but not exclusively.[4] Union activists are increasingly specialized, as recent laws have transformed them into specialists of negotiation and "social dialogue." During my investigations, for example, many activists have incidentally explained how they had to become experts in labor law, learning and sleeping with the Labor Code to assume their mandate and their role. For safety officers in the world of science, the requirement for a high level of knowledge and expertise, as well as an ability to think about how to use it and implement the rules, is similar. At West University in the United States, for example, where I investigated in 2014 and 2016, I witnessed how the health and safety office has recruited more and more safety officers with PhDs in chemistry or biology. It is expected that these actors are able to understand the researchers and share their experiences to increase their effectiveness in implementing the safety regulations developed by the university. At another university, Huising and Silbey (2011) described and analyzed this reflexivity and "relational regulation" by which safety officers managed to implement a very complex environmental and health monitoring system. Finally, forensic economic experts must also be well-versed in the rules of procedure and reflect on their relations with both litigants and judges. Since 2004, to have the right to be included on national lists of experts from which judges select their judicial experts, they have to prove every five years that they master procedural knowledge. In short, the first result is clearly the growing importance of these actors, not only in their diversity and number, but also in their training, reflexivity and possible power. They increasingly have to master develop strategic skills to make the most of the rules that surround them.

Paradox: Legal Intermediaries and the Legal Professional Roles

A second result is a paradox concerning the role of the legal intermediaries analyzed in these studies. Indeed, even though they are not legal professionals, legal intermediaries act more or less as legal professionals. This does not mean that they mimic the legal professionals with whom they interact. But their treatment of legal rules put them in a similar position as legal actors. To a certain extent, they act indeed simultaneously as legislators, judges, lawyers, inspectors, cops and even as clerks. This is additional reason for seeing a continuum between their role and those taken up by legal professionals. As Nelson and Nielsen (2000) have pointed out, corporate lawyers in large law firms – which are also not at the heart of the legal field – act as cops, counsels or entrepreneurs. Similarly, we have found that our legal intermediaries frame legality following those different legal roles, despite being sometimes very far from the legal field. Edelman and Suchman (1999) also proposed the idea that organizations act as internal legislators, judges, lawyers, and cops during the process of legal endogenization.

As legislators, legal intermediaries all contribute to the production of legal rules, which shape the practical legal environment for which, or with which, they work. As Talesh (2015) stated, "rule-intermediaries filter the meaning of the law through competing logics and, in so doing, act as legislators." They act as legislators by directly producing legal rules, such as HR staff and unions' activists in companies, through collective bargaining and collective agreements. For other legal intermediaries, it is more indirect. But, through their interpretation and reconstruction of the meaning of legal rules, the act of helping the unemployed, supervising compliance with safety rules in scientific laboratories, or helping the judge to understand and resolve business conflicts, they act as legislators. In some cases, these intermediary rules can be recognized by the legal order. Safety officers at universities produce memos and various documents, describe good practices, and disseminate standards to other contexts. Judicial experts draft reports and propose solutions, which are often adopted by the judge, thus contributing to case law. Acting as a legislator does not even require the presence of a written rule. The job counselors, during their weekly meetings with the unemployed and with their colleagues at the job center, develop "secondary rules" (Lascoumes, 1990) and like a practical jurisprudence to implement the decree, which frames the experience of OCT's clients.

As judges, even if they mobilize other principles of justice, legal intermediaries develop judgment activities based on legal rules. This is particularly salient for job counselors, who constantly judge their public, the behavior of the unemployed or the quality of their project and their training, by referring to the rules of the OCT program but also to other principles (equity or equality, need to work, gender and its naturalization on the type of work for men and women, logic of the labor market, etc.). Forensic economic experts could also be particularly qualified as "judges of a small technical trial" (Charrier & Pélisse, 2012). They provide reports to the judge, but in reality, they do a lot more during their expertise: because they organize meetings, request documents, and require the parties to plead their claims, the expertise process itself transforms the case. They often "clarify" the conflict and "drain" the case, acting as a judge, even if their contribution is limited to the technical dimension of the dispute. Safety officers also decide and judge in situation. They authorize an experiment or not, evaluate the risks in a room, and decide whether to evacuate it or not. These decisions are based on technical knowledge, but also on legal categories such as liability, potential guilt, or the precautionary principle. Union activists and HR managers, however, act less frequently as judges than others legal intermediaries. Yet, the employer is a judge in his own company. He has the right to enforce internal rules, which can go as far as terminating someone's job contract. Incidentally, both HR members and union activists are sometimes judges in the local labor tribunals.

Third, as lawyers, legal intermediaries raise cases, defend interests, and provide strategic advice. They mobilize, interpret, and manipulate the rules of law to defend their clients, who are their audiences, their employers, their voters. They can also choose to defend the "public interest." In the field of labor law, HR members are, in a way, lawyers for their employers and managers, while union's activists use the law to defend the interests of employees. Through the OCT program, job counselors defend the general interest and proper allocation of public funds. They are also the defenders of the unemployed, helping them to find a job, arguing their qualities before potential employers or training organizations and their funders. In a similar vein, safety officers are always mandated by the director of the laboratory or university and defend the cause of safety against other logics. For their part, judicial expert seeks the technical truth of the facts. These mandates require them to represent interests, defend cases, and use legal rules to achieve strategic objectives. In this sense, legal rules are specific tools for them, as they are for lawyers. Legal intermediaries obviously have other resources and logic than legal rules, such as their technical knowledge, experiences, and the legitimacy to represent employees. They infuse other professional logics than the legal logic to do their job, contributing to filter the law through their professional knowledge and practices.

Fourth, as cops, legal intermediaries monitor compliance of practices with legal rules. They inspect systems, procedures, and practices. The specific legal intermediaries on whom I have focused don't only advise on and interpret the meaning of the law, but also defines what is compliant with the law. They all enforce the rules and monitor compliance. This is clearly the case for job counselors and safety officers (the latter being often called cops by the scientists), as well as economic forensic experts who check whether litigants give them access to information, figures and documents, and are often considered as the judge's sword arm by the litigants. Legal intermediaries channel behaviors and seek compliance, like union activists who want the Labor Code to apply in their companies and often play the role of enforcers. HR members act less like cops than the others. Nevertheless, they rarely share the point of view of the managers and supervisors totally, carrying on the gaps between practices and legal rules of the Labor Code and underlining often the importance to respect the rules.[5]

Finally, as clerks, legal intermediaries increasingly report on how they implement and use the rules. They become registrars of law and legality, formalizing the situations they have to manage, implementing legal rules through formal procedures and sometimes through software and written reports, which allow them to control their audience. I observe this process among different legal intermediaries, such as job counselors or safety officers – some of them are even called "paper engineers" by safety representatives in French and American scientific labs. Faced with an increasing proceduralization of their activity, under the effect of the growing presence of corporate lawyers and "forensic accountants," judicial experts in economics have also described how they record and account for all their activities, in particular by paying attention to the calendar and deadlines. As for HR members and union activists, they increasingly have to account, write and report how they negotiate, what they said when they meet, etc. Like the clerk during the trial, legal intermediaries record what the rules say, how they are implemented, what their effects are, because they must be responsible and trace responsibilities, as the law itself promises. From a Weberian perspective, legal intermediaries are perhaps one of the most invisible, but effective agents of the diffusion of the legalistic state (Epp, 2009) and of formalization, if not rationalization of our daily life.

DISCUSSIONS AND CONCLUSION: FRAMING LEGALITY THROUGH INSTITUTIONAL, CONTENTIOUS, AND UNCERTAIN DIMENSIONS

With these results, we can open a discussion of how legal intermediaries shape ordinary legality. The line of questioning moves away from what they do in practice (as legislators, judges, lawyers, etc., as shown above) and must now assess the consequences of those practices on our legal consciousness. We can now analyze whether and how legal intermediaries managerialize the law or legalize organizations, and whether they contribute to more substantial or symbolic effects in the process of legal endogenization, to frame the question like L. Edelman does in her latest book (Edelman, 2016). For example, trade union activists are primarily motivated by the legalization of organizations. As Selznick (1969) pointed out, they attempt to transform industrial relations systems to fight arbitrariness, establish general rules to protect employees, and advance workers' social rights. On the contrary, HR members are more likely to contribute to the management of law and regulation, to use legal rights to promote their managerial interests, and to construct the meaning of law in a way that is compatible with their managerial values of efficiency, rationality, and productivity. But the issue is not just about compliance and how they interpret, implement, legalize or managerialize laws, it is about understanding how they shape legality through their everyday work, which involves legal rules and other forms of normativity, and their interactions with various audiences. We must therefore take into account the power dimensions described above and analyze how they contribute to an institutional process rather than a political process, if we use again the analytical notions proposed by Edelman and her co-authors. With this distinction, Edelman and Stryker (2005) emphasize that:

> Two processes are at work in linking law and the economy: *institutional process* that involve the production and widespread acceptance of particular construction of law and compliance, and *political process* that help to shape which constructions of law are produced and became institutionalized and who benefit from this construction. (Edelman & Stryker, 2005, p. 933)

> Neo-institutional theories of organizations can be modified to emphasize both institutional conditions under which taken for grantedeness is likely to prevail and in which these conditions could be fragile, such latent conflicts of meaning, values and interests evolve into manifest conflict. (Edelman & Stryker, 2005, p. 938)

How do legal intermediaries influence the construction of what is taken for granted and considered as an institutional reality, or, on the contrary, how do they contribute in more controversial ways to shaping legality?

One hypothesis could be formulated here: when intermediaries play an important role in framing legality (they have the power, legitimacy, capacity to control and construct the meaning of legal rules), they further strengthen the institutional process described above. When they perform various legal roles with legitimacy, they participate in "the production and widespread acceptance of a particular construction of law and conformity," to quote Edelman and Stryker (2005). By contrast, when legal intermediaries are weaker, less legitimate and less connected, when they are more constrained by rules than the strategic actors who use them, the process of legal intermediation is less institutionalized, more political and contentious. Considering my four cases could be a test for this hypothesis and a step forward in understanding how different legal intermediaries act during the legal intermediation process and with what kind of consequences on day-to-day legality.

On the side of job counselors, their power and legitimacy vis-à-vis unemployed jobseekers are clearly high, particularly for the majority of the unemployed who are in a situation of relative dependency (lack of financial resources, low qualification, age, etc.).[6] Thus, job counselors try to change behaviors: jobseekers should market themselves on the labor market, improve their skills and adapt their vision of employment. One main contribution of the job counselors is to transform labor conventions, by shifting the expectations of jobseekers from the notion of "lifelong employment" to that of "sustainable employability" (Brun et al., 2012). By doing this, they transform certain aspects of legality. They redefine popular conceptions of what "looking for a job" and "a good job" stand for, what skills are useful in the labor market. They convince jobseekers that nowadays it is necessary to change one's job regularly, through flexible contracts and permanent adaptations. In other words, employment counselors clearly contribute to an institutionalized process of legal intermediation. Obviously, their public is temporary rather than captive: unemployed people find a job, or stop looking for one (especially for health reasons). The program I studied gives them consistent support only for one year. This time period is sometimes not enough to transform the situations and identities of the unemployed. But the job counselors have the means during this year to influence their situations and, because the experimentation lasted seven years in all, they contributed, among others, to alter the collective beliefs regarding job search, "reasonable" jobs and the role of vocational training in finding a new job. In a nutshell, they influenced those constitutive categories in an institutional way, which are less officially legal than shaping informally legality.

Turning to union activists and HR members, I found that they are mainly concerned with the regulatory environment: the legal rules that matter to them are mainly statutes that regulate work organizations and workplace practices. These rules determine wages, working time, training time, job classifications, health, safety and working conditions, etc. Moreover, HR members and union activists are often conflicting with each other. They defend competing interests, yet they have to cooperate to make organizational life possible. Because negotiations and conflicts are ultimately always about rules – procedural or substantive – both HR and union members influence constitutive norms. In doing so, they contribute both to the institutional and political forms of legal intermediation. Their interactions are highly institutionalized and even ritualized, especially when the union's activities and legitimacy are recognized by employers, mostly in large companies. But this institutional framework, largely regulated by the Labor Code, creates interactions that are structurally contentious. In these interactions, the parties contest each other's legitimacy, especially when they act as legal intermediaries. Thus, when they act as judges, inspectors or cops in companies, the other parties often contest their conclusions. And when they invent rules through collective bargaining, it is always through agreements that are often seen as a temporary armistice in the "cold strike" that bind and oppose them (Morel, 1980; Pélisse, 2019). Finally, they also shape legal consciousness in the workplace, influencing day-to-day legality and the constitutive categories of what is a job and a company, what is work, wages or "normal" working time. But this influence is often controversial, especially in France where the conflict dimension of labor relations is often and always topical.

For safety officers at university, the legal environment is also made of regulations: those rules allow certain types of experiments and prohibit others, regulate the use of chemicals, and establish a precautionary principle. Nevertheless, these legal intermediaries are clearly dominated in laboratories by the expertise of researchers and the scientific logic. This is particularly the case for internal safety representatives who lack power, can rarely sanction and call upon outside authorities. Paradoxically, they seek to be forgotten by scientists: they are more successful in implementing safety practices in laboratories when they do not have to remind scientists of the rules and can disappear behind their other roles (scientists themselves in American laboratories, or technicians helping with experiments in French laboratories) (Pélisse, 2017). Outside safety officers are closer to mid-level bureaucrats: they have a clearer and deeper understanding of the rules. Their status as university bureaucrats and inspectors (even when they inspect labs only once a year) gives them authority. They translate the legal regulations into the organization of the university and the scientific labs, interacting with legal professionals like OSHA, EPA inspectors or in-house lawyers at university. Beyond these differences, they share nevertheless the same position vis-à-vis scientists and the same role in the legal intermediation process. They seek to institutionalize this process, through what they call "a living safety culture," but are often seen by scientists as "too political": scientists often blame them for referring to external rules that they consider too bureaucratic, formal, and irrelevant.

Finally, judicial experts in economics are immersed in a judicial environment shaped by very precise procedural rules, and also by very contentious relations. They are called by judges to assist them in particularly contentious and complex situations. They do not act directly or formally as judges, but they organize their activities like them, meeting with the parties, requesting documents, listening to their arguments and ruling what the decision on the technical dimension of the trial might be. They, thus, try to "empty" and "drain" the conflict of its technical aspects, by observing where the parties have complied or not, by judging how they defend their interests and by seeking a technical truth. And when they succeed – for example, when the parties accept their authority and find their relationships and reports fair – it is because they convince and shape the perceptions of those parties. As we have shown (Charrier & Pélisse, 2012), judicial experts in economics shape the social and moral conventions of a fair business relationship, not only for judges but also for litigants. They thus contribute to the institutionalization of certain interpretations of the interaction between business and law (and justice), even when the context and initial situation are highly controversial.

Legal intermediaries are therefore immersed in various legal environments and have unequal leverage over these environments and in their interaction with their audiences or legal professionals. As summarized by Table 2, they contribute mostly in some cases to the institutionalization of legal intermediation and rather to politicizing in other cases.

The role of legal intermediaries is complex, depending on the legal environment and the rules they deal with on a daily basis, their relations with their

Table 2. How Do Legal Intermediaries Participate to the Legal Endogenization Processes and How Do They Shape Ordinary Legality?

Figures of Legal Intermediaries	Job Counselors	Union Representatives and Human Resource Members	Safety Officers (in or Outside the Labs)	Judicial Experts in Economy
More institutional or political process of legal endogeneization?	*Institutional*	*Variable but mostly political and contentious*	*Will institutionalize but perceived as actors politicizing safety in the labs*	*Institutional but in intrinsic contentious context*

audiences and legal professionals, their authority, power and legitimacy in the situations at hand. However, the variability is not fortuitous, and, in each case, legal intermediaries have a major impact on legality, whether it is the unemployed, workers and managers, scientists in their laboratories or litigators in commercial cases. I argue that it is essential to consider their role in how organizations build legality that frames our daily lives and identities. Taking them into account aims at understanding how the legal and economic spheres interact and how this interaction varies according to specific issues, rules, and contexts. This approach constitutes a promising avenue for systematizing the analysis of these interactions, the processes that take place there, and their consequences on the ways the law is constructed and acts in our daily lives.

A final general remark on their intermediate position could be made because they are brokers between the legal and organizational fields, health and safety regulation and scientists, the business logic and legal rules in litigation, employees and employers, or unemployed and potential employers. These actors are both weak and strong, in-between and nowhere, in-between and everywhere. They are somewhere between the formalism of the legal field and its legal professionals and the informal phenomena pertaining to this field. Legal intermediaries can thus escape the logics of formalization and proceduralization, as well as they can legalize organizations and our daily lives. In this sense, their intermediate positions undoubtedly imply an intrinsic uncertainty. This uncertainty weakens their legitimacy to use the law and develop their various legal roles. But uncertainty is also a source of power, as Crozier and Friedberg (1977) have shown. Thanks to their intermediate position, legal intermediaries play with the rules, use different logics, cross borders, even more in different ways than legal professionals. Legal professionals have, indeed, abide to the logic of the legal field, which is very powerful, competitive, and source of a strong "illusion," as explained by Bourdieu (1987). Legal professionals, much more than legal intermediaries, are partly dominated by their professionalism, the effects of competition and reputation and their professional rules, which imply a particular form of legal liability concerning them. The power is developed by legal intermediaries, thanks to their intermediate position that is probably more informal than formal, more fragile, contested or politicized than institutionalized. But informality could be stronger than formality to participate in the process of legal endogenization, shape our legal consciousness, influence what is taken for granted, and frame ordinary legality in our social world.

NOTES

1. As explained by Silbey (2005, p. 347), the term legality refers to the meanings, sources of authority, and cultural practices that are commonly recognized as legal, regardless of who employs them or for what purposes. [...] The analytic construct "legality" names a structural component of society, that is, cultural schemas and resources that operate to define and pattern social life (Sewell, 1992). Through repeated invocations of legal concepts and terminology, as well as through imaginative and unusual associations among schemas, legality is constituted through everyday actions and practices.

2. Institut national de la recherche sur la sécurité au travail (INRS); Scientific Committe on Emerging and Newly Identified Health Risks (SCENIHR); National Institute on Occupational Safety and Health (NIOSH); Occupational Safety and Health Administration (OSHA); Environmental Protection Agency (EPA).

3. See Billows (2016), who emphasizes this crucial dimension of the more or less ambiguity or formalized characteristics of the legal rules, to understand the various strategies of regulators, as the strategies of in-house counsels in retail sector.

4. For example, 27% of the HR respondents to the surveys that I use in my inquiry (REPONSE) had a high diploma (between a bachelor and a master degree) or more in 1999. They are 41% in 2011 in the survey. This survey shows also the increasing time dedicated to legal counsels reported by unions' activists during these years.

5. Charles Epp (2009) emphasizes, for example, the role of these actors, who contribute to the legalization and bureaucratization of various administrations or companies, by overstating the judicial risks of illegal or not compliant behaviors.

6. That is not the case of all the unemployed, even if they are dismissal for economic reasons: some of them search alone a job and feel them not dependent of the job counselors or the OCT program. Even if this is very rare, others refuse the device of OCT, because they refuse to meet their job counselors every week and, precisely, to be dependent of the OCT program and their job counselor.

ACKNOWLEDGMENT

Thanks to Sebastian Billows, Lisa Buchter, and John Cioffi for their help and comments on earlier drafts of this chapter, as for the anonymous reviewers for their suggestions.

REFERENCES

Abbott, K., Levi-Faur, D., & Snidal, D. (2017). Theorizing regulatory intermediaries: The RIT model. *The Annals of the American Academy of Political and Social Science*, *670*(1), 13–35.

Albiston, C. (2010). *Institutional inequality and the mobilization of the family and medical leave act: Rights on leave*. Cambridge: Cambridge University Press.

Battilana, J., Leca, B., & Boxenbaum, E. (2009). How actors change institutions: Towards a theory of institutional entrepreneurship. *The Academy of Management Annals*, *3*(1), 65–107.

Bergeron, H., & Castel, P. (2016). Les habits neufs du néo-institutionnalisme? La redécouverte de l'ordre mésologique et de l'agency. *L'Année sociologique*, *66*(1), 31–72.

Bessy, C. (2014). Économie des conventions et sociologie. *Revue Française de Socio-Économie*, *13*(1), 259–265.

Bessy, C., Delpeuch, T., & Pélisse, J. (Eds). (2011). *Droit et régulations des activités économiques: Perspectives sociologiques et institutionnalistes*, Paris, coll. Droit et société, LGDJ.

Biland, E., & Steimetz, H. (2017). Are judges street-level bureaucrats? Evidence from French and Canadian family courts. *Law and Social Inquiry*, *42*(2), 298–324.

Billows, S. (2016). La politique de l'ambiguïté juridique. Quand l'Etat tente de réguler les échanges entre la grande distribution et ses fournisseurs. *Sociologie du travail, 58*, 8–31.

Bourdieu, P. (1987). The force of law: Toward a sociology of the juridical field. *The Hasting Law Journal, 38*, 805–853.

Brun, F., Corteel, D., & Pélisse, J. (2012). Counselling redundant employees in the framework of the occupational transitional contract program: Expertise and experience. *Revue Française de Sociologie, 53*(3), 287–315.

Buchter, L. (2019). "Companies can do better than the law": Securing rights for minorities as an insider activist in French corporations. In Billows, S., Buchter, L., & Pélisse, J. (Eds.), *Legal intermediation: A processual approach to law and economic activity. Studies in law, politics, and society* (Vol. 81, pp. 11–45). Bingley: Emerald Publishing Limited.

Callon, M. (1986). Eléments pour une sociologie de la traduction: La domestication des coquilles Saint-Jacques et des marins-pêcheurs dans la baie de Saint-Brieuc. *L'Année sociologique, 36*, 169–208.

Cavalcante, P., & Lotta, G. (2015). *Middle-level bureaucrats: Profils, trajectories, performance*. Brasilia: ENAP.

Charrier, E., & Pélisse, J. (2012). Conventions at work: On forensic accountant's intermediation. *Economic Sociology (European Electronic Newsletter), 14*(1), 31–40.

Crozier, M., & Friedberg, E. (1977). *L'acteur et le système. Les contraintes de l'action collective*. Paris: Points Seuil.

Delpeuch, T. (2011). Les interfaces entre le juridique et l'économique: concept de couplage et intermédiaire du droit. In Bessy C., Delpeuch T., Pélisse J. (Eds.). *Droit et régulations des activités économiques. Perspectives sociologiques et institutionnalistes* (pp. 127–133). Paris: LGDJ.

Demazière, D., & Jouvenet, M. (2013). The market work of football agents and the manifold valorizations of professional football players. *Economic Sociology (European Electronic Newsletter, 15*(1), 29–40.

Di Maggio, P. (1988). Interest and agency in institutional theory. In L. Zucker (Ed.), *Institutional patterns and culture* (pp. 3–22). Cambridge: Ballinger Publishing Company.

Dobbin, F. (2009). *Inventing equal opportunity*. Princeton, NJ: Princeton University Press.

Dodier, N. (1993). *L'expertise médicale. Essai de sociologie sur l'exercice du jugement*. Bruxelles: Métailié.

Dubois, V. (2010). Politiques au guichet, politiques du guichet. In Borraz O., Guiraudon V. (Eds.), *Politiques publiques 2. Des politiques pour changer la société* ? Paris: Presses de Sciences-po.

Edelman, L. (1992). Legal ambiguity and symbolic structures: Organizational mediation of civil rights law. *American Journal of Sociology, 97*, 1531–1576.

Edelman, L. (2016). *Working law: Courts, corporations, and symbolic civil rights*. Chicago, IL: The University of Chicago Press.

Edelman, L., Erlanger, H., & Lande, D. (1993). Internal dispute resolution: The transformation of civil rights in the workplace. *Law & Society Review, 27*, 497.

Edelman, L., Fuller, S., & Mara-Drita, I. (2001). Diversity rhetoric and the managerialization of law. *American Journal of Sociology, 106*(6), 1589–1641.

Edelman, L., & Stryker, R. (2005). A sociological approach to law and the economy. In N. J. Smelser & R. Swedberg (Eds.), *The handbook of economic sociology* (pp. 527–551). Princeton, NJ: Princeton University Press.

Edelman, L., & Suchman, M. (1999). When the 'Haves' hold court: The internalization of disputing in organizational fields. *Law & Society Review, 33*, 941–991.

Edelman, L., & Suchman, M. (2007). The interplay of law and organizations. In L. B. Edelman & M. Suchman (Eds.), *The legal lives of private organizations* (pp. i–xxxi). Aldershot: Ashgate Publishing.

Engel, D. (2012). Vertical and horizontal perspectives on rights consciousness. *Indiana Journal of Global Legal Studies, 19*(2), 423–455.

Epp, C. (2009). *Making rights real: Activists, bureaucrats and the creation of the legalistic state*. Chicago, IL: University of Chicago Press.

Ewick, P., & Silbey, S. (1998). *The commonplace of law. Stories of everyday life*. Chicago, IL: University of Chicago Press.

García Villegas, M. (2003). Symbolic power without symbolic violence? critical comments on legal consciousness studies in USA. *Droit et société*, *53*(1), 137–163.

Gendreau, C. (2005). 'Légitimation' et 'délégitimation' du droit de l'État: le cas des pratiques professionnelles des intermédiaires du droit dans le contexte du divorce. In Coutu M. et Rocher G. (dir.), *La légitimité de l'État et du droit. Autour de Max Weber*, Laval, Presses de l'Université Laval.

Guillaume, C. (2015). Understanding the variations of unions' litigation strategies to promote equal pay: Reflection on the British case. *Cambridge Journal of Economics*, *39*(2), 363–379.

Haveman, H., Habinek, J., & Goodman, L. (2012). How entrepreneurship evolves: The founders of new magazines in America, 1741–1860. *Administrative Science Quarterly*, *57*(4), 585–624.

Hennion, A. (1989). An intermediary between production and consumption: The producer of popular music. *Science, Technology, & Human Values*, *14*(4), 400–424.

Hoffman, E. (2003). Legal consciousness and dispute resolution: Different disputing behavior at two similar taxicab companies. *Law and Social Inquiry*, *8*(3), 691–716.

Huising, R., & Silbey, S. (2011). Governing the gap: Forging safe science through relational regulation. *Regulation and Governance*, *1*, 14–42.

Hupe, P., Hill, M., & Buffat, A. (2015). *Understanding street-level bureaucracy*. Chicago, IL: University of Chicago Press.

Juston, R. (2016). *Le corps médico-légal. Les médecins légistes et leurs expertises, thèse de sociologie*. Saint-Quentin en Yvelines: Université Versailles Saint Quentin en Yvelines.

Karpik, L. (2000). Le Guide rouge Michelin. *Sociologie du travail*, *42*(3), 369–389.

Karpik, L. (2010). Valuing the unique. *The economics of singularities*. New York, NY: Princeton University Press.

Lascoumes, P. (1990). Normes juridiques et mise en úuvre des politiques publiques. *L'Année sociologique*, *40*(3), 43–71.

Lascoumes, P., & Lorrain. (2007). Trous noirs du pouvoir. Les intermédiaires de l'action publique. *Sociologie du travail*, *49*(1), 1–9.

Lawrence, T., & Suddaby, R. (2006). Institutions and institutional work. In S. Clegg, C. Hardy, T. Lawrence, & W. Nord (Eds.), *The sage handbook of organization studies* (pp. 215–254). London: Sage.

Lazega, E. (2014). *Réseaux sociaux et structures relationnelles*. Paris: Presses Universitaires de France.

Lejeune, A., & Orianne, J.-F. (2014). The construction of workers' rights consciousness through legal intermediations: The case of employment discrimination in Belgium. *International Journal of Discrimination and the Law*, *14*(4), 221–243.

Levi Faur, D., & Starobin, J. (2014). Transational politics and policy: From two-way to three-way interactions. Working Paper 62. Papers in Regulation & Governance, Jerusalem.

Lipsky, M. (1980). *Street-level bureaucracy, dilemmas of the individual in public services*. New York, NY: Russell Sage Foundation.

Marchal, E. (2015). *Les embarras des recruteurs. Enquête sur le marché du travail*. Editions de l'EHESS, Paris.

Maynard-Moody, S., & Musheno, M. (2004). *Cops, teachers, counselors: Stories from the front lines of public service*. Ann Arbor, MI: University of Michigan Press.

Maynard-Moody, S., & Portillo, D. S. (2010). Street-level bureaucracy theory. In Robert F (Ed.), *The Oxford handbook of American bureaucracy*. Oxford: Durant Editions.

McCann, M. (2012). Expanding the horizons of horizontal inquiry into rights consciousness: An engagement with David Engel. *Indiana Journal of Global Legal Studies*, *19*(2), 467–488.

McCann, M. W. (1994). *Right at work: Pay equity reform and the politics of legal mobilization*. Chicago, IL: University of Chicago Press.

McCann, M. W. (2006). On legal rights consciousness: A challenging analytical tradition. In B. Fleury-Steiner & L. B. Nielsen (Eds.), *The new civil rights research: A constitutive approach* (pp. ix–xxx). Burlington, VT: Ashgate Publishing.

McCann, M. W., & Haltom, W. (2004). *Distorting the law, politics, media and the litigation crisis*. Chicago, IL: University of Chicago Press.

Merry, S. (1990). *Getting justice and getting even: Legal consciousness among working-class Americans*. Chicago, IL: University of Chicago Press.

Meyer, M. (2010). Les courtiers du savoir, nouveaux intermédiaires de la science. *Hermès La Revue*, *57*(2), 165–171.

Morel, C. (1980). *La grève froide. Stratégies syndicales et pouvoir patronal*. Toulouse: Octarès.

Nelson, B., & Nielsen, L. B. (2000). Cops, counsel, and entrepreneurs: Constructing the role of inside counsel in large corporations. *Law and Society Review*, *34*(2), 457–494.

Pélisse, J. (2004a). *A la recherche du temps gagné. Sens et usages du droit autour des 35h, these de sociologie*. Marne la Vallée: Université Marne la Vallée.

Pélisse, J. (2004b). From negotiation to implementation. A study of the reduction of working time in France (1998–2000). *Time and Society*, *13*(2–3), 221–244.

Pélisse, J. (2006). Time, legal consciousness and power: The case of France's 35-hour workweek laws. In B. Fleury-Steiner & L. B. Nielsen (Eds.), *New civil rights research: A constitutive perspective*. Aldershot: Ashgate/Darmouth Editions.

Pélisse, J. (2005). A-t-on conscience du droit ? Autour des Legal Consciousness Studies. *Genèses*, *59*, 114–130.

Pélisse, J. (2014). Le travail du droit. Trois études sur la légalité ordinaire. *Mémoire d'Habilitation à Diriger les Recherches*, Paris, Sciences Po.

Pélisse, J. (2017). Gérer les risques par le droit: articulation et intermédiation dans les laboratoires de nanosciences en France et aux Etats-Unis. *Droit et société*, *96*(2), 321–336.

Pélisse, J. (2018). Travailler le droit. Lectures et perspectives sociologiques. *Revue française de sociologie*, *59*(1), 99–125.

Pélisse, J. (2019). Une grève froide inversée? Eléments sur les mutations des relations professionnelles dans l'entreprise en France (1968–2018). *Négociations*, *31*, 61–81.

Portillo, D. S., & Rudes, S. (2014). Construction of justice at the street level. *Annual Review of Law and Social Science*, *10*, 321–334.

Sarat, A. (1990). "The law is all over": Power, resistance and the legal consciousness of the welfare poor. *Yale Journal of Law & the Humanities*, *2*(2), 343–379.

Sarat, A., & Kearns, T. (1995). *Law in everyday life*. Ann Arbor, MI: University of Michigan Press.

Selznick, P. (1969). *Law, society and industrial justice*. New York, NY: New York University Press.

Silbey, S. (2005). After legal consciousness. *Annual Review of Law and Social Science*, *1*, 323–368.

Silbey, S. (Eds.). (2008). *Law and science*. New York, NY, Routledge.

Spire, A. (2008). *Accueillir ou reconduire. Enquête sur les guichets de l'immigration*. Paris: Raisons d'agir.

Spire, A., & Alpes, J. (2014). Dealing with law in migration control: The powers of street-level bureaucrats at French consulates. *Social & Legal Studies*, *23*(1), 261–274.

Spire, A., & Weidenfeld, K. (2011). Le tribunal administratif: une affaire d'initiés ? Les inégalités d'accès à la justice et la distribution du capital procédural. *Droit et société*, *79*(3), 689–713.

Stovel, K., & Shaw, L. (2012). Brokerage. *Annual Review of Sociology*, *38*, 139–158.

Stryker, R. (2011). L'intermédiation scientifique dans la mise en úuvre des lois anti-discrimination américaine. In C. Bessy, T. Delpeuch, & J. Pélisse (Eds.), *Droit et régulations des activités économiques. Perspectives sociologiques et institutionnelles* (pp. 183–202). Paris: LGDJ.

Stryker, R., Docka, D., & Wald, P. (2012). Employment discrimination law and industrial psychology: Social science as social authority and the co-production of law and science. *Law and Social Inquiry*, *37*(4), 777–814.

Talesh, S. (2009). The privatization of public legal rights: How manufacturers construct the meaning of consummer law. *Law & Society Review*, *43*, 527–562.

Talesh, S. (2015a). Rule-Intermediaries in action: How state and business stakeholders influence the meaning of consumer rights in regulatory governance arrangements. *Law and Policy*, *37*(1–2), 1–32.

Talesh, S. (2015b). Legal intermediaries: How insurance companies construct the meaning of compliance with antidiscrimination law. *Law and Policy*, *37*(3), 209–239.

Talesh, S. (2017). Data breach, privacy, and cyber liability insurance: How insurance companies act as "Compliance Managers" for businesses. *Law and Social Inquiry*, *43*(2), 417–440.

Talesh, S., & Pélisse, J. (2019). How legal intermediaries facilitate or inhibit social change. In Sarat, A. (Ed.), *Studies in law, politics, and society* (Vol. 79, pp. 111–145). Bingley: Emerald Publishing Limited.

Teubner, G. (2011). *Networks as connected contracts. International studies in the theory of private law* (Vol. 7). Oxford: Hart Publishing.

Vincent, F. (2019). A multi-level approach to legal intermediation: The case of the 12-hour work derogation in French public hospitals. In Billows, S., Buchter, L., & Pélisse, J. (Eds.), *Legal intermediation: A processual approach to law and economic activity. Studies in law, politics, and society* (Vol. 81, pp. 69–100). Bingley: Emerald Publishing Limited.

Watkins-Hayes, C. (2009). *The new welfare bureaucrats: Entanglements of race, class and policy reform*. Chicago, IL: University of Chicago Press.

Zalio, P. P. (2013). Sociologie économique des entrepreneurs. In P. M. Chauvin, P. Steiner, & P. P. Zalio (Eds.), *Traité de sociologie économique* (pp. 601–634). Paris: Presses Universitaires de France.

DISMANTLING MANAGERIAL VALUES: WHEN LAW'S AMBIGUITY MEETS ORGANIZATIONAL COMPLEXITY

Alina Surubaru

ABSTRACT

Based on an in-depth case study in the French nuclear industry, this chapter describes what happens when law's ambiguity meets organizational complexity. While regulation studies suggest that organizations assign managerial values (such as efficiency or flexibility) to their compliance structures, this research focuses on the mixed role of purchasing managers in these processes. Constituting the missing link when explaining the legal regulation of economic activities, these intermediaries defend a financial conception of the firm against a more technical performance oriented solution. This financial conception did not emerge from nowhere, but resulted from the institutionalization of a particular meaning of business regulation within the nuclear industry. However, if values guide organizational behavior, the behavior of the actors can under no circumstances be reduced to these values. Conflicts, misunderstandings, and mistakes are a constitutive part of these process, too.

Keywords: Managerialization of law; organizational complexity; conflicts; intermediaries; contracts; subcontracting

A common outcome of regulation studies concerns the managerialization of the law: to comply with the law, researchers claim that organizations attribute managerial values (such as efficiency or flexibility) to their compliance structures

Legal Intermediation: A Processual Approach to Law and Economic Activity
Studies in Law, Politics, and Society, Volume 81, 129–150

ISSN: 1059-4337/doi:10.1108/S1059-433720190000081006

(Edelman, Riggs Fuller, & Mara-Drita, 2001; Gilad, 2014). In doing so, organizations do not simply act as "rational wealth maximizers" who look for the largest possible payoff at the least possible cost. In fact, organizations actively co-construct the law, as the state's legal system progressively assimilates the managerial meanings, values, and norms. From this perspective, organizations are considered to be "cultural rule-followers" who look to the law "for normative and cognitive guidance, as they seek their place in a socially constructed cultural reality" (Edelman & Suchman, 1997, p. 482). Legal intermediaries (whether inside or outside organizations) play a central role here, because they directly contribute to translating the law's meaning from one field to another (Abbott, Levi-Faur, & Snidal, 2017; Edelman, Abraham, & Erlanger, 1992; Talesh & Pélisse, 2019). As Pélisse reminds us in his contribution to this special issue, legal and non-legal professionals are both determinant in shaping the law-in-action. The law remains, however, constantly ambiguous and highly complex.

This theoretical framework helps us to understand the close relationship between law and organizations. Still, several questions about legal regulation are unanswered and call for more careful analytical attention. Among them, the question of the law's ambiguity is particularly salient. Edelman brilliantly shows how formal rules' characteristics create the structural conditions for the organizational mediation of law (Edelman, 1992). Drawing on the example of equal employment opportunities and affirmative action in the United States, she explains why the lack of a clear legal definition of "discrimination," as well as the law's emphasis on procedures had given organizations the opportunity to interpret what is at stake in different procedures.

Despite its interest, this account nevertheless misses one point: not all organizations react in the same way to the ambiguity of the law. Some of them adopt a rigid interpretation, others a more flexible one. Some organizations devote a great deal of energy to finding the "flaws" in the legal system, while others seek to explicitly influence the very maintenance of these "flaws." Some organizations mobilize subsequent resources for this purpose, while others do not. For this reason, the managerialization of the law is a much more blurred process than the current literature claims.

This chapter argues that the diversity of responses to the ambiguity of law is primarily related to organizational complexity. More specifically, organizational complexity constantly challenges the work of legal intermediaries, thus questioning the meaning of the values they convey through their practices. The organizational complexity refers to the existence of different "emergent, dynamic and self-organizing systems that interact" (Urry, 2005). In the case of firms, this general definition suggests the existence of a plurality of internal processes that interfere in ways that no particular actor can reasonably pretend to control. These processes concern human resources (pregnancy, illness, mobility, death, etc.) and also the productive and the commercial processes (delays, dysfunctions, etc.). Managers have the necessary resources to handle the variety of these situations, but their ability to act is not unlimited.

The new institutionalism admits this complexity, but generally ignores its effects on the legal intermediaries' capacity to "filter" the law (Edelman et al., 1992).

Thus, in their pioneering paper, Meyer and Rowan (1977) draw our attention to the structural inconsistencies that affect any organization that relies primarily on isomorphism with institutionalized rules:

> First, technical activities and demands for efficiency create conflicts and inconsistencies in an institutionalized organization's efforts to conform to the ceremonial rules of production. Second, because these ceremonial rules are transmitted by myths that may arise from different parts of the environment, the rules may conflict with one another. These inconsistencies make a concern for efficiency and tight coordination and control problematic. (Meyer & Rowan, 1977, p. 355)

These authors suggest several solutions to "solve the inconsistencies," but these solutions seem to be disconnected from economic life. The gap identified by sociologists between the formal organizational structure and the day-to-day working activities is never filled in. Whereas some professionals will always defend inside firms what Meyer and Rowan call "the ceremonial rules of production," others will systematically be more concerned with demands of technical efficiency. Because myths that nourish these ceremonial rules are heterogeneous and provide inconsistent incentives for action, internal conflicts are inevitable: first, between managers and employees, then among managers themselves.

By focusing on these internal conflicts, this chapter offers a more balanced account of the managerialization of the law. Inside organizations, managers are not necessarily a homogenous group that shares the same meaning of their company's performance. They may agree together on some common goals, but can change their opinion afterwards. They often make decisions that are better suited to their career plans than to their organizations, but they can be genuinely convinced that they are "doing so in the collective interest." Managers are also men and women with different professional skills and experience who do not always agree on technical issues, despite their common professional identity. Diplomas and status do not systematically produce shared meanings, even though they obviously facilitate internal cooperation.

Therefore, conflicts (more or less publicized) are frequent inside organizations (Crozier & Friedberg, 1977; Selznick, 2012; Stark, 2009). Whatever the causes of these conflicts might be (personal rivalry, search for legitimacy, divergent conceptions of corporate control, etc.), their consequences are the same: organizations do not behave rationally, despite their representatives' attempts to provide rational accounts of their behavior. Organizations are not individuals, but individuals dealing with other individuals in an institutionalized context. From a methodological viewpoint, this means that sociological research should pay more careful attention to misunderstandings, uncertainties, and frictions within economic organizations, because these processes are also constitutive to the mediation of law. This would then help dismantling the power of managerial values (like "efficiency") that previous research identified as key for the mediation of law. If business goals are constantly reinterpreted in context, their actual influence on actors' behavior is thus limited. More precisely, their influence depends on the conjunction of several processes that the existing literature does not shed sufficient light on.

Given this research question, the most appropriate method to capture what happens when legal ambiguity meets organizational complexity is the case study. By describing how a large industrial company manages a conflict with one of its subcontractors, this chapter reveals how French subcontracting law (law no. 75–1334 of December 31, 1975) is applied today.[1] Although this case study cannot be considered representative of all French subcontracting relationships, it nevertheless has the merit of highlighting the structuring effects of organizational misunderstandings (i.e., competing definitions of the situation) on the performance of a contract. Thus, beyond the particularities of this industrial company, the case study serves above all to better understand the law of subcontracting in action (Belley, 1998).

The starting point of this case study is a rather frequent, but quite disturbing industrial situation: a technical device (a "stubborn" crane bridge) is not repaired within the given deadlines. Several actors are concerned about this problem, but they do not agree upon the technical solution that might help them solve the problem. The key actor in this affair is the purchasing manager, because he is the one who decides what are the most efficient solutions for this problem. Unfortunately, his solutions turn out repeatedly to be a real organizational imbroglio and the crane bridge remains out of service for several years. The second part of the chapter explains why the purchasing manager's solution was problematic in this organizational context. By choosing to subcontract this activity to an inexperienced company (against the will of his company's engineers), the purchasing manager defended a financial conception of the firm against a more technical performance oriented solution (Fligstein, 1996). This financial conception did not emerge from nowhere, but resulted from the institutionalization of a particular meaning of business regulation within the nuclear industry. The third part of the chapter goes further into the analysis of these processes, by showing where the purchasing managers' organizational power comes from.

The purchasing managers are in fact the missing link when explaining the economic activity's legal regulation. Although they have no legal training, they are the main guardians of formal corporate commitments (Belley, 1998, pp. 42–44). They negotiate the terms of agreements with suppliers and define what is acceptable and what is not. To do so, they must apply business law, as well as all security rules. Their hierarchy often encourages them to avoid any personal interpretation of the laws and asks them to stick to the procedures defined in advance by the lawyers. In reality, their organizational autonomy is relatively important and their role as legal intermediaries is much more decisive than it seems.

THE "STUBBORN CRANE BRIDGE" AND THE RELUCTANT MAINTENANCE TEAM

A crane bridge (or an overhead crane) is an industrial installation that serves to move very heavy things quickly from one place to another. It consists of parallel runways with a traveling bridge spanning the gap. The crane's lifting component, known as the "hoist," travels along the bridge. Unlike mobile or construction cranes, overhead cranes are generally used for industrial applications where efficiency or minimal downtime are critical factors.

Verne Company[2] has a long experience of using this type of industrial installation. Verne is a European group (with a major part of its capital being held by the French State) that designs, produces, supports and dismantles very complex defense equipment, including nuclear weapons. Leader in this domain, the group is present in 18 countries such as Brazil, Canada, Ireland, Saudi Arabia, India, Malaysia, Singapore or Australia. In France, the Verne Company possesses 10 industrial facilities, spread all over the country, and employs more than 11,000 people.

The "stubborn" crane bridge that interests us is located in one of the biggest Verne Company industrial facilities, in the small city of Dearest (France). This industrial facility is strategic for the business development of the company, because all innovative equipment is produced in this city. However, the crane bridge is used by a peripheral division of Verne, in charge of the dismantling of the decommissioned equipment. This activity is highly sensitive because of the nuclear risks, but it does not represent an investment priority for the top management. Indeed, the dismantling of the decommissioned equipment is not considered to be profit-oriented as compared with the production of new defense equipment.[3]

From a legal point of view, the old nuclear equipment together with the industrial installation (including the crane bridge) that serves for the dismantling activity is the French State's property. Every three or four years, the State organizes a competitive tender for the dismantling project, but Verne Company never had any competitor because it is the original manufacturer of the nuclear equipment. In spite of this monopolistic situation, Verne's top management fears that the company could eventually lose this market, if they do not achieve the contractual objectives:

> Once you know that there is a call for tender, you are not sure to win. The State can always split the contract in two parts: the dismantling yard, on the one hand, and on the other hand, the maintenance activities. Regularly, they threat us to give the dismantling yard to somebody else, especially when they are not happy with our work. (interview, Manager, July 2013)

This is why the management of Verne's Dismantling Division values above all the ability of its teams to achieve financial performance, without jeopardizing nuclear safety. They define here the "economic performance" as the ability to "keep to the budget and the contractual deadlines" (interview, manager, October 2013). The "budget" is negotiated with the State's representatives when the contract is signed. The profit margin for this type of contracts is not every high (around 5%) and Verne Company's top management does not really expect to "earn" money with the dismantling yard. On the contrary, they simply try not to "lose money," by anticipating very carefully the schedule of their operations. This means that the main incentive for the maintenance personnel is to keep to the deadline. If they keep to the deadline, they manage to keep to the budget, too. Sometimes, unexpected activities (discovering asbestos inside the defense equipment, etc.) may delay the operations and generate additional costs. In this case, the State generally accepts to pay for it, but only if the public experts are convinced that the company could not really have anticipated the problem.

The "stubborn" crane bridge was both a technical and an organizational problem. Initially, the crane should only have been maintained for two months (October to December 2009), but finally, the repair work lasted three years (2009–2012). As a result, the budget soared and Verne was forced to pay two and a half times the initial price (without any additional costs being reimbursed by the State). This situation was highly problematic for the top-level managers who did not understand why such an "insignificant story" became a "big issue": in 2012, Verne got involved in a legal dispute with the subcontractor who failed to repair the crane bridge. The litigation was finally abandoned, but today the history of the "stubborn crane bridge" is still alive in the minds of Verne's leaders. What happened?

By the end of the 2000s, Verne Company decided to outsource several maintenance works, including the crane bridge revision. These maintenance works do not concern the dismantling yard itself, but the industrial installations that keep the workplace safe. For the maintenance manager, the externalization decision was coherent with the dismantling division's industrial strategy: "We didn't have the right skills to do these operations. Outsourcing was the only solution. Outsourcing was the only possible industrial choice" (interview, maintenance manager, October 2013). As far as the timing of the decision was concerned, the maintenance manager explains that they "had to comply with the safety standards. There was no rush, but the job had to be done" (interview, Maintenance Manager, October 2013).

At that time, the crane bridge was not out of service. Like many other installations, the crane bridge was simply not in compliance with safety standards and required revisions. The external technical experts who checked the crane bridge every year repeatedly stated that the company had to comply with the regulations, but they never explicitly asked Verne's management to stop using it. They only advised the manager "to take all necessary steps to comply with the safety regulations" (e-mail, 2007). The maintenance personnel regretted that the external experts had not put pressure on their management to comply with the law:

> The crane bridge's operation is strategic, as it concerns the nuclear safety of the dismantling site. The crane lifts and moves nuclear waste, so it's better for everyone not to have problems with it. (interview, Maintenance Technician, October 2013)

For this reason, the maintenance team took this problem very seriously and started to discuss informally with Technics about a possible revision. This company was the original manufacturer of the crane and had a long work experience at Dearest. After several meetings in 2008–2009, Technics stated that the dysfunction was probably caused by "an improper alignment of the crane bridge's runways." The company did not do all the necessary calculations, but it was convinced that this was the crane bridge's problem. For this reason, the Verne maintenance personnel decided to include in the next general maintenance contract the "troubleshooting of the crane bridge's runways."

The purchasing department opened the call for tender for this contract in June 2009. They received six different commercial proposals (including one proposal from Technics). After a very short selection process, they decided to award the contract to Presto Company. Presto Company already worked for Verne as a subcontractor, but it was the first time that it won a contract on the dismantling yard. Leader in industrial maintenance and related services in France, this company was a subsidiary of one of the most important European energy groups and employed at that time more than 4,500 people.

The Verne maintenance personnel did not welcome the choice of this subcontractor. The Presto financial proposal was so competitive that they were very circumspect about the quality of their service:

> We wonder if Presto really understood our technical needs. We have also doubts about their capacity to fulfill the contractual documentary obligations (fulfilling the necessary documents before and after the maintenance operations). (e-mail, July 2009)

For this reason, they repeatedly expressed to the purchasing department, both orally and by e-mail expressed their dissatisfaction. This situation was problematic because the Verne maintenance personnel were supposed to work together with the subcontractor. More exactly, the Verne maintenance personnel had to validate the subcontractor's work procedures, survey the execution, and then, authorize the payment. If they did not trust the subcontractor, one could legitimately expect that their cooperation would not to be effective during the execution of the contract.

Unsurprisingly, supporting work relationships based on trust was not the main concern of the purchasing department. More focused on reducing costs, the purchasing officer in charge of this affair did not take into consideration the internal technical debates. She rapidly compared the six commercial proposals and despite her maintenance team's explicit recommendations, she decided to award the contract to the less technically qualified company. Her decision was all the more problematic since Verne's maintenance personnel played an important role before and during the call for tender: first, it was these personnel who defined the technical specifications of the contract and knew best what the company really needed in order to perform the maintenance activities safely. Second and most importantly, the maintenance personnel were asked informally by the purchasing officer to compare all the commercial proposals and to make an initial choice. The maintenance staff did this job, but the purchasing officer finally rejected their choice. Ironically, when the bridge crane was finally repaired in 2012, it was Technics (the company initially chosen by the maintenance team) who succeeded and not Presto.

The purchasing department's decision in favor of the lowest bidder is not so surprising. Like all purchasing departments, its role is to guarantee the best value for money (Belley, 1998; Lonsdale & Watson, 2005; Pettigrew, 1975; Reverdy, 2009). The purchasing officers evaluate suppliers, negotiate contracts and check the service quality according to the general purchasing strategy of their company. When this strategy is too general or too ambiguous, the local purchasing department's manager defines the main purchasing priorities and allocates the necessary human resources for implementing them. In the case of the crane bridge, the purchasing manager did not consider this contract as a priority. The officer in charge of this affair was negotiating other contracts, including the renewal of a very important one. This "big deal" needed careful attention and for this reason, she was often out of office, on business trips.

When she had to open the call for tender for the maintenance activities, she was quite annoyed by the lack of experience of the internal customer[4]:

> They did not know how to write down the technical specifications. It was either too specific, or too general. I did not blame them, it was the first time that they had to do it, but it is so tiring to repeat all the time the same things. (interview, Purchasing Officer, November 2013)

Then, when confronted with the final choice, she was convinced that she was doing the best thing for her company:

> the internal customer is always trying to have the Rolls Royce. I mean the best technical proposal. They wanted Technics. OK, Technics is fine, but Technics did not really meet our expectations. It is my job to find the best value for money. Presto is a serious company, Presto is a big resourceful company, so I had no serious doubt about them. (interview, Purchasing Officer, November 2013)

To avoid further problems, a pre-contractual meeting was organized in July 2009 between the subcontractor and Verne's maintenance team. This meeting was supposed to facilitate the exchange between the two parties and make their future collaboration easier. At first sight, all parties were satisfied and Verne's technical personnel were ready to make a new start with the subcontractor. The purchasing officer closed the file and switched to another occupation. From that moment, she was no longer concerned with the maintenance activities, including the crane bridge. In January 2010, she left this purchasing department position.

During the next three months, nothing particular happened on the crane bridge side. Presto was supposed to start the work in September 2009, but they had one month and a half of delay. Then, the subcontractor did not manage to send Verne a satisfactory report about its operation methods[5] and this situation created the first interorganizational conflict. The report's problem was apparently related to the subcontractor's work methods. The Presto manager was constantly asking for information by e-mail from Verne's maintenance technician, who was not really happy about it:

> They asked me to do their job, the job they were paid for. First, I was doing the job, but after a while, I had enough. It was not my job to look for this information, they should have come and read it personally on site. (interview, Maintenance Technician, October 2013)

Verne's maintenance personnel felt "trapped" by Presto's manager:

> He was acting like a cowboy. He won the contract, so he probably thought that he could do anything he wanted. It was really not comfortable to work with him. (interview, Maintenance Technician, October 2013)

Several unexpected processes aggravated these conflicts. First, the Verne maintenance team experienced successive changes. Pierre, the maintenance technician who had the mission to supervise the subcontractor's activity was out of the office half the time, from September 2009 to March 2010. Pierre was doing training to become an executive and for this reason, he was not always very reactive to Presto's demands. Besides, François, the maintenance technician who did not appreciate working with Presto's manager, got sick and was hospitalized between November 2009 and February 2010. The management did not replace these persons, but asked Victor, the manager in charge of the general planning of Verne's maintenance activities to take the lead.

Victor had already a very busy agenda and did not have time to go through all the technical debates with subcontractors:

> Back then, I was doing a hundred other things at the same time. Inside organizations, multitasking is a pain in the ass; it's like asking 9 women to do a child in one month. [...] We are constantly solicited to sign things, we sign papers without really reading them, and we are never able to do what we have planned to do. With time, it is obvious that the crane bridge was a technical problem that needed more high-level expertise. But in 2009–2010, we were just furious about Presto's work because they were unable to repair correctly the engine. They were expecting us to tell them what to do [...] what a joke! When you bring your car to the garage, you do not tell the garage what to do! (interview, October 2013)

This last statement summarises very well the Verne's shared understanding of the situation: the subcontractor failed in the contractual obligations of results, as it was unable to find a technical solution within the given timeframe.

The last important change during the fall 2009 was the creation of a new function at Verne's top-level management. Antoine, a former manager of the dismantling yard and project manager for the construction of the new nuclear equipment, became Verne's chief engineer for nuclear projects. This new transversal function gives him the opportunity to follow both the construction and the dismantling yards, which means that he becomes responsible for the nuclear safety of the whole Dearest's industrial facility. As soon as he got into this function, Pierre and Victor informed him about Presto's delays. Therefore, Antoine became very attentive to the crane bridge situation and starting from December 2009, he got directly involved in this affair. However, his intervention made the exchanges with the subcontractor even more complex because the nuclear safety requirements were now the main priority.

REFRAMING THE PROBLEM: "WHAT PROBLEM? THERE IS NO PROBLEM!"

According to the contract, the crane bridge should have been back in service by the end of December 2009. When the deadline came, maintenance work had not even begun because the two organizations could not agree on the best technical solution. Indeed, Verne's nuclear safety engineer considered that the subcontractor's calculations were incorrect and asked them to check again in order to "comply with the safety rules" (e-mail, October 28, 2009). Presto agreed to check these calculations again, but sent an invoice for extra work. Verne refused to pay the bill and since then the two organizations had been in open conflict. According to Pierre, this invoice was the proof that Presto was not honest since the beginning:

> They are voluntarily delaying their work. Then they put pressure on the client to get more money. Everyone knows that they have very competitive commercial proposals, but after winning the tender, they make significant changes to the contract. That's their business strategy. (interview, October 2013)

However, not all of Presto's employees were comfortable with this situation:

> The maintenance technicians were stressed during the coordination meetings. I think that Presto's management was not very comprehensive and the employees had to face the problems by themselves. (interview, François, October 2013)

Whatever the explanation for this situation, the consequences were critical: the crane bridge maintenance was at a standstill. At the same time, the other maintenance operations that Presto should have done according to the contract (upgrading the ventilation system and installing dry riser pipes) were not executed either. On December 14, 2009, Antoine alerted his superiors: "I think that the subcontractor has no technical or financial control of the situation" (e-mail, December 14, 2009). The purchasing department's manager tried however to find a convenient issue to the situation, by organizing a high-level meeting in January 2010. He invited two Presto managers (the general manager of the industrial maintenance department and the project manager in charge with the contract) to discuss together with him, Antoine and Verne's legal advisor. The maintenance technicians (either client or subcontractor) were still not invited.

This meeting helped building a temporary consensus, without putting an end to the tense relationships between the two working teams. Communication continued to be difficult and actors from both sides were suspicious of each other. One month later, a new problem ignited the conflict. The subcontractor decided to modify the crane bridge's structure without Verne's authorization. Apparently, Pierre was aware of this decision, but he didn't inform Antoine in time for him to intervene. Antoine became angry and immediately sent an alarming email to his superiors:

> I'm really worried about the consequences of the crane bridge case. This case is really jeopardizing the safety of the dismantling site personnel, but also our ability to maintain the budget. (e-mail, February 19, 2010)

Antoine was afraid that the subcontractor's operation made made risk assessments more difficult risk assessments, as no calculations were available at that time.

In this particular context, Verne decided to organize on 4th March a technical meeting with Presto's project manager. This time, the Verne maintenance personnel (Pierre, François et Victor) participated in the meeting, but the subcontractor's employees were once again not invited. Without surprise, the meeting's results were not conclusive, whereas Antoine criticized the subcontractor's general technical performances (including other maintenance projects), Presto's project managers reaffirmed that they were perfectly complying with the safety and security standards and thus, "there was no problem."

At this point, it seems obvious to everyone that this story is more of a dialogue of the deaf than a cooperative business relationship. The customer is not satisfied with the quality of the subcontractor's service, but the subcontractor tries to minimize the complaint's importance. Given the importance of this industrial facility, it is to be expected that the client's management will defend its interests by all possible means (repairing the crane as soon as possible). Furthermore, given the unsatisfactory quality of the subcontractor's work, the decision to terminate the contract would be understandable. But as surprising as this might seem, Verne's management does not even consider this option before several months. Why?

When the sociologist asks the actors to explain why they had not considered this option, the actors do not know what to say. Some of them simply think "it is not in the customs to cut ties with one's partner, even if that partner is a pain in the ass" (interview, Manager, October 2013). For the purchasing department manager, breaking a contractual agreement is "always legally complicated, so it is best to try to avoid reaching the point of no return." In other words, the right to break a contractual commitment does not seem self-evident to all actors, whereas in theory, it has long since been acquired (Barbour, 1917).

Regardless of thinking in terms of "rights," there are two different ways of analyzing the possibility of breaking an unsatisfactory formal agreement: the rationalist perspective and the ethical framework. These two perspectives fall within distinct disciplinary fields, each with its own vision of causality. According to the rationalist perspective, breaking a contractual agreement is a matter of cost-benefit calculation (Birmingham, 1970; Coase, 1978; Posner, 1977). Because economic actors are seen as rational and self-interested persons who are seeking satisfactory solutions to their problems, some people consider that injuries caused by breach can be fully compensated by damages (Posner, 1977). Even when analysts are paying attention to transaction costs, they are indirectly focusing on calculations, too (Goetz & Scott, 1977; Kennedy & Michelman, 1980; Kronman, 1978). They think economic actors are evaluating breaching a contract by taking into consideration both the settlement of a contract dispute (contract damages, attorneys' fee, etc.) and the expenses related to the search for a new business partner (call of tender, negotiation, etc.). If transaction costs are too high, it is likely that actors prefer not to break the contract.

Contrary to this perspective, the ethical framework states that breach of contract is immoral:

> Because the legal construct of contract is tied so closely to the moral notion of a promise, breach of contract would seem to fall into the same category of moral harm as a broken promise. (Wilkinson-Ryan & Baron, 2009)

A broken promise leads to a loss of trust between partners, which in the long run can be very damaging in terms of reputation. Since Stewart Macaulay's pioneering article in 1963, it is established that reputation is a very important dimension of contractual relationships: even though contracts help business people to plan their exchange carefully, the exchange itself is essentially sustained by "a man's word in a brief letter, a handshake or common honesty and decency" (Macaulay, 1963, p. 6). As a result, "disputes are frequently settled without reference to the contract or potential or actual legal sanctions" (Macaulay, 1963, p. 10), because business customs have regulatory power and force actors to honor their commitments in all circumstances. Macaulay does not suggest that people do not calculate, but rather that calculations are not always a matter of economic gains. When faced with a performance problem, most businessmen try to make things "right," willing to compromise in order to preserve the trusting relationship.

Despite their divisive nature, these two perspectives can be used jointly to describe what is at stake in a dispute between two organizations. Indeed, whatever the context of the exchange, economic actors are always concerned by the material and symbolic aspects of their commitments. They can calculate the economic costs of breaching a commitment, but have a strong fear of the long-term effects of this relationship breakdown. They may threaten their partner to go to court and, at the same time, try to "settle" things informally. Analytically, this contradictory behavior cannot be understood without defining the term actor. Although the actors described by these two theories are clearly organizations, they are thought to act as individuals. As said previously, organizations are not individuals, but individuals dealing with other individuals in an institutionalized context. Organizations are certainly led by people who have values and interests, but the organizations themselves do not have homogeneous values or interests. The ability of an organization to act as if it was an individual depends on the situation.

Given these considerations, the research concerning breaking a contractual agreement should focus on the framing process rather than calculations (Goffman, 1974; Snow & Benford, 1988). At first glance, the problem with the crane bridge was due to a poor anticipation of the subcontractor's skills. Once the contract was signed, breaking it could be very costly, both financially and in human terms. In reality, this explanation of the crane bridge problem is unsatisfactory because it does not take the subcontractor's point of view seriously. When Presto's manager says that there is no "problem" with his work, one can assume that he is convinced of it. Even if Verne staff believe that the subcontractor was deliberately lying, the correspondence from these organizations rather indicates that they did not share the same definition of the situation. Finally, the problem with the crane bridge is that not all actors see it as a "real" problem: "What problem? There is no problem."

Since Goffman, framing problems is an ongoing process that provides actors with the "practical rules that they must follow in order to find their way around the situation and to act in a correct and responsible manner" (Cefaï & Perreau, 2012, p. 245). Frames are more than subjective perceptions or discursive resources that actors mobilize to defend their interests in a given situation. Frames "organize experience and guide action, whether individual or collective" (Snow, Rochford, Worden, & Benford, 1986, p. 464). However, the same situation can have conflicting interpretations because actors do not always share the same representation of their common interest. Even an artefact as standardized as a contract (Suchman, 2003) can be interpreted very differently by the actors involved: some of them use the contract to plan resources rationally, while others regard it as the formalization of a moral obligation to deal in good faith with unforeseen events.

Frame alignment is not a necessary condition for the establishment of a business relationship. Economic actors who work together do not need to agree on everything. They do not even need to agree on the definition of the exchange situation. A business relationship is always fragile, in the sense that it is always in danger of breaking down because of the partners' divergent interests or because of their conflicting values (Surubaru, 2014). As Chantelat put it, business relationship is mainly based on "the coordination of appearances, on minimal and shared convictions, without the actors ever being certain that they are really shared" (Chantelat, 2002). However, business partners must have (or succeed in creating) a minimum agreement on unforeseen events during the performance of the contract.

Unforeseen events are part of industrial life. Regardless of their origin (technical, human, political, etc.), they disrupt activities and force actors to agree on the definition of the situation. Contrary to popular opinion, it is not their seriousness that encourages actors to react in order to reach a consensus. Nor is it their exceptionality that explains the construction of a possible compromise. In reality, however serious or frequent they may be, unforeseen events are characterized by their ability to bring points of view closer together, by erasing temporarily the differences. They force actors to speak the same language, even when they have never really spoken together.

In the crane bridge case, the first series of unforeseen events are related to the technical definition of the situation. When Verne decides to outsource this work, all the actors are convinced that the main purpose of the contract is the "troubleshooting of the crane bridge's runways." This particular meaning of the subcontracting relationship delimits the scope of the possibilities for managing contingencies that arise during the performance of the contract. The contract does not concern the general maintenance of the crane bridge, but the repair of one of its components (the crane bridge's runways). Presto is therefore concentrating its efforts on the runways, but apparently these efforts are not producing the expected results. Since the subcontractor considers that they are doing what is necessary to repair this component as requested by the contract, they do not seem to accept the client's criticism.

One may consider that Verne's maintenance personnel made a mistake when they asked to Technics to evaluate the crane bridge's failure without signing together a formal agreement. In doing so, Verne was constrained to take for granted the Technics's definition of the "problem," without having the possibility to challenge it. As a result, Verne accused the subcontractor of not being "professional," but they did not realize that the technical definition of the problem actually prevented the subcontractor from being professional. As Verne's technical specifications stated that the purpose of the contract was to troubleshoot the crane bridge's runways, Presto could not have imagined that the problem came from elsewhere. It is only two years later that actors finally identified the "real" origin of the system malfunction. Contrary to what Technics had suggested in 2008–2009, it was not the runway that needed to be repaired, but the end carriage. However, when this new way of defining the situation appeared, nobody incriminated Technics or even the Verne maintenance team who had asked for their advice. On the contrary, Technics has once again been actively involved in identifying the "real" origin of the system malfunction.

Was it a mistake on Verne's part to ask Technics to evaluate the crane maintenance problems in 2008–2009 without signing a contract? A mistake violates the "formal design goals and normative standards and expectations," and for this reason, it belongs to the "dark side of organizations" (Vaughan, 1999, p. 14). Generally, a mistake produces "unexpected adverse outcomes with a contained social cost" (Vaughan, 1999, p. 14). The formal procedures of the Verne purchasing department explicitly condemn doing business without a contract and call repeatedly for vigilance with regard to such informal exchanges:

> Under no circumstances may the services start before the signing of the contract or an order. The liability of the Verne person who authorized the start of the work is individual. (Verne Procurement Best Practices, internal document, 2008)

In spite of these procedures, the informal exchanges with Technics in 2008–2009 were not considered to be a mistake by anyone. This type of informal exchange is quite frequent at the field ground level. Since Technics carried out other work on the dismantling site, the teams knew each other personally and could exchange ideas outside the contractual framework. The purchasing department was not necessarily aware of the existence of this type of informal exchange, but neither was it seeking to be informed of it. In fact, in 2009, the technical team and the purchasing officers had very few opportunities to meet or to discuss outside contract negotiations. The purchasing department was located in an administrative building far from the industrial workshops and purchasing officers almost never moved from their offices.

But beyond this aspect, the technical diagnostic is not a real topic of interest for the purchasing department. The internal customer is supposed to know the "needs" of the company and the purchasing manager has nothing to say about this, except formal aspects:

> It was the first time that our department was doing this kind of technical specification. We learned it along the way, at our expense, through the critical remarks of the Purchasing Department. [...] For example, they advised us to replace the term "subcontractor" with the term "supplier." Sometimes they would rephrase our sentences, but nothing important. (interview, Victor, October 2013)

Two and a half years after signing the contract with Presto, Verne took the case to court. To establish each company's share of responsibility, a technical expert was appointed on this occasion. This expert reviewed the technical specifications of the contract and stated that the contract did not provide sufficient information on the company's requirements. The expert did not criticize the diagnosis by Technique, nor Verne's "mistake." He simply stressed the "poor" quality of the technical specifications as a whole. But Verne's maintenance team strongly rejected this accusation:

> If we listen to the expert, the technical specifications should be as thick as the Bible. I can't do that, it's obvious [...] but the expert doesn't care, he doesn't live in the real world. In the real world, we are not experts [...]. Because I needed technical advice from my supplier, I explicitly asked the buyer to specify in the contract that the supplier has an obligation of result. An obligation of result means that the supplier must do everything possible to solve the problem. (interview, Pierre, October 2013)

People who make and keep contracts alive are caught in the middle of their organization's flow. They are not "experts" because they do not treat technical malfunctions as if they were mathematical puzzles. They treat them as practical problems, which means they know that the information they need to solve the problem can be vague or uncertain. They also know that information depends on the context and sometimes, on the person. Practical problems do not have single solutions and actors are generally aware of it. However, they usually take shortcuts. In the case of the crane bridge, the simplest way to proceed was to refer to a legal obligation of performance (a "promise of result") supposedly embedded in the contract. According to Verne, the "result" was simple to measure: at the end of the subcontractor's work, the crane bridge had to be functional. As Victor said: "When you take your car to the garage, you do not tell the garage what to do!" Therefore, Verne simply expected Presto to repair the installation on time. However, comparing the two situations is not innocent, mostly because a bridge crane is not a car. The following paragraph analyses the meaning of this metaphor and shows why it unexpectedly created a conflict trap.

THE COST KILLERS, THE "PROMISE OF RESULT" AND THE CONTRACT

The story of the "stubborn crane bridge" illustrates what happens when law's ambiguity meets organizational complexity. Verne is a large company that develops, produces and then dismantles arms systems, including nuclear ones. Like many other companies, Verne outsources a large part of its activities, especially the least profitable of them. It also outsources activities that may have a negative impact on workers' safety (like the decontamination of facilities containing asbestos). In 2013, when this research was carried out, a well-known economic magazine ranked this company among the largest French industrial companies. Verne also received public awards for its "responsible purchasing policy and general management of jobs and skills." Although the total number of Verne subcontractors is not officially known, the various internal sources indicate the existence of several thousand subcontractors. Of these, around 30 are considered to be "major subcontractors," in so far as they achieve annual turnover with Verne in excess of €1 million.

Verne's subcontracting policy is therefore under high scrutiny. Since the mid-2000s, top management has intensively formalized its subcontracting management strategy and implemented numerous procedures to comply with law. An "army of lawyers" has been hired to define these procedures (interview, in-house lawyer, October 2013). Since Verne was a public company until recently, this major investment in the formalization of subcontracting relationship management procedures actually corresponds to the opening of its capital to private investors. As a consequence, in 2013, more than 160 formal documents concerning purchasing procedures were recorded at a group level. While external observers congratulate the top management on the quality of these procedures, Verne employees are more skeptical: "When it comes to subcontracting purchases, always wait for the counter-order of the counter-order," joked one interviewee in January 2013.

At the same time, the opposite trend seems to be taking place. By the end of the 2000s, the new CEO was advocating a "simplification of structures and purchasing procedures" (press release, CEO, 2009). His main objective was to "increase the company's turnover by 50–100% over the next ten years, i.e. 3.5 to 5 billion (against 2.5 billion in 2008)" (press release, CEO, 2009). In fact, this simplification process makes internal procedures even more complex:

> Each new CEO has his own idea of change. The purchasing manager also has his own ideas. As a result, our procedures change every two or three years and everything becomes even more complicated. Procedures change, but we don't really change the way we do things. (interview, Dearest Purchasing Manager, December 2012)

This remark is not surprising because the functioning of an organization is always:

> the product of a mix of formal and informal prescriptions, supporting each other, where formal prescriptions are rooted in a power structure and informal exchange and negotiation processes for which they in turn provide arguments and resources. (Friedberg, 1993, p. 161)

This mix of formal and informal rules influences the contractual management of subcontracting relationships, especially with regard to the technical prescribers' behavior:

> The prescriber is not a real prescriber, but he is a man who knows that one day or another he will have to manage purchases. He does not anticipate his needs and when he thinks he needs something, he rarely follows procedures. (interview, Dearest Purchasing Manager, December 2012)

Therefore, the drafting of the technical requirement (also called "specification") represents a very important moment in the outsourcing process, which can take various forms:

> Some prescribers send you a 3-page dossier, others a 150-page dossier. In both cases, this is problematic. When the prescriber does not define his need, the buyer cannot do his job, so he must ask him questions to get to better specify (but this wastes time, then it does not fall within the buyer's remit). When it's too thick, you get lost in reading and you don't understand what he wants, you get the impression that he wants to buy a car, but that's not what he needs, considering the budget, but a factory. (interview, Purchasing Officer, October 2013)

But what seems even more problematic is the difficulty of capitalizing on past experiences:

> We had a contract negotiation six months ago. I invited the technical prescriber to all the meetings; he seemed to understand very well how it works. But today he has forgotten everything; I have to explain everything to him again. The other day, a guy hung up on me on the phone, accusing me of being very hard on my e-mails. Yes, I was a little bit hard with him because I'm tired of repeating things. (interview, Dearest Purchasing Manager, December 2012)

Despite this generalizing statement, certain activities to be subcontracted (such as the maintenance of the lifting installations) nevertheless undergo a routinization process: "We have had a single partner for years, it has the monopoly. As a result, we anticipate quite well our needs and we never had any problem together" (interview, Purchasing Officer, October 2013). As for the crane bridge, its maintenance had never been outsourced. Consequently, learning the purchasing process was inevitably done gradually, through successive trial and error.

However, misunderstandings or ignorance of formal rules do not mean that actors do not share some common representations of what the "right procedure" should be. Nor does it mean that the formal rule is not a major causal constituent of the regularity of activity. On the contrary, the greater the organizational complexity, the more actors try to make it intelligible through binary oppositions or explanatory shortcuts. When this complexity meets the inherent ambiguity of legal devices, the shortcuts end up having the force of evidence. In other words, actors orient their behavior according to what they believe the formal rule is (Weber discussed by Coutu, 2013). By doing this, they actively participate in the construction of the empirical legal orders inside corporations (Belley, 1998).

However, a legitimate question now arises as to the source of the actors' representations: where do they come from? How do these explanatory shortcuts emerge inside organizations? To answer this, an interesting avenue of investigation concerns the legal intermediation activity of purchasing managers. These actors are the missing link when explaining the legal regulation of economic activities. Indeed, if in-house lawyers first translate the law into standard internal procedures, purchasing managers then give them the force of economic evidence. Thus, the daily use by the purchasing department of legal devices makes the law alive in every commercial transaction (although this can also be a source of organizational conflict).

In this respect, the case of outsourcing operations is representative. Every time they negotiate a new contract, Verne's purchasing officers have to fill in a lawfulness form. The in-house lawyers provided this form and they are updating regularly (Table 1).

At the bottom of this table, a bold sentence states: "A single negative answer leads a priori to consider the contract unsatisfactory." "Unsatisfactory" here means "not complying with the law." Because the legal terms may be far too ambiguous for Verne's purchasing team, a one-page document provides a brief explanation on this subject. Here is how the formalization of a clear objective in contracts (the third question) is justified:

> This obligation is compulsory for industrial works (Court of Cassation, Criminal Division, 1984). This may be an obligation of means (Court of Cassation, Criminal Division, 1981) only in the case of studies, advice or other intellectual services, but in this case the task must nevertheless be clearly defined. [...] In any event, it goes without saying that a time limit must be systematically prescribed. (internal document, accessed 2012)

As for the supervision of the subcontractor's teams, this question "warns against the risk of illegal lending of labor (Court of Cassation, 1997)."

Table 1. Verne's Lawfulness Form, Internal Document, Accessed 2012.

Questions	Answer	
	Yes	No
(1) Is it necessary that the work be done inside Verne?		
(2) Does the subcontractor have the standard resources and personnel to carry out the work itself?		
(3) Is there a clear formalization of an objective to be achieved (with an agreed time frame)?		
(4) Is there real permanent supervision of the provider's teams by one of his managers and not integration of these teams into ours?		
(5) Are the contractual provisions for the receipt of services strictly defined?		

This one-page document does not dwell much on the judgments of the Court of Cassation. However, their mere mention seems to have a particularly strong binding power, insofar as this institution is the highest court of the French judiciary and plays a fundamental role in the harmonization of case law. For this reason, the lawfulness form becomes a resource for economic action, even though the purchasing officers are not necessarily aware of it:

> Not knowing the law is a real asset for the company, because if all the purchasing officers knew it, none of them would dare act. [...] Imagine someone who wants to steal an apple and asks a lawyer if he can do it. The lawyer will surely answer "You are free to do what you want, but this is what can happen to you if you are arrested for theft." Most people are stunned by this answer and won't do anything anymore. They no longer even ask themselves the question of theft. (interview, In-house Lawyer, October 2013)

Without suggesting that purchasing officers are all potential thieves, what does the "apple theft" metaphor mean? One interviewee explains that subcontracting relationships are always tricky:

> When you estimate the cost of an outsourced service, you always think of the wage cost, the cost of the man doing the work. You add a margin and you get your real cost. When you negotiate, you keep this in mind and then systematically try to lower it. (interview, Purchasing Officer, January 2013)

The problem with this way of reasoning is precisely the outsourcing's legal framework:

> While everyone buys men, the law prohibits it. As a result, we must be very vigilant in the way we negotiate and draft our contracts. The legal department helps us to formulate things differently, even if in reality, the reasoning remains the same, we always buy men. (interview, Purchasing Officer, January 2013)

This method of evaluating the subcontracting cost is problematic because purchasing departments pay little attention to other costs associated with the work (staff training, documentation, acquisition of specific tools, etc.). In the long run, a race toward the lowest bidder is settling in and companies consider this quest for economic performance inevitable. Most subcontractors cannot resist the pressure exerted on prices by major contractors. It is only the large subcontractors that succeed in doing well, in particular because they are implementing the same types of massive cost reduction strategies.

Considering this, the purchasing managers appear to be the new-armed wings of capitalism, defending a financial conception of the firm against a more technical performance oriented solution. Long considered by management as mere logistical support for the other departments, they generally enjoyed a reputation as "bean counters." In the early 1990s, few purchasing managers were involved in negotiating contracts and their participation in the strategic decision-making was rather limited. In the 2000s, the situation changed and the economic press welcomed the rise of the "purchasing function." In a context of market stabilization and reduced sales, the need to have better control on the operating expenses seems to become a general priority. The public reputation of purchasing officers is also changing, the vulgar "bean counters" becoming now true "cost killers." Finally, the training offer has evolved significantly: for example, in 2010, France had more than 800 master's graduates in purchasing management per year. Whereas at the beginning of the 1990s, people became purchasing officers through internal promotion, today business school training seems on the contrary to be the best key to join this service.

These structural changes have an impact on the company's representations about outsourcing. In the case of the crane bridge, it seems obvious that technical prescribers are driven by the belief that Presto has a "contractual obligation of result." Although the contract clearly formalizes "an objective to be achieved (within an agreed period)," the traditional doctrinal distinction between "obligation of result," and "obligation of means" is not always clear (Fabre-Magnan, 2016; Plancqueel, 1972). More precisely, depending on the economic situation, the courts may judge this distinction very differently (Jourdain, 2016). Non-legal professionals of course largely ignore these legal subtleties and simply think that contractors should keep their "promise" whatever the situation.

To say that a subcontractor must keep his promise of result whatever the situation is in reality misleading. In fact, technical prescribers and purchasing managers mix law and economic interest, which is defended through legal means. Given the complexity of the technical problem to be solved, Presto could not repair the crane bridge as planned by the contract. They had put in place the means they had to do so, but their efforts were inconclusive. The metaphor best suited to this situation is not that of the garage owner, but rather that of the doctor who tries unsuccessfully to cure his patient.

To this is added a second structural difficulty. The crane bridge contract concerns work in a nuclear environment. While the case law requires autonomy for subcontractors (which means separate working teams, no direct monitoring, etc.), the nuclear safety and security regulation contradict this requirement. The nuclear operator always remains responsible for his installation and that is why the Verne maintenance team (Antoine in particular) exerted a continuous control over Presto's activities. While some members of Verne's maintenance team considered that the subcontractor had an "obligation of result," others monitored its work very closely, constantly questioning the technical repair solutions. For these reasons, the representations that the actors of the exchange had could only keep them in a vicious circle of conflict.

Concluding Remarks: Dismantling Managerial Values?

After examining this case study, one can ask oneself what are in reality the values defended by Verne's management. Does flexibility or efficiency explain how this company complies with the law? The answer is not simple, because values guide organizational behavior, but actors' behavior cannot be reduced to these values. Moreover, the very definition of what a value is is subject to debate in the social sciences, as the concept does not always have a sufficiently precise explanatory scope.

In the case of the bridge crane, flexibility is obvious important, especially in relation to the workforce. The way in which subcontractors are selected clearly indicates a search for flexible business management processes. Instead of hiring maintenance technicians capable of repairing complex installations, management prefers to outsource this work. Even if the search for flexibility is not made here at the expense of the company's employment (there are no layoffs, for example), we can assume that, in the long term, the repeated use of subcontractors impacts the careers of Verne employees. Subcontracting relationships are nevertheless defined by a set of formal rules (partly established by the case law of the Court of Cassation and embedded in contractual devices), which make the reciprocal commitments of the players more complex than one might think. In Durkheimian terms, "not everything in the contract is contractual."

In a capitalist economy, the search for flexibility is linked to the search for efficiency. "Efficiency" means the pursuit of maximum results with minimum means. In the case of nuclear weapons, outsourcing maintenance activities can optimize budget. But this strategy does not always take into account the consequences of outsourcing on working conditions or nuclear safety. The case of the crane bridges teaches us that the causal links between values and behavior are always difficult to establish. Despite the increasingly important role of "cost killers" within companies, nuclear safety engineers still have an influence on decision-making processes. In the future, these actors could defend a logic of different efficiency, more concerned with environmental or labor issues, but only if they manage to understand the real scope of the intermediation work of legal and purchasing services.

NOTES

1. This study is part of a university-industry research partnership. The main objective of this partnership has been to analyze the impact of subcontracting relationships on nuclear safety. For this, between 2012 and 2014, I carried out intensive fieldwork in a large French company located in a small town in northern France. I had access to internal documents (negotiation files, e-mails, expert reports, etc.), and I was able to conduct in-depth interviews with some 20 employees, subject to data anonymization. The interviews were recorded and transcribed. Some employees were interviewed several times during the

research. I have not met the subcontractors of this company, but I have read their correspondence (e-mails) with this company.

2. In order to protect people's confidentiality, all names are changed.

3. Dismantling defense equipment is not a regular activity. Moreover, the public budget for this activity depends on many political factors that limit the company's ability to anticipate future calls for tenders.

4. The "internal customer" is an indigenous term that defines the entity that needs to purchase goods or services, through the mediation of the purchasing department, also called "technical prescriber."

5. This report was compulsory.

REFERENCES

Abbott, K., Levi-Faur, D., & Snidal, D. (2017). Regulatory intermediaries in the age of governance. *The Annals of the American Academy of Political and Social Science*, *670*, 1–288.

Barbour, W. T. (1917). The 'Right' to break a contract. *Michigan Legal Review*, *16*, 106–109.

Belley, J.-G. (1998). *Le contrat entre droit, économie et société*. Cowansville: Les Éditions Yvon Blais Inc.

Birmingham, R. L. (1970). Breach of contract, damage measures, and economic efficiency. *Rutgers Law Review*, *24*(2), 273–292.

Cefaï, D., & Perreau, L. (Eds.) (2012). *Erving Goffman et l'ordre de l'interaction*. Paris: CURAPP-ESS/CEMS-IMM.

Chantelat, P. (2002). La nouvelle sociologie économique et le lien marchand: des relations personnelles à l'impersonnalité des relations. *Revue française de sociologie*, *43*, 521–557.

Coase, R. H. (1978). Economics and biology: Evolution, selection and the economic principle: Discussion. *The American Economic Review*, *68*, 244–245.

Coutu, M. (2013). Weber reading stammler: What horizons for the sociology of law? *Journal of Law & Society*, *40*(3), 356–374.

Crozier, M., & Friedberg, E. (1977). *L'acteur et le système. Les contraintes de l'action collective*. Paris: Le Seuil.

Edelman, L. B. (1992). Legal ambiguity and symbolic structures: Organizational mediation of civil rights law. *American Journal of Sociology*, *97*, 1531–1576.

Edelman, L. B., Abraham, S. E., & Erlanger, H. S. (1992). Professional construction of the legal environment: The inflated threat of wrongful discharge doctrine. *Law and Society Review*, *26*, 47–84.

Edelman, L. B., Riggs Fuller, S., & Mara-Drita, I. (2001). Diversity rhetoric and the managerialization of law. *American Journal of Sociology*, *106*(6), 1589–1641.

Edelman, L. B., & Suchman, M. C. (1997). The legal environments of organizations. *Annual Review of Sociology*, *23*, 479–515.

Fabre-Magnan, M. (2016). *Droit des obligations. Contrat et engagement unilateral*. Paris: PUF.

Fligstein, N. (1996). Markets as politics: A political cultural approach to market institutions. *American Sociological Review*, *61*, 656–673.

Friedberg, E. (1993). *Le pouvoir et la règle. Dynamique de l'action organisée*. Paris: Le Seuil.

Gilad, S. (2014). Beyond endogeneity: How firms and regulators co-construct the meaning of regulation. *Law & Policy*, *36*, 134–164.

Goetz, C. J., & Scott, R. E. (1977). Liquidated damages, penalties and the just compensation principle: Some notes on an enforcement model and a theory of efficient breach. *Columbia Law Review*, *77*, 554–594.

Goffman, E. (1974). *Frame analysis: An essay on the organization of experience*. Cambridge, MA: Harvard University Press.

Jourdain, P. (2016). Quel avenir pour la distinction des obligations de résultat et de moyens? *La Semaine juridique, édition générale*, *36*, 1557–1559.

Kennedy, D., & Michelman, F. (1980). Are property and contract efficient? *Hofstra Law Review*, *8*, 711–770.

Kronman, A. T. (1978). Specific performance. *The University of Chicago Law Review*, *45*, 351–382.

Lonsdale, C., & Watson, G. (2005). The internal client relationship, demand management and value for money: A conceptual model. *Journal of Purchasing & Supply Management*, *11*, 159–171.

Macaulay, S. (1963). Non-contractual relations in business: A preliminary study. *American Sociological Review*, *28*, 1–19.

Meyer, J. W., & Rowan, B. (1977). Institutionalized organizations: Formal structure as myth and ceremony. *American Journal of Sociology*, *83*(2), 340–363.

Pettigrew, A. M. (1975). The industrial purchasing decision as a political process. *European Journal of Marketing*, *9*, 4–19.

Plancqueel, A. (1972). Obligations de moyens, obligations de résultat. *Revue Trimestrielle de Droit Civil*, *334*, 336.

Posner, R. A. (1977). *Economic analysis of law* (2d ed.). Little: Brown and Company.

Reverdy, T. (2009). Mettre en concurrence ses fournisseurs-partenaires. Comment les acheteurs reconfigurent les échanges interindustriels. *Revue française de sociologie*, *4*, 775–815.

Selznick, P. (2012). *TVA and the grass roots: A study of politics and organization. A study in the sociology of formal organization*. London: Forgotton Books.

Snow, D., Rochford, E., Worden, S., & Benford, R. (1986). Frame alignment processes, micromobilization, and movement participation. *American Sociological Review*, *51*(4), 464–481.

Snow, D. A., & Benford, R. D. (1988). Ideology, frame resonance and participant mobilization. *International Research Movement Research*, *1*, 197–217.

Stark, D. (2009). *The sense of dissonance – accounts of worth in economic life*. Princeton, NJ and Oxford: Princenton University Press.

Suchman, M. C. (2003). The contract as social artifact. *Law & Society Review*, *37*, 91–142.

Surubaru, A. (2014). *La fragilité des liens marchands. Sociologie de la sous-traitance international*. Paris: Pétra.

Talesh, S., & Pélisse, J. (2019). How legal intermediaries facilitate or inhibit social change. In Sarat, A. (Ed.), *Studies in law, politics, and society* (Vol. 79, pp. 111–145). Bingley: Emerald Publishing Limited.

Urry, J. (2005). The complexity turn. *Theory, Culture and Society*, *22*(5), 1–14.

Vaughan, D. (1999). The dark side of organizations: Mistake, misconduct, and disaster. *Annual Review of Sociology*, *25*, 271–305.

Wilkinson-Ryan, T., & Baron, J. (2009). Moral judgment and moral heuristics in breach of contract. *Journal of Empirical Legal Studies*, *2*, 405–424.

CONTRACTS AS COMPLIANCE MECHANISMS: LEGAL INTERMEDIATION AND THE FAILURE OF FRENCH RETAIL REGULATION

Sebastian Billows

ABSTRACT

The legal devices crafted within large organizations are a key component of legal endogeneity theory (LET). While symbolically complying with legislation, legal devices allow organizations to infuse managerial logics into the legal field, which eventually diverts law from its initial political goals. Although the LET has considered legal devices such as anti-discrimination guidelines and grievance procedures, this chapter argues that contracts also constitute a locus of symbolic compliance and contribute to the eventual endogenization of regulation. Supplementing LET with a focus on legal intermediation, this chapter explores how contracts are crafted and used by large organizations to respond to regulatory pressure. While other legal instruments are unambiguously managerialized from the outset, contracts are highly versatile legal objects that perform the seemingly opposite functions of symbolically complying with regulation and serving substantive commercial purposes. This discussion of the role of contracts as compliance mechanisms is based on an in-depth empirical study of the French retail industry and its response to a set of regulations that aimed at making their business practices fairer.

Keywords: Contracts; retail; business relations; business regulation; legal endogeneity; in-house counsel; France

Legal Intermediation: A Processual Approach to Law and Economic Activity
Studies in Law, Politics, and Society, Volume 81, 151–174

ISSN: 1059-4337/doi:10.1108/S1059-433720190000081007

INTRODUCTION

In the sociolegal literature on contracts, it is a commonly held view that private agreements predate legal contracts and that those legal contracts predate state intervention. It is true that legal contracts are not the unique way of securing private agreements (Macaulay, 1963). Certain business communities never make use of these legal devices and systematically use informal dispute resolution mechanisms (Bernstein, 1992). This view of contracts is supported by the fact that courts, and public authorities in general, exercise discretion in enforcing private agreements. To become legally binding objects, contracts must meet a set of formal criteria, such as legibility or the presence of the signature of both parties at the bottom of the document. The criteria are also substantial: a judge may strike down a contract if some clauses fail to conform to the standards of fairness mandated by statutes or case law (Knapp, 2013). The notion that legal contracts predate state intervention is also tangible in the way that sociolegal scholarship addresses regulation. In labor law, for instance, the term "collective bargaining" entails that a standardized contract replaces a wide array of potentially unfair individual contracts (Bessy, 2008). An aspect of this notion is that public intervention in private business relations has political goals, such as the protection of weaker market players against those who can use contractual freedom to their advantage (Talesh, 2009).

In this chapter, I put forth an alternative view of contracts and regulation. Rather than agreements that might or might not lead to public intervention, I consider legal contracts that arise in response to regulation. In such cases, one wonders whether regulation still achieves its goal of protecting weaker parties. To address this issue, I draw on the conceptual framework and empirical methods of legal endogeneity theory (LET) (Edelman, 2016; Edelman, Fuller, & Mara-Drita, 2001; Edelman, Krieger, Eliason, Albiston, & Mellema, 2011). Inspired by neo-institutional sociology and organizational theory, LET provides a model to understand how large organizations respond to legal regulation. Rather than adhering to the initial political goals of regulation, organizations infuse their own managerial logics into the legal field. This process can eventually lead to endogenization, whereby organizational interpretations of compliance shapes case law and new legislation. Part of this process is driven by compliance mechanisms, which refer to the objects that organizations craft to comply with regulation. I argue that contracts constitute one of those compliance mechanisms and contribute to the process by which organizations internalize and endogenize the regulations targeted at them.

Edelman (2016) argues that compliance varies along a continuum from symbolic and substantive to merely symbolic. Due to their commercial importance, the role of contracts is rarely entirely symbolic. They play key substantive functions of commercial nature such as framing how firms interact with their strategic partners. This dual nature points to the paradoxical aspect of the rise of contracts as compliance mechanisms: these legal documents symbolically comply with legislation that aims at protecting weaker players and, at the same time, serve a key function in a firm's business strategy. Solving this paradox requires a departure from the field-wide approach that neo-institutionalist scholars have used so far. This chapter supplements the aforementioned approach with the legal intermediation perspective, paying close attention to how compliance mechanisms are crafted within organizations and to the different nuances of legality they contribute to produce.[1] In doing so, I shed light on the work of in-house counsel workers who craft those contracts. As they navigate complex organizational structures, those legal intermediaries struggle to maintain their legitimacy and to promote their framing of how their firms should comply with regulation (Pélisse, 2014; Pélisse, Bessy, & Delpeuch, 2011; Talesh, 2015; Talesh & Pélisse, 2019).

To outline the rise of contracts as compliance mechanisms, this chapter relies on a theoretically-informed case study. It surveys the evolution of anti-trust legislation targeting French food mass retail. Faced with the increasing market power of French mass retail, suppliers successfully lobbied the state into protecting them. Starting from 1996, the French legislature intervened by introducing a new set of rules (known as "Title IV") that specifically targeted the annual bargaining process between retailers and suppliers. The explicit aim of lawmakers was to force all retailers, regardless of their economic power, to sell their suppliers' products at the same price. This plan, however, dramatically failed. I argue that the contracts designed by the retailers in response to regulation were a key factor in the latter's internalization, endogenization, and eventual failure. As puzzling as it may seem, contracts were both a form of symbolic compliance which contributed to the endogenization of French anti-trust law and a strategic legal tool that helped retailers pressurize their suppliers into giving them more rebates. The key factor of the rise of contract as a compliance mechanism is intra-organizational. Hence, this chapter devotes close attention to the work performed by the staff of retailers' own legal departments.

THEORY AND RESEARCH DESIGN

The evolution of French retail regulation is typical of legal endogeneity, a process by which private organizations comply with regulation, but eventually alter the meaning of what compliance means. Once legislatures pass laws to promote fair business practices or to fight against discrimination, large businesses respond by assigning new meanings to those legal mandates. Then, as Edelman and Talesh (2011) put it, those:

> institutionalized conceptions of law and compliance [...] become widely accepted within the business community and eventually [...] come to be seen as rational and legitimate by public legal actors and institutions. (p. 103)

By holding court on their own, managerial terms (Edelman & Suchman, 1999) and by "internalizing the judicial function" (Pélisse, 2011), businesses have increased their legitimacy and turned scrutiny from official legal institutions away from them. Based on this approach and using the case of US anti-discrimination policy, neo-institutionalist scholars have covered multiple aspects of how large private organizations reinterpret and thus circumvent official legal norms and institutions (Edelman, 1992; Edelman et al., 2001; Edelman et al., 2011; Talesh, 2009). The remainder of the theoretical section discusses the scope and limits of LET. The first subpart argues that LET can be extended beyond the typical empirical case of US anti-discrimination law. The second part identifies theoretical and methodological limitations of LET that have to be overcome to fully understand contracts and legal work within organizations.

LET Beyond the Case of US Anti-Discrimination Law

The proponents of LET have applied their theoretical framework to US anti-discrimination law, a highly political issue in the US since the civil rights era (McAdam, 1989). Due to the political implications of US civil rights law, some scholars have combined the analysis of the bureaucratic enforcement of civil rights on the workplace with a study of social movements (Lieberman, 2015; Stryker & Pedriana, 2004, 2017). Recently, Shauhin Talesh investigated the endogenization process of Californian consumer law protecting consumers against car manufacturers (Talesh, 2009). He claimed that this area of regulation pertained to "public legal rights" and thus could be analyzed through the lens of endogenization. Although public legal rights are not directly at stake, regulation promoting "fair practices" in business-to-business relations (the empirical object of this chapter) is an area of regulation with political implications. As Bruno Amable has suggested, debates about market competition and economic policy have moral undertones (Amable, 2011). Analyzing those debates is important to uncover the "moral-political conflicts" that underlie capitalism (Fourcade, Steiner, Streeck, & Woll, 2013). As I have shown in a previous publication (Billows, 2016a), large food manufacturers have developed since the early 1980s, a political narrative blaming the "unfair" business practices of retailers and calling for a halt to destructive price competition. Later on, this political agenda was taken up by mainstream French parties.

A second extension to the LET literature I make relates to enforcement. According to the literature, the key factor explaining legal internalization and the subsequent endogenization of regulation is the lack of strong enforcement agencies acting on behalf of disadvantaged social groups. The neo-institutional literature views the equal employment opportunity commission (EEOC), the federal agency in charge of enforcing Title VII, as weak. While some authors described its unorthodox approach to anti-discrimination law and its alliance with social movements as sources of strength (Lieberman, 2015; Stryker & Pedriana, 2004), most stressed its lack of resources and its fuzzy legal mandate. Contrary to Title VII where private enforcement prevails, French law protecting suppliers was backed by DGCCRF,[2] a powerful regulatory agency. By US standards, the human resources of DGCCRF were plentiful. On January 1, 1997, 3,715 officials worked for DGCCRF. By contrast with EEOC, whose agents "cannot file a lawsuit in every case where discrimination has been found,"[3] DGCCRF has an aggressive litigation branch with extended powers to sue retailers on behalf of their suppliers. In my view, this does not preclude me from applying the endogenization framework to the case at hand. Actually, failure, the eventual outcome of this regulation attempt, becomes even more surprising. Why did DGCCRF fail to settle the economic imbalance between retailers and their suppliers *despite* a clear legal mandate, significant material resources, and broad enforcement powers?

Consistent with recent literature (Talesh, 2009, 2014), this chapter proposes a third extension of LET by studying the interplay between institutionalized logics and political mobilization and lobbying. Similar to Talesh, I take into account the efforts made by business interests to alter legislation. Contrary to US anti-discrimination law, where the US Congress rarely changes legislation, legislation targeting French retail has changed many times during the time period I investigate. While Edelman's contributions dealt mainly with courts and judges, the evolution of French retail regulation and its eventual endogenization results from the recursive interplay between lawmaking and how law is implemented by the organizations and institutions it targets (Halliday & Carruthers, 2009; Mallard, 2014).

Legal Intermediation: A Reassessment of Compliance Mechanisms and Legal Work within Organizations

As shown above, the main features of the case of French retailer-supplier relations are consistent with the main premises of LET. However, regardless of the specifics of the case, I claim that a full understanding of how contracts are crafted and used by large businesses, requires two departures from the concepts and methods commonly found in LET.

The first departure regards contracts themselves. A key component of this theoretical framework is the fact that organizations, in response to regulatory pressure, craft internal legal devices which act as compliance mechanisms. An empirical example is how US companies responded to anti-discrimination laws. They established their own codes of conduct and formal grievance procedures (Edelman, Uggen, & Erlanger, 1999). By introducing those internal compliance mechanisms, large organizations symbolically complied with anti-discrimination laws but failed to adjust their actual business practices. Once those compliance mechanisms became widespread across the organizational field, they started permeating official legal institutions and eventually weakened their scope. Over time, the legal practices of the industry have become the official standard by which compliance is measured. It has been shown, for instance, that courts are more lenient towards firms who have adopted those mechanisms than toward those that have not, regardless of their actual record in hiring women or members of ethnic minorities (Edelman et al., 2011).

Whether it is labor law, consumer law, or the promotion of fair business practices, contracts have been a locus of regulation since the Industrial Revolution. These legal objects are at the heart of the tensions between individual freedom (and freedom to do business) and the social movements representing weaker parties in contractual relationships, such as workers in labor contracts (Weber, 1978, p. 886). Despite their importance, contracts have been seldom addressed by the LET literature.[4] Yet, as compliance mechanisms, contracts obey a logic that is similar to the legal devices described in the LET literature. They are designed within organizations but have an official legal status in the outside world. (Theoretically, they can even be enforced by courts.) As the empirical case presented in this chapter will demonstrate, they can contribute to the internalization of regulation by organizations, and even to its eventual endogenization. Yet a key characteristic of the other legal devices addressed in the LET literature is missing. The latter features legal devices that give more autonomy to corporations *because* they play little more than a symbolic role. The ability of large organizations to circumvent anti-discrimination law has lied in the intrinsic weakness of those legal devices. By contrast, since they determine with whom and how they collaborate, contracts are at the heart of large corporations' business strategy (Dietz, 2012; Granovetter, 1985; Li-wen & Whitford, 2013). Standing between the public and the private legal orders, contracts are inherently ambiguous legal objects that perform symbolic compliance and key business functions at the time.

To move beyond the symbolic role of compliance mechanisms, one has to investigate whether and how they shape business relationships. This is in line with the constitutive approach to legal objects put forth by Robin Stryker, who argues that "law provides tools that help actors attribute meaning, existence, desirability or undesirability to their economic activities and environment" (Stryker, 2003, p. 349). To apply this principle, I draw inspiration from the legal realist scholarship on contracts (for a review essay, see Brooks, 2013). Stuart Macaulay laid the foundations of this literature 50 years ago, in one of the most cited papers in the history of US sociology (Macaulay, 1963). Ever since Macaulay's seminal contribution, taking a realist approach to contractual relations means challenging the legal fiction that contracts are ubiquitous. Consistent with this principle, the legal realist perspective insists on the diversity of business arrangements (Bernstein, 1992; Li-wen & Whitford, 2013; Marotta-Wurgler & Taylor, 2013; Teichman, 2010). Not all businesspeople use formal, legal contracts to protect their commercial dealings. And, even when they do so, the problems that arise during a business relationship are hardly ever solved through litigation. This chapter builds on those principles to address standardized agreements. There are many empirical examples of standardized contracts ("boilerplates") produced by large organizations (Bessy, 2008; Davis, 2006; Kahan & Klausner, 1997; Marotta-Wurgler & Taylor, 2013). Yet, those contributions have failed to open the organizational black box and to investigate how and by whom standardized agreements are crafted and why in some cases they are used by businesspeople and not in others.

Understanding how compliance mechanisms are crafted and used, entails an analysis of professional work within and outside organizations (Abbott, 2005). Here lies my second departure from the LET literature. Proponents of LET have described how various professional groups define compliance. Empirical examples include managers (Edelman et al., 2001), human resource professionals (Dobbin & Kelly, 2007), and insurance staff (Talesh, 2015). Although "legal intermediaries" (see Pélisse & Talesh, in press) are a core concern in this chapter, the methodology I use differs from LET. Most of the research on how professionals shape compliance, analyzes how professional groups operate *outside* large organizations. Rather than the daily interactions between professionals and their clients, scholars have focused on the professional literature (such as magazines) and gatherings (such as conferences). By contrast, I take a close look at the "division of labor [...] in the cubicle" (Abbott, 2005) and analyze daily interactions *within* a large French retailer between In-House-Counsel and commercial staffers who are in charge of sourcing (i.e., doing business with suppliers). Behind this methodological choice lies a theoretical claim. I predict that the framing of what compliance means can happen at the industry- and organization-level rather than at the level of the profession at large. This is consistent with other contributions that show that a compliance expert's professional background is not, in itself, a predictor of the advice they deliver to specific market players (Pélisse, Protais, Larchet, & Charrier, 2012; Suchman & Cahill, 1996). On top of professional dynamics, the specific culture of the market players and the contingent power relations between laypeople and compliance experts also matter. One has to also take into account the material context in which the contract is produced (Suchman, 2003): as the empirical case addressed in this chapter will show, the fact that contracts are ensconced in corporate software has an impact on how laypeople use them.

To reflect on the role of in-house Counsel in the French retail business, I draw from a rich literature on lawyers.[5] On the one hand, as suggested in a classical account of the legal profession, lawyers are likely to promote "legal casuistry" and "high logical sublimation," two core aspects of the formal rationalization of law (Weber, 1978, p. 655). Compared to other legal intermediaries, they are closer to the core areas of the legal field (see Pélisse's contribution in this special issue). As such, they are more likely than others to use the symbolic resources of the legal field (Bourdieu, 1987) and to insist on procedural conformity rather than substantive conformity to regulation.[6] In his account of how US firms interpreted and conformed to anti-discrimination law, Franck Dobbin claims that due to their focus on formal legal procedure, lawyers retreated from compliance altogether, and recommended that their clients did nothing until courts clarified their interpretation of ambiguous legal mandates (Dobbin, 2009). On the other hand, in specific business contexts, it was found that lawyers put their professional norms aside and adapted to the commercial demands of their clients (Suchman & Cahill, 1996). In such cases, rather than narrow compliance with the law, they focused on creating trust among business partners. The work of Nelson and Nielsen (2000) provides a summary of those hypotheses.[7] Based on an in-depth survey of 50 "in-house" lawyers in large US corporations, the authors identified three different roles taken up by legal staff. As cops, legal departments "are primarily concerned with policing the conduct of their business clients" (p. 463). As counsels, they are closer to "businesspeople" and take part in commercial decisions. As "entrepreneurs," lawyers give up giving legal advice entirely and act as general business advisers.

DATA

The data I collected aimed at understanding the evolution of French retail regulation between 1996 and 2008 (from its inception to its eventual failure). Using an intra-organizational viewpoint, I look into how retailers complied with the legislation.

To survey the evolution of legislation and the shifting attitude of bureaucrats towards retailers, I examined state archives and six semi-directed interviews with high-level DGCCRF officials. The archives were part of the holdings of the Center for economic and financial archives (*Centre des archives économiques et fiancières*) located at Savigny-Le-Temple. The documents I examined were memos, policy briefs, draft regulations produced by DGCCRF and the cabinet of the French Minister for Financial and Economic Affairs. The documents span across the 1996–2004 period and provide a comprehensive view of changes in crafting and enforcement of French anti-retail policy. Some documents report about investigations on retailers' practices and thus provide direct information about compliance strategies.

Yet the main findings about how retailers complied with the legislation are drawn from participant observation. In 2013, the legal department of Superchain,[8] a large retailer in France for fast-moving consumer goods, hired me as an intern for three months. I was assigned tasks directly connected to contractual relationships, such as answering the formal requests for amendments sent by Superchains' suppliers. The legal department was aware that I was conducting research on Superchain. The legal staff allowed me to attend numerous meetings, including some involving interaction between lawyers and the commercial staff. I also conducted formal interviews with members of the sourcing department who interacted with the legal team. These commercial workers were tasked with leading the annual negotiation process with suppliers for a given product category. During my internship, I gained access to Superchain's boilerplate contract as of 2013 and to some of the previous versions (the boilerplate is revised annually). I also had access to other internal documents, such as correspondence between the legal staff and DGCCRF staff investigating Superchain, and a document reporting about each legal change since 1997 and how Superchain should comply with it.

Although most of my data comes from observation and interviews at Superchain, I conducted eight additional interviews with lawyers and members of commercial staff who work or have worked for other retailers listed in Table 1 and for their major suppliers. Other interviews were conducted with employees of business organizations representing either retailers or suppliers. Retailers, rather than suppliers, were the best site to explore how contracts were designed and enforced. Because of their high market power, retailers can unilaterally impose their own standardized contracts on their suppliers.

The French market for fast-moving consumer goods is an oligopsony. A few retailers act as mandatory intermediaries between a large number of suppliers and the end-consumers. In 2013, the year I conducted observation within Superchain, I found out that their suppliers had little economic leverage on

Table 1. Market Shares of the Main French Food Retailers, as of 2017 (in %).

E. Leclerc	21.0
Superchain	20.9
Intermarché	14.1
Casino	11.4
Auchan	11.0
Système U	10.3
Lidl	5.3
Other	6.0
TOTAL	*100.0*

them. The combined weight of the 100 biggest suppliers represented a mere 60% of their annual turnover. By contrast, one retailer can represent up to 25% of the annual turnover of a supplier on the French domestic market. This economic power translates into contractual power. As stated earlier, the task I was assigned was to handle the requests for contractual amendments made by suppliers. I was asked to turn down most of them.

FINDINGS

In the present section, I outline the major steps by which French retailers internalized the legislation targeted at them and eventually contributed to its endogenization. The approach chosen here is both processual and analytic. I start with a description of the main characteristics of the harsh legislation set up in the late 1990s and early 2000s in order to make retailers' business practices fairer. In a second paragraph, I describe the subsequent rise of standardized contracts, which helped retailers strategically comply with legislation protecting suppliers. Then I explain the intra-organizational origins of this unlikely compliance mechanism: legal departments, which had emerged as the key legal intermediary between legislation and retailers, chose contracts as a way to solve dilemmas regarding their intra-organizational status. Finally, I exhibit how this type of compliance influenced the content of new regulations drafted by French regulators.

Voluntary Legal Ambiguity

Retailer-supplier relations had been a contentious issue since the inception of French mass retail in the 1950s (Billows, 2016a; Jacques, 2016). At first, suppliers were reluctant to sell their products to the nascent mass retailers. They feared that price wars between retailers would bring their margins down and affect their brand image. The French state, however, had been supportive of mass retail. The *Circulaire Fontanet*, a regulation passed in 1960, mandated suppliers to sell their products to all retailers, even those that sought to reduce consumer prices. The late 1990s saw a reversal of state policy. In the 1980s and early 1990s, the retail industry entered a phase of heavy consolidation. In 1995, seven players dominated the mass retail market, down from 30 in the early 1980s. Such concentration allowed supermarket chains to exercise higher levels of pressure on their suppliers. Supermarket chains could set the price of grocery products unilaterally. No matter their size, suppliers had no choice but to comply: retailers would retaliate against suppliers who didn't bring their price down by removing their products from their shelves. The pressure put on suppliers was driven by competitive dynamics: large retailers were waging a price war against each other and expected the suppliers to pay its costs.

A legislative battle that lasted between 1995 and 1996 introduced stringent legislation against retail. A key contributor was Jacques Chirac, a conservative politician who was elected President in 1995. In 1996, he publicly declared that "mass retail had a negative impact" on society.[9] Before serving two terms as President of France, he had served two terms as mayor of Paris. Back then, he actively used his planning powers to prevent large retail chains from opening new outlets in the city.[10] French politicians such as Jacques Chirac feared that large retail chains could undermine the French food industry, a vital part of the economy. Another contributor to this anti-retail policy was ILEC (Institut de liaisons et d'études des industries de consommation),[11] the business group representing the largest suppliers. Thanks to its resources and the solidarity among its members, it outcompeted FCD (Fédération du commerce et de la distribution),[12] the business group representing the major food retailers. The Galland Act of 1996 was the outcome of this phase of political mobilization. The main provision of the Act ensured that the final price paid by the retailer should match the basic rate set by the supplier. This rule is similar to the one introduced in the US by the Robinson-Patman Act of 1936, which outlawed "price discrimination." Suppliers hoped that it would put an end to the costly price war between retailers and would provide them with higher margins.

When the Galland Act of 1996 came into force, retailers complied with the rule mandating them to buy and sell their products at rates that had been set by suppliers. As intended, the main outcome of the Galland Act was the virtual freeze of price competition between retailers. But this piece of legislation had an unintended effect: that of boosting "back margins." Because virtually all products were sold at a price close to the basic rate set by the supplier, retailers' "front" margins became very low. Instead, retailers requested higher back margins, that is, fees paid directly by the supplier. Formally, this transaction was performed in exchange for services to the supplier, such as placing their product on the top shelf in the supermarket. In fact, these services were largely fictitious and were a mere outcome of retailers' economic pressure. No matter what suppliers needed, retailers sold more and more of these dubious services to them. Such commercial behavior sparked furor among suppliers and prompted the French Parliament to take action again.

In response to the rise of back margins, the French Parliament passed new legislation in 2001. The new economic regulations (NRE) Act introduced a blanket ban on obtaining "disproportionate advantages." Although its primary target was back margins, the ban was drafted in ambiguous terms on purpose. The state officials who drafted the ban wanted to create as much legal uncertainty as possible (around "commercial cooperation") in order to anticipate future legal inventions made by retailers (see Billows, 2016b):

> We looked at the facts and we try to have an open wording, because you can't imagine beforehand what retailers will do [...]. Enumerating specific behaviors, would be counterproductive, because you'd assume that behaviors that are not listed are legal. In that case, you'd have to convince the judge that although the behavior presented before him is not listed, it can be still considered as abusive. (Senior official, DGCCRF, 1998–2005)

Those ambiguous statutes made the legal environment uncertain. Another source of legal uncertainty was broad and aggressive enforcement. DGCCRF, the French regulatory agency in charge of fair business practices and food safety had played a major role in drafting the new regulations. It was also in charge of enforcing those rules. The NRE Act of 2001 increased state officials' enforcement powers. The Act allowed DGCCRF to bring civil cases before commercial courts, on behalf of suppliers.[13] The NRE Act allowed courts to order retailers to reimburse the fraudulent back margins to the supplier. This proved very costly for some retailers. In 2007, a commercial court requested that Super U, a retailer, reimbursed €72 million to various suppliers.

The Rise of Contracts as a Response to Retail Regulation

Retailers were infuriated by the back margins system. Despite lucrative back margins, they feared that the freeze of price competition would drive consumers away from the large superstores they had been building since the 1960s in order to achieve economies of scale. To fight against the Galland and NRE Acts, retailers' lobbyists created a two-sided narrative. On the one hand, they reframed the rise of back margins as an inevitable side-effect of unrealistically anti-competitive legislation. On the other, they argued that their huge commercial power was an asset to offer lower prices to the consumer. Retailers initiated a series of media campaigns against the Galland and NRE Acts stressing their inflationary effect. In July 2001, the (yearly) rate of inflation for food prices attained 6.5%.[14] Between 1997 and 2002, France moved from fourth to second costliest country in Europe (Colla & Lambert-Pandraud, 2007, p. 31). In their media campaigns, retailers targeted consumers directly, warning them of the negative impact of legislation on their purchasing power (*pouvoir d'achat*). At the height of this campaign, in 2003, E. Leclerc commissioned 20,000 billboards across the country to publicly attack back margins.[15] The mottos used an anti-elite rhetoric, with some advertisements stating: "opinion leaders can always talk about your purchasing power, they don't have the same as yours."

Despite those quasi-political media campaigns, the battle fought by retailers against the Galland and NRE Acts was mostly a legal one. The most conspicuous change triggered by pro-supplier legislation was the rise of standardized contracts. Retailers responded to the NRE provision that prohibited "disproportionate advantages" by coercing their suppliers into signing "agreements" where they spelled out the different "services" offered by the retailer and their "compensation" by the supplier. Archives from an investigation performed in 2002 by DGCCRF officials gave a detailed picture of the contractual practices that one of the main French retailers set up in response to the NRE law. Each supplier was requested to sign several contracts. One contract, the "National Retail Policy Agreement" was national. It compensated the fact that the supplier's product was listed by the retailer's central purchasing body. The price tag varied from 1% to 12% of the total turnover. A second contract, the "Regional commercial and promotional agreement" was signed at the level of the 16 regional branches of the retailer. It compensated services such as the "assortment agreement," which defined where the supplier's products were placed on the shelf, or the "marketing agreement," which provided for the placement of products in the free leaflets given out by the retailers to the consumers. During the 2000s, those boilerplate contracts and the internal procedures linked to them kept growing both in size and in level of detail. In 2012, the last year Superchain sold "commercial cooperation" services to its suppliers, the retailer took and stored pictures that proved that the "service" was performed at the shop level.

In the 2000s and 2010s, such contracts were an institutionalized feature of the French retail market. As shown above, the leaders of the retail market both put contracts at the center of their compliance strategy. The smaller retailers listed in Table 1 had similar practices.[16] Suppliers took those standardized contracts for granted and accepted that the only way to do business with retailers was to sign them.

> Because they are huge and well organized, [retailers] have always anticipated and established a certain number of [legal] documents. [...] The only purpose of those documents is to say "this is how I buy your products, this is how I receive them, this is how I want our relationship to function. And of course, you owe me penalties if you don't deliver the products the way I want". There is no room for negotiation [...]. Those are contracts of adhesion: either you sign them or you don't. (Head of legal, large supplier)

This quote illustrates the institutionalized nature of contracts in that market. It also shows the double nature of those legal documents. Their primary role is to incorporate the harsh legislation targeting retailers and to extract "commercial cooperation" payments from suppliers. On top of this, contracts acquired a secondary role, that of micromanaging the suppliers' behavior and streamlining their logistics to conform to the operational demands of retailers.

Turning Business Relations into Contractual Relations

Consistent with the legal intermediation perspective, I view different forms of compliance as the result of an intra-organizational process. Legal intermediaries are the key contributors: depending on their socialization, the structure of their relationships with other intra-organizational actors, legal intermediaries shape different forms of legality. In the case at hand, the legal staff hired by retailers in response to the Galland and NRE Acts are a critical group of actors to understand why and how contracts were used as a compliance mechanism. While this subsection focuses on Superchain, I will provide evidence that similar patterns happened at the other retailers listed in Table 1.

Within retailers, in-house counsel swiftly became the key legal intermediary who participated in the interpretation and the framing of compliance. When I conducted most of my fieldwork, in 2013, I realized that the biographies of the senior legal staff at most retailers were intertwined with the history of Title IV legislation. Franck Le Vern,[17] who was still the head of the commercial legal department at Superchain as of 2013, started his career in 1997 at another retailer. Faced with increased pressure from Title IV legislation and DGCCRF lawsuits, his former employer requested him to create a legal department from scratch. He had been fortunate enough to write his master thesis on this subject, back in 1996, when he graduated from law school.

> To complete my masters, I had to write a small thesis and an internship report. I wrote my master thesis on the parliamentary debates that took place back then and which sought to regulate supplier-retailer relations, the first time this happened since the Balladur ordinance of 1986. My internship report was on the Galland Act. It's funny when I think about this, I didn't imagine that it would become the founding piece of legislation of a job I'm still doing. […] I was fortunate to take part in all the debates of the following laws. The first one of them took place in 2001. This was the NRE Act. (Franck Le Vern, head of the commercial legal department, Superchain)

As he arrived at Superchain in 2005, he became the head of the commercial legal department. He hired more lawyers, who specialized in supplier-retailer relations. Observation and interviews showed similar career trajectories at the legal departments of other retailers. The head of legal at Superchain's biggest rival was also recruited in the 1990s. At first, she was alone. Then, as legislation became harsher, she hired more and more staff. In 2014, she supervised a team of nine lawyers. All those legal departments had one thing in common. Although members of staff specialized in various areas of commercial law, the heads of legal always spent most of their time on retailer-supplier relations. In the interviews I conducted with them, they presented this area of law as their top priority.[18]

Far more resources were dedicated to Title IV than other areas of legislation, such as consumer law. This is surprising since retailers conduct millions of daily transactions with consumers, who are defended by regulators and consumer organizations alike. Why did Title IV attract more attention than those other areas of legal expertise? The lawsuits introduced by DGCCRF in the aftermath of the NRE Act of 2001 and the extreme levels of legal uncertainty constituted a rhetorical resource for lawyers who were directly employed by retailers. Rather than responding to lawsuits and court decisions on a case by case basis, they emphasized the general risk of litigation. One of my respondents, a legal counsel for Superchain's biggest rival, told me that DGCCRF's lawsuits constituted a "legal hazard." By framing lawsuits as an almost-inevitable danger, those lawyers behaved similarly to the human resource professionals described by Frank Dobbin (2009) or the US legal insurance staff depicted in Shauhin Talesh' work (2015, p. 221). The yearly training sessions, where a few members of the legal department gave talks to the entire commercial staff, provide a good illustration of the risk-based framing of Title IV. Those training sessions were held in a big lecture hall at Superchain's headquarters. During the one I attended,

Franck Le Vern presented the main provisions of Title IV legislation and the precautions that the commercial staff should take in their dealings with suppliers. First, he emphasized legal risks: the lawsuits that Superchain had faced in the past and how illegal behavior could lead to harsher legislation in the future. Prescriptions came later: they were presented as the only way to mitigate the legal threat posed by DGCCRF's lawsuits. This focus on legal risk was combined with boundary work outlining the rift between the daily business activities of the commercial staff and the legal activities of Superchain's in-house counsel. Representatives of the legal department created anxiety by mentioning specific legal provisions or court cases, although the commercial staff was unfamiliar with this terminology. During the training session I attended, Franck Le Vern displayed a PowerPoint slide featuring a judge's hammer, a symbol of the power of the judiciary.

Going back to Nielsen and Nelson's typology (see part 2), the preferred role of lawyers working for retailers was that of counsel. They enjoyed situations where the commercial staff brought them problems that could only be solved; thanks to the intervention of a lawyer. In those cases, lawyers could perform diagnosis, inference, and treatment (Abbott, 1988), three steps that define professional work. Yet due to their framing the Galland and NRE Acts as "legal hazard," most of the time they took up the role of cop. As I have shown above, this allowed them to increase their resources. This role, however, had its pitfalls. Acting like a "cop" put lawyers at risk of excluding themselves from decision-making altogether:

> During my fieldwork, I interviewed a commercial worker who sought Franck Le Vern's advice about how he could rapidly remove a supplier which did not sell as much as in the past. Following common practice in his department, the commercial staffer suggested writing a letter to the supplier stating that due to a glitch in the IT system, all new orders would be suspended. Franck Le Vern knew that no matter how it was covered-up, the brutal suspension of a supplier was illegal.[19] Case law interpreting a vague provision of the Galland Act mandated a period of prenotification of up to three years, depending on the length and the volume of the business relationship. He had even set up an internal procedure so that people in his department could pre-screen the suspension of an established supplier. In the case in point, Le Vern faced a dilemma. One option was to act as a "counsel" and to use his legal expertise to help the commercial staffer covering up the suspension of his long-time supplier. But this would jeopardize his status as a credible "cop." Yet he did not go as far as reminding the commercial staffer that the proposed business practice was illegal and could affect Superchain as a whole in the unlikely event of a lawsuit triggered by the supplier. He knew too well that the commercial staffer would ignore his prescription and would proceed with his plan of suspending the supplier anyway. Instead, all Franck Le Vern had to say was "Yes it's a common practice, no it's not legal."

Due to lawyers taking up the role of cop, their relational resources were scarce. Close relationships with commercial staffers were so difficult to build that there were subject to infighting within the legal department:

> I witnessed an argument between Franck Le Vern and his boss. Franck Le Vern was the head of the commercial legal department, one of the several entities under the supervision of François Oussé, Superchain's Of Counsel. Le Vern was invited to attend the annual convention organized by the commercial staff. He had not let Oussé know about this. As Le Vern

> was driving to the convention, he got a phone call from an infuriated Oussé, who had just found out about the event being held that morning.

This incident shows that even top managers of the legal department can be sidelined. Since he arrived in 2005, Franck Le Vern had struggled to build and maintain relationships with laypeople in key business functions. Those relationships were so precious to him that he did not want to share them with his boss.

For Superchain's lawyers, standardized contracts represented a way to combine the advantages of the roles of "cop" and "counsel." Rather than designing a specific contract for each supplier, lawyers created a standardized document to be used with all suppliers. From a material standpoint, it would have been impossible, anyway, to negotiate each contract separately. Only three people at the legal department specialized in sourcing. Therefore, providing individualized advice to all members of commercial staff involved in transactions with suppliers was simply impossible. In 2012, Superchain signed 1,650 deals with suppliers, and that only included fast-moving consumer goods.

Due to the legal nature of contracts, nobody within Superchain contested the fact that lawyers would chair the committee in charge of updating the standardized contract every year.

> Very early in the year, around end of April, early May, right when negotiations are over, we convene a committee to prepare the negotiations of the next year. In this committee, we try to have people representing all the stakeholders who have a say in the decision-making process. [...] We make sure it's people high in the hierarchy enough. If a director cannot make it, we try to get his or her deputy. We make sure that we implement what we decide in committee meetings. So we have a representative of all the commercial departments. Those are the core members of the committee, because they are at the heart of the negotiations with suppliers. (Franck Le Vern)

In this committee, lawyers translated the commercial strategy decided by "businesspeople" into legal, contractual provisions. The legal nature of the contract allowed them to perform efficient gatekeeping (Nelson & Nielsen, 2000) and to keep laypeople at bay. At Superchain, once the main provisions were decided over, commercial staff had little say in the last stages of contractual design. Superchain's standard agreement was written in "legalese" (Hill, 2001), which made it difficult for laypeople to participate. As an intern at Superchain, the hardest task for me had been learning the legal language used in contractual documents. The drafts I gave my supervisors were sent back to me because they didn't seem "legal" enough. Although it is hard to define what "legal" parlance stands for exactly, it differs from the vernacular language in several respects. One of the specificities is the use of capital letters to refer the parties ("the Parties," and "the Retailer").

During the annual revision process of the standardized agreement, lawyers at Superchain sent around the draft to make sure other departments agreed with the changes they made. According to Célestine Lejoyeux, the lawyer in charge of emailing the draft version, very little people even bothered to open the attachment. In the end, because the contract was considered a "legal" document, lawyers were the ones who performed the final editing and polishing of the draft. This formal prerogative gave them some degree of control over the substance of the contract. During my internship, Julie Holstein and Charlotte Pépin oversaw the editing of the final version of the boilerplate to be used in the following year. They complained to Frank Le Vern (their supervisor) that Superchain's insurance people asked them to introduce a clause forcing suppliers to buy an insurance policy covering up to €5 million in potential damages. Julie Holstein and Charlotte Pépin reckoned that such a clause would alienate suppliers too much and would lead to too many amendment requests sent to the legal department: "for grocery products [where suppliers are very big] I get it, but for non-grocery products [where many smaller suppliers operate], we'll be flooded with amendments." Eventually, Franck Le Vern decided to take away the clause without letting the insurance people know about it.

As the standardized contract was built into Superchain's IT infrastructure, retailers were able to keep the commercial staff at bay while exercising control over them at the same time. All, commercial staff at Superchain in charge of procurement used BCP Simu, a computer program that assisted them in their dealings with suppliers. The computer program divided the annual negotiation process into different temporal stages. The supplier's "tariff" was used as a starting point in the negotiation. (Retailers and suppliers never negotiated directly the final price tag of the product.) Then they negotiated different types of back margins which were listed in the standardized contract. Once the negotiation was over, the buyer entered the different margins they obtained and BCP Simu generated the contract automatically.

By delineating and naming each phase of the negotiation, BCP Simu performed two forms of control. First, it ensured that commercial staff conformed to company-wide policy that symbolically complied with pro-supplier legislation:

> We have an entire system to monitor whether the contracts are signed and the progress of negotiation. We don't want to end up on February 28th with 70 unsigned contracts.[20] That would look bad. [...] We are very careful with legal matters [...]. We [the management] can always find whether a contract is signed or not. (Dairy products category manager, Superchain)

But it was not just direct compliance with Title IV legislation that was monitored through BCP Simu. Using the different types of back margin that were defined in the contract, managers of the procurement staff could directly monitor their commercial performance:

> At first, you enter your annual targets in BCP Simu. As the negotiation progresses, you're going to update the data on BCP simu. You also enter the appendices. This allows management to directly monitor the negotiation process. (IT manager, Superchain)

As this example illustrates, the commercial strategy (the definition of annual targets *vis-à-vis* suppliers and how the negotiation should be conducted) was translated into legal terms by the legal team. Through the IT infrastructure, those legal categories became a core aspect of the commercial work performed by laypeople. In other words, the legal categories crafted by legal departments became constitutive of the buyers' cognitive environment (see Stryker, 2003, p. 733). At the company level, due to the involvement of in-house counsel, the legal strategy (finding the best way to symbolically comply with Title IV) and the commercial strategy became deeply intertwined. While keeping commercial staffers at bay and imposing their legal framing of compliance, legal departments gained a high level of influence on strategic business decisions.

The head of legal at another, smaller retailer provides a similar account of her involvement in crafting standardized contracts:

> Let me explain to you the process of drafting the annual agreements. In June or May, we settle down, we look at how the negotiations went [They typically end in March]. We look at the evolution of regulation, we exchange views with the products chief, with the marketing division, with the actors of company. The CFO is also involved, to look at where we're going in 2015 [the interview was conducted in summer 2015]. In June or July, we start to have a good view, and starting in September we're all set, we know how the next negotiation phase will be structured. So we have documentation, we have the paper document, the agreement. Then we have the commercial-legal direction [*l'axe commercial-juridique*] [...]. There are strategies. During this May-June period, we specify our legal strategy but also our commercial strategy based on what our competitors do and the context, on how we interpret what happened in the previous negotiation phase. (Head of legal, smaller retailer)

The quote reflects a deep entanglement of commercial and legal concerns. As in the case of Superchain, the legal department sets the agenda and the priorities of the negotiation strategy for the following year. Those priorities are reflected in the annual contract that the legal department is in charge of drafting.

From Symbolic Compliance to Endogenization

This last paragraph of the empirical section assesses the impact of the institutionalization of standardized contracts on further attempts by the French state to settle the economic imbalance between retailers and suppliers. As I have shown, the contracts set up by their legal departments allowed retailers to formally comply with the Galland and NRE Acts without substantively changing their business practices. In response to this, new regulations were drafted by the French state, which triggered similar forms of compliance based on contracts. This cycle of new legislation and symbolic compliance contributed to the endogenization of French retail regulation. Over time, bureaucrats working for the DGCCRF drafted new regulations which recognized contracts as a legitimate locus of compliance. The contractual framing of business relations as an equal relationship between "business partners" made its way into French statutes. I argue that retailers' legal departments played a key role in both stages of this process (symbolic compliance *and* endogenization). The infusion of the logics of the legal profession into compliance shifted policymaking debates from ethical and economic concerns to purely legal and technical ones.

In 2001, the NRE Act introduced an openly worded blanket-ban on "disproportionate advantages." Despite this broad prohibition and tough court decisions against retailers, state officials failed to significantly reduce back margins. Starting in 2003 with the Dutreil Regulation, DGCCRF officials dramatically changed course and decided that the best strategy against back margins would be drafting very detailed legislation. In 2003, DGCCRF issued a *circulaire*, a regulation that had less legal standing than an Act of Parliament, but could still be used in courts to (re)interpret current statutes. This text was known as the Dutreil regulation.[21] Despite not having full legal standing, the regulation had a lasting influence. Its content inspired the Dutreil Act of 2005.[22] As explained above, early on, the law and legal decisions produced by DGCCRF were unorthodox. In order to fight dubious "commercial cooperation" contracts, officials drafted the NRE law in ambiguous terms. Starting from 2003, regulation started drifting towards more precise and more technical provisions. Gradually, the commitment to help suppliers at any cost declined and was replaced by a cool-headed approach to regulation as a technical field of expertise.

Like the NRE Act of 2001, the aim of the Dutreil regulation was to reduce the use of commercial cooperation and thus decrease the amount of back margins. However, the new regulation differed from the strategy used in the NRE Act, which had introduced a broad prohibition of all "disproportionate and uncompensated advantages." By doing this, it regulated supplier-retailer relations using an ethical principle of proportionality between the compensation for a service and its intrinsic value. In the NRE Act, DGCCRF refused to clearly define what sufficient "counterparts" were, for fear that retailers would circumvent those rules. By contrast, in the Dutreil regulation, bureaucrats gave commercial cooperation a clear legal definition, based on two decisions made by the *Cour de cassation*, one of the three French supreme courts. The rationale was the following: retailers requested too much back margins from their suppliers. As of 2003, most of those back margins were made of "commercial cooperation" agreements. By narrowing the definition of "commercial cooperation," DGCCRF hoped that retailers would find it harder to "sell" back margins to their suppliers. The regulation specified that services pertaining to "commercial cooperation" should have a positive impact on the supplier's sales. This new narrow definition excluded from commercial cooperation the mere resale of statistics or vague "merchandising plans."

DGCCRF officials expected two things from the Dutreil regulation: reducing back margins and cutting inflation rates. However, defining commercial cooperation precisely, as the regulation did, was not successful in lowering the use of back margins by retailers. Between 2003, the year the Dutreil regulation was released, and 2005, the rate of back margins rose from 33.5% to 35.3% (Colla & Lambert-Pandraud, 2007, p. 34). Retailers' legal departments circumvented the Dutreil regulation by changing the legal qualification of the back margins they sold to suppliers. Rather than reducing back margins, they preferred to develop new kinds of "services." The nature of those "specific" services was diverse.[23] The only thing they had in common (and the only thing that really mattered) was that they did not fit in the legal definition of "commercial cooperation." The Dutreil regulation restricted commercial cooperation to the services that could boost sales. Yet the retailers developed new services that rather than boosting sales, aimed at improving commercial relations through other means. The most typical example of this was the resale of statistics to the supplier.

To circumvent the Dutreil regulation, the lawyers who worked for retailers did not go for pure illegality. They didn't ignore the legal mandate spelled out by DGCCRF in the Dutreil regulation, but they complied with it creatively. The creation of those "specific" services was an initiative of retailers' legal departments. They were mentioned by Franck Le Vern, the head of the commercial legal department of Superchain. The quote below helps to understand the role played by lawyers in developing those services. From a legal standpoint, they framed certain services as *distinct* from commercial cooperation. This legal qualification led to the contractual planning of services that were already performed by retailers, yet on an informal basis. As the following quote shows, lawyers also covered up the creation of those "services" by emphasizing the economic "interest" suppliers had in buying them:

> One understands well that retailers accumulate a lot of data and have the capacity to conduct surveys. We have big research departments to analyze the behavior of the customer and the needs of the customer. (Franck Le Vern)

The other category of services that came about were the "international services." Retailers set up legal entities abroad. Then they requested the supplier to sign a contract with this entity. By signing this contract, suppliers were bound to pay a certain rate of their annual sales to the retailer's international entity. Those legal devices allowed increasing the amount of back margins without altering the contract signed by the French entity. "International" back margins were no longer under the DGCCRF's jurisdiction. Like "specific" services, "international" services were an outcome of retailers' legal departments' expertise. During my observation at Superchain, one of the lawyers mentioned the creation in the early 2000s of a legal entity based in Geneva, Switzerland.

The Dutreil regulation was not the only example of DGCCRF's failure to contain back margins by using more precise legal language. A similar process unfolded after 2005, when the Parliament passed the Dutreil Act that defined back margins in even more precise terms than the Dutreil regulation did. During that time, DGCCRF's emphasized "formalism" as its top enforcement priority.[24]

> Guillaume Cerutti, director general of DGCCRF, is less satisfied. Not of the Dutreil Act, but of its application: "There is not enough compliance to the 'formalism' mandated by the Act [...]. Commercial relations have become more transparent. However, compliance to formal requirements is not high enough. Rather than commercial cooperation, retailers use 'distinct' services more and more. [...] Formalism is not anecdotical. It allows to have rules of the game".

What does the enforcement of "formalism" mean? Instead of capping back margins (to reduce the economic power of retailers), the aim of DGCCRF became retailers' narrow compliance with the formal requirements listed in the Dutreil Act. A clear sign of legal endogeneity, DGCCRF officials now viewed retailers' contracts as the main locus of compliance. The word "formalism" was not specific to DGCCRF. Over the years, it became a key notion for all the actors concerned with Title IV.

> This term was used for instance by in-house counsel who worked for retailers. In his memo that synthesized all the major changes in legislation, Franck Le Vern used the word

"formalism" for the first time when the Dutreil Regulation came out: "The regulation emphasizes the formalism that must be followed in the commercial cooperation contracts and in invoicing." In subsequent memos drafted in 2005 and 2008, he used this term 5 times to describe the impact of the Dutreil and Chatel Acts on the standardized agreements used by retailers with their suppliers.

The Chatel Act,[25] drafted and discussed starting from 2007 and passed by Parliament in January 2008, was consistent with this new goal of increasing the formal requirements regulating commercial negotiation instead of paying attention to the economic imbalance between suppliers and retailers. Its main provision was to integrate into a single agreement all the "services" (and hence back margins) that were negotiated between suppliers and retailers. Once the Chatel Act was passed, article 441-7 of the Commercial code provided that commercial partners should sign a contract listing:

> the commitments made by the retailer towards the supplier [...] aiming at improving the commercialization of his products and which do not merely arise from the operators' status as sellers and buyers.

As it increased the formal requirements enforced on the commercial agreements, DGCCRF now framed supplier-retailer relations as a normal business relation where each party had a say in defining the terms of the relationship:

> It was better to have only one contract and to make sure that when people meet around the table, they discuss both the front [margins] and the back [margins] at the same time. This way they can reach a win-win agreement. (Senior official, DGCCRF, 2006–2008)

CONCLUSION

The major steps in the recent history of French retail regulation are the following: during the 1990s, business relations between retailers and suppliers became politicized. Suppliers and their allies accused retailers of unfairly taking advantage of their tremendous size, which led the French Parliament to pass harsh legislation. Those ambiguous statutes triggered the rise of standardized contracts, which became retailers' preferred form of compliance with the new regulation. In-house Counsel was at the forefront of retailers' efforts to ensconce their business relationships in legally binding agreements. Complying through contracts was detrimental to suppliers in two ways. First, while they applied the principles laid out in retail regulation, they also served as a coercion mechanism against suppliers, making them pay more and more back margins and streamline their operations. Second, the legal nature of those agreements and their compliance towards specific legal mandates protecting suppliers gave retailers a sense of symbolic legitimacy. As they became institutionalized, contracts became viewed by regulators as an inevitable form of compliance. Their language started permeating legislation up to a point where the French state deemphasized the economic imbalance between suppliers and retailers.

In those respects, the fate of French retail regulation is consistent with what legal endogeneity theory predicts (Edelman, 2016): organizational responses to regulation lead to institutionalized forms of compliance that can eventually undermine its scope. Similar to the cases described by Talesh (2009, 2014) institutionalized and political logics go hand-in-hand: large organizations diffuse and legitimize specific practices and also exercise direct pressure on political and bureaucratic officials. Yet in its current form, legal endogeneity theory would not have been able to capture certain aspects of the endogenization of French retail regulation. Legal intermediaries are key actors in the emergence of institutionalized conceptions of compliance (Talesh & Pélisse, 2019). While LET emphasizes professional dynamics, my case shows that interactions within organizations, or even "within the cubicle" (Abbott, 2005), are also crucial in shaping how organizations comply with regulation. Compliance professionals, including lawyers, show a great deal of adaptation to the local business norms of their clients (Suchman & Cahill, 1996). The role of ambivalent legal objects such as contracts should also be reassessed. It is their double-sided nature that allows the legal staff to act simultaneously as "cops" and "counsels" (Nelson & Nielsen, 2000). Standardized contracts gave lawyers access to strategic decision-making, while allowing them to keep laypeople at bay. The organizational dimension of contracts is also relatively downplayed in the legal realist literature (Brooks, 2013; Macaulay, 1963). Although it moves away from legal orthodoxy, this literature still views contracts as a reflection of how reflexive business partners decide to secure an ongoing relationship. Such a view cannot be applied to the asymmetrical "agreements" that French retailers created.

NOTES

1. The paper introducing the current special issue contains a thorough presentation of the legal intermediation perspective and in what respect it differs from LET.
2. DGCCRF stands for *Direction générale de la concurrence, de la consommation et de la répression des fraudes* (General Directorate for Competition, Consumption, and the Repression of Fraud)
3. EEOC official website – https://www.eeoc.gov/eeoc/litigation/procedures.cfm
4. In her latest book, Lauren Edelman mentions how organizations "contract and manage around legal risk" (Edelman, 2016, p. 136). Yet contracts themselves play a secondary role in her theory. There are two occurrences of contracts in that paragraph of Edelman's book. The first refers to the contracts with insurance companies by which firms outsource compliance by buying employer practice liability insurance (EPLI) (see Talesh, 2015). The second refers to the mandatory arbitration clauses in work contracts which prevent workers from going to court. In both cases, the focus is not on the contracts as such but on other compliance mechanisms that they carry with them.
5. French bar associations deny membership to those who work directly for corporations. In France, about 16,000 people have received formal training in law but are not considered as proper lawyers ("juristes d'entreprise"). Only those (58,224 as of 2013) who work in single practices or in law firms can claim full membership in the legal profession ("avocats").
6. As Bourdieu wrote in the "The Force of Law" (1987), "the establishment of properly professional competence, the technical mastery of a sophisticated body of knowledge that often runs contrary to the simple counsels of common sense, entails the disqualification of the non-specialists' sense of fairness, and the revocation of their naive understanding of the facts, of their 'view of the case'" (p. 828).

7. In the paper published in the current issue, Jérôme Pélisse uses a similar typology to describe the roles of legal intermediaries in various organizational and economic settings.

8. The name of the retailer was changed for confidentiality reasons.

9. Statement made by Jacques Chirac during a visit of the Rungis market on May 1, 1996. *L'Express*, May 15, 1996. The statement drew a lot of media attention. See also: "Chirac rajoute un couplet anti-hypers. Le Président n'en finit pas de stigmatiser la grande distribution", *Libération*, 2 mai 1996; "Grandes surfaces: l'accusation de Chirac", *Le Figaro*, 2 mai 1996.

10. Nowadays, Paris has only one "hypermarché" (hypermarchés are the biggest type of mass retail stores in France).

11. "Institut de liaisons et d'études des industries de la consommation" ("Institute of Liaison and Study of Consumer Industries").

12. "Fédération du commerce et de la distribution" ("Federation of Commerce and Distribution")

13. The suppliers, even the largest among them, refused to sue retailers themselves. A lawsuit by a supplier would have resulted in an immediate cancellation of all orders by the retailer. This could have disastrous consequences: for a given supplier, a retailer could represent up to 30% of the total sales. The reverse was not true: there were only seven or eight major retailers as opposed to dozens of suppliers. Lawsuits by DGCCRF represented an actual threat to retailers. Lawsuits targeted "commercial cooperation" contracts where the retailer failed to perform the intended "service," or charged unreasonable prices for those "services".

14. Figures available online on the INSEE website: https://www.insee.fr/fr/statistiques/serie/001761326. Accessed April 4, 2018.

15. Pierre Kupferman, "Michel-Edouard Leclerc s'affiche en héraut de la France d'en bas", *La Tribune*, 10 février 2003.

16. The interviews I conducted with the legal counsel of one of those smaller retailers and with various lobbyists confirm this.

17. For confidentiality reasons, I refer to members of Superchain's legal department using pseudonyms.

18. This also applies to the legal counsel of a third retailer that I interviewed. When prompted to describe her daily activities, she focused on contracts.

19. This was another important provision of the Galland Act of 1996.

20. One of the legal mandates of Title IV legislation is that contracts should be signed before March 1st every year.

21. Circulaire du 16 mai 2003 relative à la négociation commerciale entre fournisseurs et distributeurs.

22. Loi no° 2005-882 du 2 août 2005 en faveur des petites et moyennes entreprises.

23. The term specific services appeared for the first time in February 2004 in a DGCCRF memo (retrieved from the French state archives, PH279-05 DGCCRF B2).

24. "Incertitudes sur les relations commerciales", *LSA*, n°1969, October 12, 2006.

25. Loi n° 2008-3 du 3 janvier 2008 pour le développement de la concurrence au service des consommateurs.

ACKNOWLEDGMENTS

I am grateful towards Lisa Buchter, Bruce Carruthers, John Cioffi, and Jérôme Pélisse for their useful comments on earlier versions of this chapter. I would also like to warmly thank the two anonymous reviewers for their insightful contribution.

REFERENCES

Abbott, A. (1988). *The system of professions*. Chicago, IL: The University of Chicago Press.

Abbott, A. (2005). Sociology of work and occupations. In N. J. Smelser & R. Swedberg (Éd.), *Handbook of economic sociology* (pp. 307–330). Princeton, NJ: Princeton University Press.

Amable, B. (2011). Morals and politics in the ideology of neo-liberalism. *Socio-Economic Review*, *9*(1), 3–30.

Bernstein, L. (1992). Opting out of the legal system: Extralegal contractual relations in the diamond industry. *Journal of Legal Studies*, *21*(1), 115–157.

Bessy, C. (2008). Pratiques contractuelles et individualisation de la rupture de la relation de travail. *Travail et emploi*, *114*, 71–93.

Billows, S. (2016a). À qui profite la "concurrence"? Modèles de concurrence et régulation de la grande distribution française (1949–1986). *Gouvernement et action publique*, *5*(4), 69–91.

Billows, S. (2016b). La politique de l'ambiguïté juridique. Quand l'Etat tente de réguler les échanges entre la grande distribution et ses fournisseurs. *Sociologie du Travail*, *58*(1), 8–31.

Bourdieu, P. (1987). The force of law: Toward a sociology of the juridical field. *The Hastings Law Journal*, *38*(1971), 805–853.

Brooks, R. R. W. (2013). On the Empirical and the Lyrical: Review of Revisiting the Contracts Scholarship of Stewart Macaulay. In Jean Braucher, John Kidwell & William C. Whitford (Eds.), *Wisconsin Law Review*, 1299–1354.

Colla, E., & Lambert-Pandraud, R. (2007). L'influence de la loi Dutreil sur la politique de prix des distributeurs et ses conséquences. In *XII° Journées de Recherche en Marketing de Bourgogne* (pp. 24–40). Dijon: IAE de Dijon.

Davis, K. E. (2006). The role of nonprofits in the production of boilerplate. *Michigan Law Review*, *104*(5), 1075–1103.

Dietz, T. (2012). Contract law, relational contracts, and reputational networks in international trade: An empirical investigation into cross-border contracts in the software industry. *Law & Social Inquiry*, *37*(1), 25–57.

Dobbin, F. (2009). *Inventing equal opportunity*. Princeton, NJ: Princeton University Press.

Dobbin, F., & Kelly, E. L. (2007). How to stop harassment: Professional construction of legal compliance in organizations. *American Journal of Sociology*, *112*(4), 1203–1243.

Edelman, L. B. (1992). Legal ambiguity and symbolic structures: Organizational mediation of civil rights law. *American Journal of Sociology*, *97*(6), 1531–1576.

Edelman, L. B. (2016). *Working law. Courts, corporations, and symbolic civil rights*. Chicago, IL: University of Chicago Press.

Edelman, L. B., Krieger, L. H., Eliason, S. R., Albiston, C. R., & Mellema, V. (2011). When organizations rule: Judicial deference to institutionalized employment structures. *American Journal of Sociology*, *117*(3), 888–954.

Edelman, L. B., & Suchman, M. C. (1999). When the "Haves" hold court: speculations on the organizational internalization of law. *Law & Society Review*, *33*(4), 941–992.

Edelman, L. B., & Talesh, S. A. (2011). To comply or not to comply – that isn't the question: how organizations construct the meaning of compliance. In C. Parker & V. L. Nielsen (Éd.), *Explaining compliance. Business responses to regulation* (pp. 103–122). Cheltenham: Edward Elgar.

Edelman, L. B., Uggen, C., & Erlanger, H. S. (1999). The endogeneity of legal regulation: Grievance procedures as rational myth. *American Journal of Sociology*, *105*(2), 406–454.

Edelman, L., Fuller, S., & Mara-Drita, I. (2001). Diversity rhetoric and the managerialization of law. *American Journal of Sociology*, *106*(6), 1589–1641.

Fourcade, M., Steiner, P., Streeck, W., & Woll, C. (2013). Moral categories in the financial crisis. *Socio-Economic Review*, *11*(3), 601.

Granovetter, M. (1985). Economic action and social structure: The problem of embeddedness. *American Journal of Sociology*, *91*, 481–510.

Halliday, T. C., & Carruthers, B. G. (2009). *Bankrupt: Global lawmaking and systemic financial crisis*. Stanford, CA: Stanford University Press.

Hill, C. A. (2001). Why contracts are written in legalese. *Chicago-Kent Law Review*, *77*(1), 59–85.

Jacques, T. (2016). Refus de vente interdit! Quand la politique de la concurrence oeuvre à la réforme de la distribution. *Gouvernement et action publique*, *4*(4), 47–67.

Kahan, M., & Klausner, M. (1997). Standardization and innovation in corporate contracting (Or "The Economics of Boilerplate"). *Virginia Law Review*, *83*(4), 713–770.

Knapp, C. L. (2013). Is there a "Duty to Read"? In J. Braucher, J. Kidwell, & W. C. Whitford (Éds.), *Revisiting the contracts scholarship of stewart macaulay: On the empirical and the lyrical* (pp. 315–343). Oxford: Hart.

Li-wen, L., & Whitford, J. (2013). Conflict and collaboration in business organization: a preliminary study. In J. Braucher, J. Kidwell, & W. C. Whitford (Éds.), *Revisiting the contracts scholarship of stewart macaulay on the empirical and the lyrical* (pp. 191–222). Oxford: Hart.

Lieberman, R. C. (2015). Private power and American bureaucracy: The state, the EEOC, and civil rights enforcement. In J. T. Sparrow, W. J. Novak, & S. W. Sawyer (Éds.), *Boundaries of the state in US history* (pp. 259–286). Chicago, IL: The University of Chicago Press.

Macaulay, S. (1963). Non-contractual relations in business. *American Journal of Sociology*, *28*(1), 1–23.

Mallard, G. (2014). *Fallout. Nuclear diplomacy in an age of global fracture*. Chicago, IL: University of Chicago Press.

Marotta-Wurgler, F., & Taylor, R. (2013). Set in stone: Change and innovation in consumer standard-form contracts. *New York University School of Law Review*, *88*, 240–285.

McAdam, D. (1989). The biographical consequences of activism. *American Sociological Review*, *54*(5), 744–760.

Nelson, R. L., & Nielsen, L. B. (2000). Cops, counsel, and entrepreneurs: Constructing the role of inside counsel in large corporations. *Law & Society Review*, *34*(2), 457–494.

Pélisse, J. (2011). La mise en oeuvre des 35 heures: d'une managérialisation du droit à une internalisation de la fonction de justice. *Droit et Société*, *77*, 39–65.

Pélisse, J. (2014). *Le travail du droit. Trois études sur la légalité ordinaire*. Sciences Po.

Pélisse, J., Bessy, C., & Delpeuch, T. (Éd.). (2011). *Droit et régulations des activités économiques: perspectives sociologiques et institutionnalistes*. Paris: LGDJ.

Pélisse, J., Protais, C., Larchet, K., & Charrier, E. (2012). *Des chiffres, des maux et des lettres. Une soicologie de l'expertise judiciaire en économie, psychiatrie et traduction*. Paris: Armand Colin.

Stryker, R. (2003). Mind the gap: Law, institutional analysis and socioeconomics. *Socio-Economic Review*, *1*(3), 335–367.

Stryker, R., & Pedriana, N. (2004). The strength of a weak agency: Enforcement of title VII of the 1964 civil rights act and the expansion of state capacity, 1965–1971. *American Journal of Sociology*, *110*(3), 709–760.

Stryker, R., & Pedriana, N. (2017). From judicial doctrine to social transformation? comparing US voting rights, equal employment opportunity and fair housing legislation. *American Journal of Sociology*, *123*(1), 86–135.

Suchman, M. C. (2003). The contract as social artifact. *Law and Society Review*, *37*(1), 91–142.

Suchman, M. C., & Cahill, M. L. (1996). The hired gun as facilitator: Lawyers and the suppression of business disputes in silicon valley. *Law and Social Inquiry*, *21*(3), 679–712.

Talesh, S. (2015). Legal intermediaries: How insurance companies construct the meaning of compliance with antidiscrimination laws. *Law & Policy*, *37*(3), 209–239.

Talesh, S. A. (2009). The privatization of public legal rights: How manufacturers construct the meaning of consumer law. *Law & Society Review*, *43*(3), 527–561.

Talesh, S. A. (2014). Institutional and political sources of legislative change: explaining how private organizations influence the form and content of consumer protection legislation. *Law and Sociel Inquiry*, *39*(4), 973–1005.

Talesh, S., & Pélisse, J. (2019). How legal intermediaries facilitate or inhibit social change. *Studies in Law, Politics, and Society*, *79*, 111–145.

Teichman, D. (2010). Old habits are hard to change: A case study of israeli real estate contracts. *Law and Society Review*, *44*(2), 229–330.

Weber, M. (1978). *Economy and society*. Berkeley, CA: University of California Press.

Printed and bound by CPI Group (UK) Ltd, Croydon, CR0 4YY

13/09/2026

14961027-0006